BILL VEECK

BILL VEECK

A Baseball Legend

Gerald Eskenazi

McGraw-Hill Book Company

New York   St. Louis
San Francisco   Bogotá   Mexico
Milan   Montreal   Panama
São Paulo   Toronto

2 3 4 5 6 7 8 9 D O C D O C 8 7

ISBN 0-07-019599-4

LIBRARY OF CONGRESS CATALOGING-IN-PUBLICATION DATA

Eskenazi, Gerald.
    Bill Veeck: a baseball legend.
    1. Veeck, Bill.   2. Baseball—United States—
Promoters—Biography.   I. Title.
GV865.V4E86   1987   659.2'9796357'0924 [B]   87-3917
ISBN 0-07-019599-4

This book is for Roz,
who knows the score
and how to keep it

Acknowledgments

Months after my book-writing was finished, I sat in Florida with Art Modell, the lighthearted Brooklyn-born owner of the Cleveland Browns. The subject of Bill Veeck came up.

"Did you know," said Modell, "that ten days before he died, Bill called me? He said, 'You know, I think I'd like to get back into baseball. What do you think my chances are of buying the Indians?'"

Of course.

That has been one of the maddening, and rewarding, aspects of working on a book about Bill Veeck. Invariably, when I mentioned to someone what I was doing, they had an anecdote for me.

I collected as many as I could, of course, and read as much as I could, and spoke to as many people as I could. I never met Bill Veeck, and never even spoke to him on the telephone. But I did wind up reporting on his memorial service in *The New York Times* and that launched this work.

Bill Veeck was more than a baseball legend. He remains a metaphor for innovation in sports, a gadfly to the Establishment, and a man who, once again, annually remains off the final ballot when it comes to nominating club executives for the Baseball Hall of Fame.

It seems clear to me that, with all his faults, his excesses, his ramshackle approach to life and the game he loved, Bill Veeck belongs in someone's hall of fame.

To try to learn and write about him, I worked with an extraordinary variety of people. Their names and titles tell something about the sort of man he was, the friends he kept, and the impact he made. So in no special order, let me thank the following:

Circus World Museum, Baraboo, Wisconsin; Marvin Davis, Denver oilman; County Clerk's Office, Los Alamos, New Mexico; Larry Doby, former Indians star; Bob Hope, entertainer and part-time baseball owner; Jimmy Piersall, former player, current announcer; Harry Caray, announcer; Gene Michael, one-time spy-in-the-sky, current manager; Lou Boudreau, ex-player-manager, Indians, now announcer; Mrs. Ellen (Veeck) Maggs, Bill's daughter, sculptor; Mrs. Will Veeck 3d, widow of Bill's first child; Peter Veeck, son of Bill, a former airline pilot with unusual insights; Mrs. Eleanor (Raymond) Veeck, ex-circus performer, ex-wife of Bill Veeck; Roger Angell, fiction editor, baseball writer, *The New Yorker*; Sidney Salomon, Jr., late influential St. Louis businessman and Democratic Party mogul; Lincoln Center Library for the Arts; Lee MacPhail, retired American League president; Max Gruber, lawyer and former owner of popular St. Louis restaurant; Dick Schaap, author, television personality; A. B. (Happy) Chandler, former governor and senator from Kentucky, and former baseball commissioner; Milt Esterow, editor, *Artnews*; Harold (Spud) Goldstein, Veeck's traveling secretary; Rudie Schaffer, Veeck's business manager; Bob Cain, former pitcher who hurled to the midget; Johnny Berardino, ex-player for Veeck, now actor (portrays Dr. Steve Hardy on *General Hospital*); Bill Gleason, former Chicago newspaperman; Peter Ruger, general counsel, Washington University of St. Louis; Calvin Griffith, former Senators-Twins owner; Bill Wrigley, head of chewing-gum company; Eddie Einhorn, president of White Sox; Cooper Rollow, Chicago *Tribune* columnist; Al Rosen, former Indians slugger, now president of San Francisco Giants; Bob Varey, former Suffolk Downs publicist; Billy Sullivan, owner of the New England Patriots and storyteller; Father Thomas J. Fitzgerald, friend of Veeck's; Roland Hemond, ex-White Sox general manager, wide-eyed Veeck admirer; Frank Mankiewicz, former press secretary for Robert Kennedy, now advertising official; Chuck Heaton, Cleveland *Plain-Dealer* columnist; Asher J. Birnbaum, editor-publisher *North Shore*; Andrew J. McKenna, Cubs official; Bob Pastin, executive sports editor, St. Louis *Post-Dispatch*; Jack Kent Cooke, Jr., Washington Redskins owner, sportsman-businessman; Thom Greer, managing editor, Cleveland *Plain-Dealer*; Robert Doepke,

Kenyon College roommate; Bob Verdi, columnist, Chicago *Tribune*; Thomas Stamp, public relations director, Kenyon College; Bob Varey, former public relations director, Suffolk Downs; Skitch Henderson, conductor, man-about-music; Lieutenant Michael F. Imsick, deputy director, public affairs, United States Marine Corps; Hedy Dunn, director, Los Alamos Historical Society; Baseball Hall of Fame; Governor's Office, New Mexico; Gabe Paul, retired multitalented baseball executive; Marty Appel, former Yankees publicist, now Bowie Kuhn's biographer and vice president, public relations, Channel 11 in New York; Arthur Chase, Veeck prep-school instructor; Cook County Clerk's Office, Chicago; Nick DelNino, former publicist, Suffolk Downs; Paul Zimmerman, football expert, *Sports Illustrated*, and former New York *Post* columnist; Bob Broeg, retired St. Louis newspaperman, columnist, and midget expert; Marsh Samuels, former partner in publicity firm with Veeck and retired baseball executive; Bob Feller, no-hit fastball pitcher and still barnstorming; Bob Fishel, longtime friend and observer and reigning expert on Bill Veeck; Bill DeWitt, Jr., who loaned the midget the uniform, former baseball executive now a financier; Al Lopez, former player, manager, and full-time raconteur.

And, of course, Tom Quinn of McGraw-Hill, for being excited about this fascinating project and slicing off redundancies, and Jay Acton, for imagining it.

Foreword

People were murmuring. It had been, after all, quite a life. There was a lot to talk about, to remember. Then silence, as the service in the cathedral began with a lone trumpeter playing Aaron Copland's "Fanfare for the Common Man."

Fittingly, people sat upstairs as well—it reminded me of the bleachers—because all the seats downstairs were filled at the Church of St. Thomas the Apostle on this chill January day in Chicago in 1986. There were grown men wearing the warm-up jackets of their youth. There were youngsters wearing baseball caps. There was even an old ballplayer wearing his White Sox uniform—all in respect for the man whose funeral services they were attending: Bill Veeck, dead at the age of seventy-one.

Throughout the church it seemed as if the services were as much a celebration of the fan in the stands as a mass for Veeck. The obituaries had described him as "maverick," "innovator," "impresario," "creative," and "provocative." Jim Murray, the wonderful columnist, had once called him "America's Gadfly."

The holy card, distributed to each of the nine hundred people who attended, contained Henry David Thoreau's homage to the man who "hears a different drummer." Veeck's widow, Mary Frances, had thought of everything. She had orchestrated this good-bye very carefully, and months later she said to an interviewer who had recalled the Thoreau quote, "You noticed it, did you?"

There was a roped-off section for the press, but the reporters who knew him preferred to sit among family and friends. The press section was empty.

Minnie Minoso—an irreverent baseball oddball who had played for Veeck at the age of fifty-seven—showed up wearing a White Sox cap, and baseball shoes, and a shirt that read "Chicago" tucked into blue warm-up pants. Of course. Minoso, after all, was honoring a baseball figure, a larger-than-life fans' owner who had touched the game with his special, crazy magic dust and changed it wherever he went.

So no one was surprised when the services were over and Minoso, looking like springtime in his uniform, discovered he was locked out of his car, which was parked right in front of the church. He yanked on the door a few times. Then he called out for help. Fans started to give him advice. Finally, a nun in the crowd—an old White Sox fan, she explained—went inside the church and got a wire hanger. When she emerged with the hanger the crowd let out a whoop—as if their favorite pinch hitter was coming to bat in a tight situation. Minoso bent and curled the hanger and maneuvered it inside the window.

"C'mon, Minnie, you can do it," bellowed a fan in encouragement. And Minoso did, too, beaming. The crowd cheered.

Greg Brown, wearing his White Sox cap, was pleased. "Bill is laughing at that," said Brown as Minoso got inside the car, signed autographs, and then sped off with his tires screeching.

Bob Fishel, a dapper little man, his hair parted down the center in the style of the 1930s, walked out of the church with his family. He was grieving. It was always one of the anomalies of baseball that Fishel, this pleasant, soft-spoken gentleman, had actually worked for the zany Veeck—had actually participated in the one event that Veeck will be remembered for beyond all others: the day the midget went to bat. Fishel had been Veeck's P.R. man. He was now the American League's executive vice president, a man who adored Veeck yet always saw his foibles plainly.

Another man, more frail than Veeck, descended the steps. He leaned on two people. It was Charles O. Finley, baseball curmudgeon, the man who had brought white shoes and orange baseballs and a mule to the game. Charlie Finley's eyes lit up like an old warrior remembering past battles when he thought about Veeck. "He really taught me how to rock the boat," said Finley proudly.

In the services the Reverend Thomas J. Fitzgerald, an old friend of Veeck's, praised him as "a genuinely religious person." Pause. Then the Father added, "Of course he expressed it as only Bill could." Laughter from the mourners.

Outside, Father Fitzgerald spoke of the tickets to tough games that Veeck used to provide to the church. The priest also reminisced at length with Charles Comiskey, whose family owned the White Sox before Veeck had taken control of the team in 1959. Father Fitzgerald told Comiskey of first going to Comiskey Park when he was eight years old. Veeck's death had stirred baseball talk, evoked the old days.

"That generation of owners isn't here anymore," said Comiskey as he was leaving the funeral. He was asked why baseball didn't show up in force for Bill Veeck's funeral.

"The new owners don't know that much about Bill Veeck," Comiskey said sadly. "There were the Macks in Philadelphia, Griffiths in Washington, the old families."

Everyone seemed to remember that Bill Veeck came from a time when baseball was played in sunlight. People left the church on this gray blustery day and smiled.

BILL VEECK

Chapter 1

Forever, Bill Veeck and the midget will be joined. And why not? What else should an owner of an eighth-place team do to attract attention to his hapless band of performers, the 1951 St. Louis Browns? It was a team so inept, it finished forty-six games out of first place, failed to boast one full-time hitter who batted above .261, and produced only one pitcher to win more than six games. In fact, an unheard-of number of twenty-two pitchers saw action for the Brownies. Along with one midget, whose name was Eddie Gaedel. Veeck sent Gaedel to bat, the midget drew a walk, the starched collar of the president of the American League fluttered and he ordered the midget's name expunged from the records, and Bill Veeck became a legend.

But William Louis Veeck, Jr., transcended the little things in life. He was the first American League owner to put a black ballplayer in uniform. As head of the Cleveland Indians, Veeck bought Larry Doby in 1947 shortly after the Brooklyn Dodgers changed the game forever with Jackie Robinson. The next year Veeck signed a wheezing relic from the Negro Leagues named Satchel Paige, who brought an irreverent, homespun grace to a hidebound league.

Veeck's baseball life was filled with these delightful oases. He hung the ivy in Wrigley Field. He brought fireworks to the home run. He produced morning baseball during World War II so the swing-shift workers wouldn't be left out of the National Pastime. His '48 Indians drew more fans than any baseball team had before.

1

Bill Veeck delighted America and its fans for more than forty years, which saw him run the minor-league Milwaukee Brewers, then burst upon the majors with the Cleveland Indians, following them with the St. Louis Browns, and, twice, the Chicago White Sox.

And yet there was something he never was able to accomplish, his failed dream, his "rosebud." Friends called it his obsession, one labeled it his forbidden "lollipop." And that was to run, to own, the Chicago Cubs—the team his revered father once had been the president of. But Bill Veeck, Jr., never was to succeed his father in running the Cubs, and Bill's excesses as an owner forever labeled him a maverick, especially when compared to the more traditional ways his father had done things.

Bill Veeck's life revolved around Chicago, and twice he ran a ball club there. He died in Chicago. But Veeck was also a man who spent his life scrounging around for other people's dollars, and there never ever would have been enough to buy the Chicago Cubs from the extraordinary wealth of the Wrigley family, whose chewing-gum empire never could be equaled by the likes of a Bill Veeck.

This obsession with money—there never was enough—also created what one newspaper writer and admirer, Cooper Rollow, describes as Veeck's "dark side." Here was a man who could spend the night—the whole night—playing charades with show-biz people, who could shut down bars drinking beer with truckers, who would sit shirtless in the bleachers, who was loved and adored by virtually all he touched. Yet he could also have his glowering moods when he realized he never would be as powerful as the New York Yankees, and never would own the Chicago Cubs.

So Veeck spent much of his life tweaking the ears of the New York Yankees. Indeed, he enjoyed seeking out and skewering the pompous. But if you were a Yankee owner, you were cut down to size by Veeck, who knew more baseball than your money would ever buy.

He also knew a lot about many things. Behind his gravelly voice—which never uttered a curse—there was a tender, philosophical soul and brain. He read everything, and frequently. He spent at least two hours a day soaking a stump of a leg that grew smaller and smaller over the years, and while he soaked he read. The stump was a legacy of World War II and the island of Bougainville, where the recoil of an antiaircraft weapon smashed his right foot and resulted, eventually, in repeated sawing-off operations.... No matter. Veeck simply threw himself a party when he got his first wooden leg, and he eventually built an ashtray into it so he could flick his cigarette into it.

This was a fabulous character. Sometimes the myth and the reality blurred. Sometimes he didn't burden friendly newspaper reporters with the whole truth. He allowed the legend to grow in all directions at once.

The city hall records show he was born February 9, 1914, in Chicago to William Louis and Grace Greenwood (DeForest) Veeck.

The elder Veeck was an extremely popular newspaperman in Chicago who in one of his many jobs wrote a column under the name of Bill Bailey. Years later newspaper stories about him contended he had been the namesake for the song "Bill Bailey, Won't You Please Come Home?" However, that song was copyrighted in 1902, many years before he used that pseudonym.

Instead, Bill Veeck, Sr., was a respected, correct man-about-Chicago. Photographs show his attention to fashion, and he invariably wore not only a neatly fastened tie but vest and jacket as well, his outfit topped by a wide-brimmed hat. His son disdained ties and got about with a shirt open at the neck, its wide collar flared. Young Bill Veeck rarely went anywhere in a topcoat, even on Chicago's most blustery days. "Sports-shirt Bill" they called him.

His father, William Louis Veeck, Sr., was an immensely popular figure with the baseball Establishment. He was born in 1877 in Indiana. His father was a wagon builder and cabinetmaker. The son worked as a printer's devil. He sold photographs on the road. He was an itinerant news-paperman. He ingratiated himself with editors at the Louisville *Courier-Journal*, where he hung around until he finally got a job. Then he married his childhood sweetheart and moved on to Chicago at the beginning of the new century.

He went through a series of newspaper jobs and finally became a columnist. In a conversation with one of the Cubs' new owners, William Wrigley, Jr., in 1918, Veeck reportedly said that his four-year-old son, Bill, Jr., as an infant could "throw his bottle farther than the team can hit."

That nettled Wrigley. He had recently bought into the team and he was looking for a dynamic person to run it. The story, passed on by Wrigley's grandson, goes that he told Veeck, "If you're so smart, why don't you see if you could do a better job?"

So Veeck left the newspaper business in 1918 and became the Cubs' vice president and treasurer. The next year he took over as president. He ran the team for fifteen seasons, until his death on October 5, 1933. The Cubs won National League pennants in 1929 and 1932.

While he was in charge he engineered the biggest deal baseball had known. Wrigley always had been fond of Rogers Hornsby, now well into his thirties as the 1928 season ended. Still, Wrigley wanted the irascible Hornsby, who was playing for the Boston Braves. So Veeck put together a package for Boston of $200,000 and six players. The money in the deal topped the Yankees' historic purchase price for Babe Ruth eight years earlier by $65,000. Hornsby helped the Cubs win their pennant.

Although Veeck was a solid businessman and unyielding disciplinarian, he also was a baseball innovator. Not all his ideas were accepted. During the early days of the Depression, with baseball attendance slumping, he urged a mid-season schedule in which the American and National leagues would play each other instead of waiting until the World Series. It was an idea the public, but not the owners, accepted.

Veeck, in fact, habitually threw out ideas to the fans and gauged their reactions. His associates often criticized him for not remaining aloof from the crowd.

Still, some aspects of his personality were distinct, and different, from those his son would acquire. Perhaps the following column, written at the death of Veeck, Sr., in 1933 by Arch Ward of the Chicago *Tribune*, puts into perspective how the baseball world viewed him:

Bill Veeck is dead. It is probable that the death of no man connected with the business end of baseball would have caused such widespread mourning.

Veeck has been president of the Cubs since 1919.... They have been the biggest money earners in the league, if not in baseball.

He put across some of the biggest deals in baseball. Seldom did he make a mistake. But he was more than a smart business man. By his subtle yet striking personality he made the Wilsons, the Hornsbys, the Hartnetts, the Cuylers...come around to his way of doing things or else they didn't stay.

Veeck tolerated no display of poor sportsmanship on or off the diamond. He was a strict but understanding disciplinarian.... You never heard of a holdout on the Cubs' squad after Veeck became chief. Few leaders could have handled so many high strung athletes with exaggerated ideas of their worth with so little friction. It took patience, restraint, and a sympathetic attitude toward the other fellow to turn the trick. Not many baseball leaders have done it. Not many would have tried.

Never have we heard the Cubs' late leader utter a derogatory word in reference to any human.

"I do things one way, the other man likes them done another way, and for all we know I may be wrong and the other fellow may be right, so why criticize?" he said recently....

Veeck was recognized as the most progressive magnate in the National League. He never was afraid to try something new if he thought it had merit....

His dismissal of Hornsby in August, 1932, was one of the most daring moves in baseball. If the Cubs had fallen further behind instead of spurting to the pennant he would have been severely criticized. But Veeck, Grimm, and the Cubs came though 100 per cent.... His honest and unyielding scruples must stand as his epitaph....

On the day of his funeral the Giants defeated the Senators and won the World Series in Washington. There were several thousand empty seats, even in the $3.30 section. Baseball was mired in the Depression.

Bill Veeck, Jr., was nineteen years old when his father died. Until the death of Bill, Jr., more than fifty years later, he always referred to his late father as "Daddy." It didn't matter if he was discussing his father with other club owners or sports writers or show people. To Bill Veeck, even at the age of seventy, his father was, simply, "Daddy"—not even "my Daddy." No possessive was deemed necessary.

At the time his father died young Veeck was already on his way to establishing the unexpected and the innovative that would mark his career in baseball. His father had put him to work early, at the age of ten or eleven, helping in the office, handling advance sales for ladies' days. Bill Veeck, Sr., is credited with creating the first Ladies' Day (although records show it was popular before the turn of the century). Young Veeck spent his summers at Wrigley Field selling peanuts and hot dogs, and in spring training on the West Coast he learned how ball fields are constructed.

"I'm the only human being ever raised in a ballpark," he liked to say. He also spent much of his time in a firehouse near the ballpark, and he was a fixture in the firehouse, considered the mascot.

But Bill Veeck, Jr., was also a studious, inquiring youngster. His father had always proffered books to him and the youngster eagerly accepted them.

A part of his life few people knew about was his education and the schools he attended. He didn't like to brag and he also liked to nurture a streetwise image. With his frizzy hair and growling voice and disdain for the shirt and tie, he did indeed appear to be a diamond in the rough.

Yet, he attended Phillips Academy in Andover, Massachusetts, one of America's elite boarding schools. He remained only eight weeks. Records there fail to indicate what sort of student he was, but a school official concedes that in those days the school was more exclusive than now.

If, however, homesickness was the purported reason he left Phillips, why would his next stint at school be in Los Alamos, New Mexico, at the tony Ranch School? He bragged that he was kicked out of the elitist school and never graduated from high school.

The Ranch School was one of the more extraordinary institutions in the history of American education. Its rollcall of students includes the authors Gore Vidal and William Burroughs, as well as Antonio Taylor, brother of Lady Bird Johnson, and the eventual corporate heads of Quaker Oats, Sears, and American Motors.

Its life was short and its creation and demise had ironic overtones. When it was founded in 1918 for grades seven to twelve, it was patterned on Thoreau's theories nurtured at Walden Pond—learning from nature. And when it ended in 1943 it was because a top-secret operation called the Manhattan Project needed buildings to house the scientists who were working on the atomic bomb.

More than forty years after the school suddenly stopped existing, Ranch School memorabilia still provide the single largest collection at the Los Alamos Historical Museum. Former students and teachers constantly forward books and notes and clippings to the museum, reports its director, Hedy Dunn.

When Bill Veeck attended the school in 1931 and 1932, he found a school so exclusive that it had only thirty-nine students. Some classes had as few as three pupils. The tuition was $2,000 a year—more than double that of Harvard. You could go to Harvard then by paying $400 a year tuition and another $9.50 a week for room and board.

Mornings in Los Alamos were for studies, but afternoons were for community service. So the young men worked at fence-mending and branding cattle.

It was at the school that Bill Veeck's trademark—the open-necked shirt—began. But not because he wanted to be thought of as informal, one-of-the-guys. Nor did he disdain ties and a buttoned shirt as a sign of rebellion.

The reason was more mundane—he had eczema, a skin condition aggravated by his asthma. Tight shirts would chafe him. And, as an asthmatic, he also had an obsession for breathing freely, to be unhindered. Looking at his later life, and his reaction to—or, more precisely, his denial of—illness, it was obvious that he had always strongly battled to defeat anything that might hold him back.

Arthur Chase was one of his instructors at the school. The pair kept in touch for more than fifty years. "He was a very individualistic kid, but in a very nice way," Chase remembers. "He wasn't really rebellious, but I'm sure he thought activities of the Ranch School were rather far out. He never went for horses and we didn't have a very heavy sports program.

"I remember the Cubs were playing the World Series that fall with Connie Mack's Philadelphia team, and of course he was crazy to listen to the ball game. But the riding program came before everything, so poor old Billy, he had to go out and curry his horse and saddle up. I remember one game the Cubs were ahead and we went out riding and Billy came back and tried to get the score and he found out that Philadelphia had rallied and taken the game, much to his chagrin."

Chase, the head of the English department, was also the school's boxing instructor. Boxing was mandatory. Because young Veeck was a little bigger than everyone else at the school, Chase decided to spar with him.

"I started in sparring with Billy, who weighed about 165 and I weighed 210. After a while he clipped me under the jaw and knocked me down and really addled my brains. He rang my bell. That was sort of not in the rules of sparring and I got pretty mad. I walloped him into a corner of the ring and gave him the what-for. But he was such a good-natured fellow that I think it was a little bit of a joke to clip the old man on the jaw."

Chase got friendly with the boy and his father, and took an interest in them. "I think the thing that brought him out there was the asthma. A lot of boys went out there for that. That flaky skin that he had, always had trouble with his skin, you know. And he never wore collars out there. I think that coming out to the West, his father thought that would help the situation. There were an awful lot of asthmatics that came out there. The dander of the horses irritated them, but they did well in that climate."

Chase also spent time with Veeck in English class. "He was a very entertaining fellow to teach. He'd come in in the morning and he had very spikey hair. His hair would stand on end. And he'd come into the classroom—there were only four or five in the class—and I'd say, 'Billy, let me see if you've got any spark in you,' and I used to rub my knuckles on his spikey hair, and he was always entertained by that and would say, 'Mr. Chase, you want to see if I've got any power today?'

"His writing had a rather colloquial style, but he was very appreciative, he could read some Shakespeare and see the humor and the pathos in it. Still, he was a rough kind of kid who spent a lot of his time in Chicago under the grandstand and the concessions and he was from sort of a different background than most kids we had.

"Most of the boys were pretty wealthy, but his father was wealthy then. His father was a big, tall, dark fellow, unlike Bill, who had sort of sandy hair. But there was no shortage of money. It was a very expensive school.

"I always admired his inventiveness. Everything he did, he did with a very joyous twinkle in his eye. He was always two jumps ahead of you. He was a very good student. I think he was a very good reader with a lot of imagination. My brother-in-law was in school with him and said he read all the time. He read all the time on his own in addition to what I assigned to him."

Wasn't this an unusual setting for a boy from such a free-wheeling background? "His attitude toward the activities of the school was anti-Establishment. To him, riding was for the birds. Every boy had a horse and took care of him, polished up the saddle. His attitude was one of, not hostility, but that this is crazy. It was a pretty tightly run school. He wasn't a complainer, but he was just amazed at what was required of him."

Yet, Chase recalls Veeck as a good student, even though Veeck liked to suggest that he was kicked out of the school. The Ranch School, though, was demanding. "All the teachers were Ivy Leaguers," says Chase. "We got an awful lot of our boys from Hotchkiss and various prep schools around the East, and also Lake Forest Academy. But the philosophy was high-grade college preparation—a lot of Latin, a lot of language. In those days practically all who graduated went to Ivy League colleges.

"Arthur Wood was there, he later became chairman of the board of Sears, Roebuck, and Roy Chapin, he was president of American Motors, and Bobby Stewart, he became chairman of the board of Quaker Oats, John Reed, who recently retired as chairman of the board of the Sante Fe Railroad."

Veeck's rebelliousness was more subtle than most. It was typical Veeck, though. "We wore a uniform out there, with the Dakota Stetson hat. And when you wore the Stetson it was pointed at the top. He wore the uniform, he sometimes dented it in the middle. You were supposed to wear it peaked like a forest ranger. But he was a very gentle fellow even though he did knock me down."

Although he had no degree, Veeck in 1932 matriculated at Kenyon College, a fine school in Gambier, Ohio. The freshman yearbook of 1932 shows, on the activities page, a Huck Finn look-alike with thick hair, narrow eyes, and high, round cheekbones above the caption "William L. Veeck." He was a blocking back on the football team and also made the basketball squad. On another page, headed "Class of 1936," there is a listing of class officers. The top line reads, "William Louis Veeck, Jr.— President."

His roommate was Robert Doepke, now the Kenyon College "agent" for the class of '36. He was also the senior-class president. Doepke's role now is to keep track of members of the class. Veeck was easy for him.

"We were members of the Beta Alpha chapter of Beta Theta Pi," recalls Doepke "We roomed together for a year. We had a lot of fun. He was a burly guy, and I often remember that he loved to have his back scratched. I never felt it was a necessity, but he thought so. We'd get into wrestling matches over this and he'd get what he called a 'death grip' on me and I'd end up scratching his back. In later years we never did get Bill to come back for a reunion. I even offered to scratch his back, but he didn't come back."

Was there an inkling in Veeck the young man of things to come? "Well, no, to be honest with you. Bill was the kind of fellow who was well liked by everybody, but any innovative ideas such as he came up with later on—I don't imagine there was too much opportunity for it back then. It was a man's college at the time. We had a very small student body because it was during the Depression. I think we had maybe 150 students in the whole school, and only about twenty or twenty-five in our class."

At the school Veeck continued the carousing that had marked at least part of his career at the Ranch School. "We had a parlor on the fourth floor of our building. This was during Prohibition, but that didn't seem to bother anybody as far as getting what you needed," recalls Doepke. "We had quite a few very active parties, and this was one of them. And Bill got out on the balcony and somehow fell off. But he really didn't hurt himself too much. It was rather amazing. I'd say he was a rugged guy."

In later years, when Veeck recalled the incident, he said he wound up at the hospital with two broken legs. In an interview with the *Kenyon College Alumni Bulletin*, Veeck said of the school, "It was during prohibition and there was a lot of action." He told the *Bulletin* his most vivid memory of Kenyon was "falling out of the window of Leonard Hall. I was getting ready to go to a spring dance. I was standing up in those windows and I waved to a fellow across campus. I made a mistake, and I waved with the hand I was holding on with; fell down like a sack of wheat; broke both my legs."

And of Kenyon in general? "It was a delightful place, even though on occasion I had to go to classes."

One newspaper account, written after Veeck's "retirement" from the White Sox in 1961, claimed that Veeck actually jumped from the balcony on purpose to win a $5 bet. That may have been in keeping with the columnist's image of a daredevil Veeck, but it was not how it happened.

Veeck did well at school despite his misadventures. But shortly after he returned for his sophomore year in 1933, he was forced to leave suddenly when his father fell ill with a disease that was spelled "leucaemia" in those days and which was a little-known killer. Young Bill never returned to Kenyon. The school's alumni bulletins are filled with items about him and he still is regarded as one of theirs.

Instead, he went to work for the Cubs. That set up an interesting series of confrontations, which probably helped set the tone for many of the authority clashes he had later. For the year before Bill Veeck's own father died, William Wrigley, Jr.—the Cubs' owner—had passed away. He was succeeded by his son, Philip K. Wrigley. And P. K. Wrigley and young Bill Veeck did not have the same respect for each other that their fathers had had. This was a classic case of the sons attempting to go their own way, indeed of attempting to rid themselves of their fathers' shadows.

Veeck recalled his struggles with Phil Wrigley as a clash between "the baseball men and the gum men." Phil Wrigley's son Bill, now the president of the gum empire, recalls it as a clash between a brash promoter—Veeck—and a more substantial operative—Phil Wrigley.

"They were more opposite," recalls Bill Wrigley from his offices at the William Wrigley Company. "Bill Veeck's father was considered a solid businessman while Bill was more a promoter, at least as my father saw it. You know, Bill Veeck had the exploding scoreboard. That's not the way we operated. In the early days there was a crossover between the Cubs and gum in terms of advertising, but the two organizations were separated. We were very careful about that. We wouldn't even take a spot on the baseball program."

Phil Wrigley loved day baseball and the sense of the game it imparted. "Dad used to say when night baseball got going that we were pioneering day baseball," says Bill Wrigley. "But when I got out of the service I did studies and it showed no need for night baseball. But Bill was promotion-oriented and he wanted the gimmick. We wanted a clean park where families could go in the daytime. These people grew up and brought their children and that's the way it was supposed to go."

Veeck and Phil Wrigley did agree that the beautification of the ballpark, Wrigley Field, was critical to keeping fans coming and keeping them happy once they arrived. It was an old park, of course, and small when looked at through today's eyes. But you look across the street and there's someone's front porch and, yes, isn't that a woman in an apron coming out after a home run has thwacked onto her house?

At Bill Veeck's death in 1986, seventy years after the Cubs moved in, the ballpark still had no lights. Baseball remained a sunny-day game there.

In an age of the multipurpose stadium, with its gently sloping aisles, the upper-deck spectator is so far from the action that the game may look no more exciting to him than on the home TV screen. Or there are stadiums built indoors. They protect fans from the weather, but no one sees a blade of grass. The ambient crowd noise is hollow. It must be what life in a glass bottle sounds like. Grass doesn't grow indoors when glass is painted to keep out the sun's rays, as they discovered in the Houston Astrodome.

Wrigley Field, though, was built for baseball in an era when fans often stood along the foul lines. Imagine how Bill Veeck would have loved that.

Wrigley Field, in Chicago's North Side, is the team's fifth home. When they moved into the park—originally built in 1914 for the rival Federal League—the stadium became known simply as Cubs Park. It held 14,000 people. Even now, after half a dozen renovations, Wrigley Field barely holds 37,000 fans. The center-field wall is only four-hundred feet from home plate. People remain close to the batter and pitcher and fielders. So do the neighbors across the street from the left-field stands, especially when the wind is blowing out and balls often wind up in people's homes.

In the early years every fan in the stands was at the same level as the action. It wasn't until 1926, when the name was changed to Wrigley Field, that the park was double-decked.

It is only a quarter block from the Addison Street Station to the park. If you haven't gone to the game, though, and you are in a passing El train, you can tell whether the Cubs won or lost. A blue flag with a white "W" flies atop the scoreboard signaling victory, and a white flag with a blue "L" means temporary despondency. In 1978 the Cubs even made a concession to the night with lights—a blue light atop the scoreboard means victory, a white light defeat.

This is the park that Bill Veeck returned to after his father's death. Phil Wrigley hired nineteen-year-old Bill as an office boy. So Phil Wrigley—in his son's words, the "solid businessman"—and Bill Veeck—"more a promoter"—began an eight-year association that ended when Veeck left to buy himself a minor-league team in Milwaukee. It was apparent that he never would advance beyond being the club's treasurer.

Still, Wrigley and Veeck worked well together on what they could agree on. The ivy, for instance. What else but green plants should symbolize a park that refuses to bow to night baseball? The ivy-covered bleachers of Wrigley Field give it a cozy summery tone as well as a distinctive look. It was the place an aging, ill, and mellowed Bill Veeck returned to in the 1980s in his last years to sit among the "Bleacher Bums," he and they shirtless under the sun.

Wrigley wanted to impart a verdant feel to his new bleachers in 1937. He asked Veeck to plant trees there. They didn't take, but the ivy did. And so the wall was covered with the clinging vines. They enabled the Cubs over the years to cling to their past as well.

By the late 1930s Veeck by now had studied engineering and accounting. He had taken extension courses from Northwestern University and attended the Lewis Institute. In addition to his burgeoning knowledge of baseball, and his longtime love for books and information, he now had become technically knowledgeable about the physical aspects of a ballpark. He probably knew more about every phase of what makes a ballpark tick—from the design of hot-dog stands to promoting their sale, to putting together a contract, to judging talent—than anyone in the Cubs' organization, if not in all of baseball.

Yet, he kept secret his accounting training. He explained years later that he thought he would have an advantage if the other owners considered him a buffoon.

The thirties was one of the great Cubs' eras, with three pennants and three second-place finishes. Never once did the team fail to finish at least fourteen games over .500. The managers were Joe McCarthy, Rogers Hornsby, Charlie Grimm, and Gabby Hartnett. The sluggers included Hack Wilson, Rogers Hornsby, and Billy Herman. Bill Lee and Lon Warneke were among the finest pitchers of that era.

As a teenager in the twenties, Veeck often had gone places with Grover Cleveland Alexander, an alcoholic. Over the years with the Cubs, young Veeck attached himself to the rowdy and the drinker, apparently fascinated by the fact that a man could stay out drinking all night and wind up playing like a future Hall of Famer the next day. The Cubs led the league in carousers.

Wrigley Field was also the the place where Babe Ruth added to his legend by supposedly calling his home run in the 1932 World Series between the Yankees and Cubs.

But the Cubs captured only one pennant in the 1940s, and none in the fifties, sixties, or seventies. They finally captured a division title in the 1980s, but within two years their manager was fired.

In this bread and circuses milieu, where life was a constant doubleheader and the popcorn always flowed, Bill Veeck met and married a Ringling Bros. and Barnum & Bailey Circus elephant trainer named Eleanor Raymond. He was twenty-one years old at their marriage on December 8, 1935. It produced three children—two boys and a girl—and ended in divorce in 1949.

She was described in *Billboard* as a "society girl of Evanston, Ill." money. She was educated, said later reports, in "fashionable Eastern finishing schools." And she liked to ride sidesaddle through rings of fire— at least the way Veeck remembered her. He said she was a bareback rider.

"I have never liked those who were cautious," Veeck said in an interview almost fifty years later. "My first wife was an equestrienne in the Ringling Brothers Circus who jumped a horse through a ring of fire sidesaddle. She was also an elephant trainer, lying under their feet. It's not true that elephants never forget. Years later, we went back to the circus and she went up to her favorite, Modock the Elephant. He swung his trunk and knocked her flat. There's a lesson in there, I suspect.

"She was a very interesting woman. The divorce was my fault. I couldn't leave baseball alone. It consumed my time. In the end, we parted on very good terms, which, of course, is the saddest way, since it means that everything we had had slithered away and been denigrated. Politeness is the end of passion."

But passion there must have been at one time. Shortly after their marriage she told an interviewer, "When I got married I thought I was all through with circuses. Apparently, I was wrong."

Veeck remained with the Cubs until 1941, a year after he had risen to treasurer. But it was apparent he would never run the ball club as its general manager. And he certainly would never own it.

His good buddy in the organization was the madcap manager whose enduring description is "left-handed banjo player." That would be Charlie Grimm. Veeck also palled around with the equipment manager, Joe Bernardi. His friends, his living habits, were varied and hardly traditional.

Veeck always had an eye out for the unusual. Roger Angell, who is a graceful baseball writer as well as a fiction editor at *The New Yorker*, enjoys telling of a Veeck-Angell conversation:

They were sitting in a restaurant in Scottsdale, Arizona, when talk got around to Veeck's early days with the Cubs and the oddments of a baseball team.

"Know what a Duker is?" asked Veeck.

"A what?" replied Angell.

"A Duker. Get up and walk past me."

Angell, who loves a mystery, stood up and walked past Veeck.

"The next thing I knew, the menu was in my hand, and Veeck says, 'You just bought a program.' That's what a Duker was. He'd put the program in your hand and you bought it."

Veeck went on to explain that a Duker would often keep some of the money for himself after stealthily selling the programs.

"And you know who the best Duker was we ever had at Wrigley Field?" Veeck asked Angell. Pause. "It was Jack Ruby."

Chapter 2

Bill Veeck had become treasurer of the Cubs by the age of twenty-seven in 1941. But it was apparent that he would go no higher. Despite his knowledge, his innovative ideas, his love for the Cubs and the game, Veeck had reached a plateau under P. K. Wrigley. And Veeck wanted desperately now to branch out, to put into effect what he had learned and developed and created. He wanted to own a ball club. The Milwaukee Brewers of the American Association were for sale. All you had to do was pay their debts, about $100,000, and they were yours.

"You may not know this," says P. K.'s son Bill, "but Dad gave Veeck a hand when he left the club and he let Charlie Grimm be his manager. Veeck wanted to run his own club in the way he wanted—which was most different from our own club."

Grimm, in addition to being the new manager of the Brewers, also had some money to invest in the team. Veeck got together assorted banks and friends and began the first of the mostly-other-people's-money deals that would land him baseball teams. He liked to say in later years that he put no money into the Brewers. His longtime business associate, Rudie Schaffer, claims that Veeck put about $40,000 into the club.

In any event, on June 23, 1941, Veeck finally had his own team. It played in Borchert Field, a rotting, unkempt wooden park that seemed a perfect home for a team that was in last place and whose attendance often literally could be counted in the dozens. The day he took over, his last-place club had already lost forty-three of its sixty-two games and were five and a half games behind the seventh-place team. That same day, Veeck often recalled, he had arrived in Milwaukee with $11 and promptly spent $10 buying rounds for the writers.

His years with the Brewers were a microcosm, and portent, of the more noted years he was to have later on. The Brewers gave him the opportunity to bring his unique outlook to the game and the way it should be sold. And it also afforded him the chance—which, of course, he never would pass up—of making fun of the Yankees (even if it was only a Yankee farm team) and also of learning to twist and bend the rules to give his team every advantage. Why, some owners might even call it cheating.

He went to work immediately, first painting and cleaning the place, and then doing a housecleaning of the players. By season's end he and Grimm had traded, sold, cut, or acquired forty-two players. Veeck told his new friends, the writers, that he had three teams: "One going, one coming, and one on the field."

The first day he looked at his team fewer than four hundred fans joined him in the stands. But word quickly spread that this new fellow, who wears an open-neck sports shirt and has a fringe of woolly hair, was interested in cleaning up the operation. Borchert Field had not been painted since 1924, seventeen years before, but Veeck spent $40,000 refurbishing the park.

Even now Rudie Schaffer enjoys reminiscing about his longtime friend and partner. Schaffer also has retained a sense of perspective and reality about Veeck.

"There came a time when he figured he ought to strike out on his own from the Cubs," says Schaffer, going back to Veeck's departure from Chicago. "At the time I was secretary and business manager of the Brewers. We struck it off right from the word 'go.' He had his own preconceived ideas of what he wanted to do promotionally. We were not very promotion-minded in Milwaukee at the time, of course. The one thing he did almost immediately was to clean up the park. We had gone into the doldrums because of money. He was concerned with hyping up the team and making it fun for people to come to the ballpark.

"When we went to war he realized there were people who were fans but couldn't come to the games because they worked at night. So he started scheduling games in the morning and they started at 8:30, and of course we served coffee and doughnuts to the people and they could come from different swing shifts right to the ball game. It wasn't a real bell ringer, but it got a lot of attention for the Brewers and a lot of favorable comment from people."

Schaffer was to go with him to the majors in Cleveland and St. Louis and Chicago, and from a business standpoint it was always the same. "He would have voting control. Sometimes he would borrow money from a bank, or he'd mortgage his own house and put his own scratch in. In addition to that, he'd always have a syndicate. It would always be people who knew his operation and gave him voting control."

And did Veeck always make money? "Yes, but it depends on how you define making money. In his last stint with the White Sox we didn't have profitable years, but in the end he sold it for more than he paid for it, so he made money."

But why was he always jumping around looking for teams? "Once he accomplished what he wanted to—or if he couldn't, if he were stymied—he'd lose interest."

But in Milwaukee there was a beginning, and Veeck loved beginnings. He also had this thing for wounded birds, and no turkey was more damaged than this minor-league team.

"Bill had a passion for taking somebody that had a problem, whether it was a drinking problem or a family problem or some physical problem, and he tried to resurrect those people," says Schaffer. "He would seek these people out from other clubs, and as it happens he'd get a bargain rate on the guy. But he had a fascination of trying to rehabilitate people. I think it went back to the time he was a kid working on the Cubs and people like Hack Wilson were with the Cubs."

Veeck's methods worked wonders in Milwaukee. Not in the first year, of course. The team was too far gone for that. But he had established the fact that someone cared for the club and its fans. And he also established baseball as fun. What happened in Milwaukee became known as "Veeck's Varieties." He cut the club's debt at the end of the season by amassing $60,000 in cash for selling three pitchers—Johnny Schmitz and Vallie Eaves to the Cubs, Dave Koslo to the Giants.

Eaves, an American Indian, had been one of Veeck's reclamation projects. Schaffer recalled Eaves as a hard-drinking performer whom other clubs had given up on. "Bill brought him along and then sold him, but once he left Milwaukee, no one gave him the same kind of attention and he went sour again," says Schaffer.

Before Veeck was finished redoing his team, he sold or otherwise got rid of all but two players from his 1941 squad. That squad had no left-handed power hitters, which distressed Veeck, since his right-field fence was only 265 feet from home plate. The rival Minneapolis team, though, had left-handed sluggers. When Veeck saw them come into his park and drill the ball over the right-field fence, he did something about it. The next time Minneapolis arrived their hitters found the fence in right field raised by sixty feet with chicken wire. Veeck had customized his ballpark to suit—rather, hinder—the enemy. But the next season, when the Brewers landed the left-handed slugger Hal Peck, the wire came down.

Yet, 1942 made Veeck a national name, perhaps the first minor-league baseball executive to create such an impact. Small wonder that with his fan gimmicks in such a relatively small market he caught the attention of Charlie Finley, who was based in Chicago and well aware of what Veeck was doing.

What Veeck did was throw the game open to the public. And each time he did, it was a surprise. He never announced in advance his plans. One day he might offer a "country store" promotion. Lucky fans would get a cake of ice, poultry, or fruit—or a live lobster. Inspired by the Olsen and Johnson vaudeville team and their zany *Hellzapoppin'* revue, Veeck also staged a giveaway with a pair of guinea pigs as the prize. Or a stepladder. Or a keg of nails.

Every day became special, honoring this lodge or that industrial group. Ceremonies included introductions and rounds of applause. The bosses loved it, their spouses loved it, and the workers loved it. In short, it made ticket buyers of them.

Veeck began his tradition of peripatetic wanderings through the stands. An account of the time describes Veeck sitting in the stands second-guessing Grimm: "I don't know what Charley's thinking of—this pitcher hasn't got a thing." Then, only after he had established a rapport with those sitting around him, he would introduce himself as the team president. Fans would leave happy and somewhat proud. On their way out there would be Veeck greeting them, shaking hands, thanking them for their business.

But he spent as much time away from the ballpark. That first winter he started making speeches—the Kiwanis, church suppers, father-and-son banquets, always with a pocketful of tickets. On one of these swings, speaking at an industrial plant, the idea hit home that many of these workers couldn't see his Brewers play because they were working the swing shift with the war under way.

So he conceived of an idea that brought him national prominence and a spot on *Fox Movietone News*: morning baseball, timed to fit the schedule of war workers. The morning of the Brewers' first swing-shift game, Veeck personally served the fans corn flakes and milk. And he dressed his orchestra (yes, bands played at every game) in nightgowns.

The game didn't start on time—the visiting team's train didn't arrive until noon because of the crazy rail traffic and changes in scheduling—but the Brewers won by 20–0.

It was a club that was getting better as Veeck continued to provide it with players. It seemed not to matter at all that the Brewers hadn't even gone to spring training in the sunshine, where every proper baseball team belongs. In past years they had trained in Ocala, Florida. Veeck, though, decided—long before Baseball Commissioner Landis had made it a wartime rule—that the club would train close to home. Instead of Ocala the Brewers trained in Waukesha, fourteen miles west of Milwaukee.

Anyway, said Veeck, "spring training is 50 percent for publicity, 25 percent for looking over rookies, and 25 percent for conditioning."

He got more publicity than even he had bargained for when sportswriters and photographers discovered that snow was still on the baseball diamond at Waukesha as the Brewers took the field. Visiting ballplayers in 1942 also found the infield very slow. It was filled with loose sand.

"Our own boys haven't been able to steal any bases," explained Veeck, "and I'll be damned if anybody else does."

Rival owners soon became nettled by his machinations, often made at their expense and egos. To kid them about their park's poor lighting, he put lanterns on the batter's cage when his Brewers were taking batting practice. Another time he was invited to speak in St. Paul, a rival city. He told the group what a miserable team the town had. He also was not a favorite in Indianapolis. With good reason.

In July of 1942 Indianapolis was leading the Brewers by 3–2 with two out in the fifth inning at Milwaukee. A storm was brewing, but one more out would make the game official and the Brewers the losers. When the next batter came to the plate, though, the lights suddenly went out. "The umpires and Indianapolis cried like a baby," said Veeck. It took fifteen minutes before Veeck's electricians could find the proper fuses. The lights came on just as the storm broke overhead.

Yet those same lights failed Veeck on the final day of the 1942 season, a campaign in which the Brewers had elevated themselves to second place and now, in fact, were fighting for the pennant. If the Brewers played two games, they had to win both. But if they could play only one—and he had only one trusted pitcher available—his team had a better chance at taking the pennant.

Just before game time, a warm summer shower hit the field. Veeck quickly put his grounds crew to work. For ninety minutes they tended the field while Kansas City cried to the umpires. Two hours later Kansas City phoned the league president. Two and a half hours later they telephoned their parent organization—yes, the New York Yankees, of course—asking for help.

The game finally did start and the Brewers had the lead going into the eighth inning. Then Kansas City went ahead. "That's when I should have turned on the light," Veeck was to recall soon afterward in *The Saturday Evening Post*. "That would have invalidated the game we were losing. Under the rules, you can't play a game partly under daylight and partly under bulbs. Then we could have started a new game, giving us a fresh chance at that one win we needed for the pennant. I just wasn't thinking."

He didn't miss much else, though. Throughout the season he put on shows, including himself. He played a slide whistle; Grimm, of course, was the left-handed banjoist, and Schaffer, the money man, played a broomstick cello. Veeck liked to describe Schaffer as having "a great background for usury." Grimm had no contract, merely a handshake, and, according to Veeck, Grimm "rarely knows how much money he is making."

This oddball approach to the game included transportation. Veeck bought a truck and commuted to the park in it rather than a car.

While Veeck did put money into the park, he was unable to fix its peculiar configuration. Somehow, the park was misshapen. Fans who were able to look at right field couldn't see left field. Fans who looked to left couldn't see right. That was fine with Veeck. He told the fans, "Got to come out twice to see the whole team."

A pretty good team it was, too, with that second-place finish. It attracted 273,000 fans—200,000 more customers than in Veeck's first season. Indeed, the Brewers had the best attendance in all minor-league baseball. Veeck was honored as the minor-league executive of the year. His fame began to spread. Of course not everything he did immediately turned to gold. But he came close.

After the 1942 season, he ran another player sale. This time he sold Eddie Stanky and Heinz Becker to the Cubs, while Peck wound up in Brooklyn. He had sold Peck for $40,000 when he got a phone call from Peck's home in Genesee Depot, Wisconsin. Rats had been marauding Peck's henhouse. One morning the outfielder set out after them with his shotgun. Now his wife was on the phone to Veeck, crying that Peck had stumbled and shot off the second and third toes of his left foot.

Veeck recalled that not only as a bad day, but as a bad night too. "We were giving a prize for speed in circling the bases," he said, "and naturally we expected to win it or we wouldn't be giving it. Well, here was the only guy we had who could run, and he shoots himself in the foot. Maybe you think we didn't have to do some chiseling with those stopwatches. There was only one thing to do with my toeless wonder. The minute that our season ended, I got right on the train and spent two days yelling myself hoarse for the Brooklyn Dodgers. I knew that Larry MacPhail was the only guy in the racket with enough moxie to take a chance on an eight-toed ballplayer."

Veeck, meanwhile, consulted orthopedists who assured him that three points of foot contact are all that a ballplayer needs—a big toe, little toe, and a heel. MacPhail, the Dodgers' president, bought that analysis only up to a point. He paid $23,000 for Peck, $17,000 less than the player originally would have brought. In other words, the accident cost Veeck $8,500 a toe.

MacPhail's son Lee was to have many more tangled dealings with Veeck in MacPhail's tenure as president of the American League. "I want you to know I liked him," says Lee MacPhail, "but he was the reason several rules were put into baseball. One of them is you can't change the fences during the season without the approval of the league. In Milwaukee and Cleveland he used to change the fences depending on what team was coming in.

"Another time in Milwaukee, he didn't have enough pitchers for a series. There had been a rain, but not that much rain, not enough to cancel a game. So he got the hose out and turned it loose on the field and turned it into a quagmire so the game was called and he got his pitchers an extra day of rest. Some people didn't cotton to those sort of things."

Veeck loved to hate the Yankees. More than that, he delighted in embarrassing them and never—never—missed the golden opportunity. Part of it went back to his life with the Cubs in the thirties, when the Yankees swept his team in four straight games in the two World Series they played in that era. "They never did like him, you understand," says Happy Chandler, who was baseball commissioner in Veeck's early major-league career.

The Yankees' poker face, their public persona, was personified by their general manager, George Weiss. "Weiss was just the opposite of Bill," recalls MacPhail. "Weiss was no nonsense, no sense of humor. And Bill just loved to do everything he could to upset George Steinbrenner.

"In 1945, Roy Hamey was running the Kansas City club for the Yankees and Bill was in Milwaukee with the American Association club. The Yankees didn't really have any kind of team in Kansas City since all the players were in the service. For the entire season they drew something like 37,000 people, and that included 7,000 on opening day.

"In the old Kansas City ballpark the office was right above the turnstiles. So now, Milwaukee's in town and Kansas City is going to draw their six hundred or seven hundred people. Roy Hamey looks out at the people coming in—and there's Veeck standing there, and Veeck's giving out dollar bills. The admission was a dollar. And Veeck is saying, 'Here's your money back. It's a shame you have to pay to see a team as bad as this.' And Hamey goes through the roof."

Veeck's dealing created a solid team, though—good enough to capture the American Association pennant for three straight years, starting in 1943. But in December 1943, at the age of twenty-nine, he enlisted in the Marines.

On his thirtieth birthday he was named the honor man of his platoon at Camp Elliott in San Diego, where he was taking basic training, even though, he was considerably older than the average recruit. Still he was one of the first in his platoon of sixty to scale the obstacle course, and he made "sharpshooter" on the firing range, although he claimed he never had fired a rifle before. He spent much of his spare time "snapping into position" with his rifle. The work paid off—he shot 302 of a possible 340.

He was trained in using an antiaircraft gun, and the hottest place for a Marine with such a skill was the Pacific. So in 1944 they sent him over. He fought on Guadalcanal and then Bougainville. Marine records show that in the spring of '44 his right foot was crushed by the recoil of an antiaircraft gun on Bougainville. If his foot was broken years earlier after he fell at Kenyon—as he often claimed—it is possible that the war injury became more serious as a result of that earlier accident. Now it meant hospitalization—confinement—a state that Veeck would not tolerate.

It was part of his battle with various illnesses—and a denial that anything was wrong with him—that continued until his death more than forty years later. Even now people who knew him will immediately recall the cigarette after cigarette that he jammed into his mouth—eighty of them a day. Or his obsession with having something to drink. For most of his life it was beer, a dozen or more daily. When he got older he switched to wine. And when he got sicker it was iced tea or a soft drink. But always there was the cigarette and the liquid. And, unless asked, he didn't talk about his illnesses. When he mentioned them it was with a derisive sneer.

Corporal Bill Veeck argued with doctors about the length of stay in the hospital and left too soon. He was told to keep off the leg, but he put pressure on it. He was fitted for a brace so that he could walk around rather than have someone push him in a wheelchair. He refused to sit around.

But he also got rid of the Brewers in 1945. A few years later he explained to people in Cleveland that his wife's health had been failing and he wanted to spend time with her. Later, though, Veeck contended that the real reason was their crumbling relationship. He blamed it on the time that baseball demanded from him. He sold the Brewers for a $250,000 profit and put much of the money into a ranch in Tucson that he dubbed the Lazy Vee.

Rudie Schaffer recalls the time and says that the long hours Veeck was on his back made him reflective as well as restless. "He had a lot of time and thought about what he wanted to do. He had been in the major leagues with the Cubs, and that was going to be his next move. He no longer was interested in running the Milwaukee Brewers and arranged to sell it. He immediately began working on buying the Cleveland Indians."

Did he think about the Cubs? "Oh, yes, yes. He would have loved that more than anything else, and as a matter of fact he tried to buy them on any number of occasions, but P. K. Wrigley and others always discouraged him by saying they had no ideas to sell."

That didn't stop Veeck from looking around. His eyes fondly embraced a team such as major-league baseball had never envisioned.

Chapter 3

Veeck had some ideas besides owning a traditional team. Indeed, he had one of the most radical ideas anyone in baseball ever came up with.

For many years he had followed the Negro Leagues and was familiar with many of the ballplayers. He had seen them play in the Midwest, a favorite region for barnstorming. Of course there never had been an acknowledged black ballplayer in the major leagues, even though some players who claimed they were Latin probably were American blacks.

What Veeck proposed in 1945 was to stock the Philadelphia Phillies—a team that produced the worst record in baseball that season—with American Negro ballplayers. He wanted to create an all-black, or mostly black, team to compete in the National League.

For several years, during the low-talent era of wartime baseball, there had been repeated stirrings to bring the Kansas City Monarchs intact into big-league baseball. But now Veeck actually told Commissioner Kenesaw Mountain Landis that he was planning to buy the Phillies and to fill the club with black talent. The Phillies were sold quickly to someone else.

On the record, Landis did not oppose Veeck. Why, when Leo Durocher, the Dodgers' manager, once had said he would employ black ballplayers if it weren't for the commissioner, Landis, all dignity, replied, "Negroes are not barred from organized baseball by the commissioner. There is no rule in organized baseball prohibiting their participation."

The 1945 Phillies seemed to have suffered the wartime player drain more than anyone else. They had won only 46 games while losing 108,

25

a winning percentage of .299. Happy Chandler, who replaced Landis as commissioner, recalls the incident this way:

"Veeck wanted to buy a black team and put it in Philadelphia. But he was not popular with the other owners. The obvious thing, of course, was that he was smarter than most of them. He was a smart baseball man. He knew the rules, and a lot of these Yankees, they were crybabies."

So Veeck did not become the first person to put a black player in a major-league uniform. That honor was to wait until 1947 and go to Branch Rickey of the Brooklyn Dodgers. But Veeck did put the second one in, as Veeck became the first American League owner to hire a black ballplayer.

With the war over, Veeck had to look to the more established channels. He learned that the Pittsburgh Pirates and Cleveland Indians were for sale. His major-league career was about to resume.

His wife was in Tucson for her health, he said. And he still loved baseball. In fact, part of the Veeck legend is that he got back into baseball because the Cubs and White Sox played a spring-training game in Tucson. His National Pastime juices again began to flow. What he needed was a baseball team, but this time a major-league team.

He came across the Indians. While they might not have been in the same funk as the Brewers when he stepped in, the Indians were hardly a baseball power. They had not won a pennant since 1920.

In 1945 they were able to draw barely half a million fans. The Indians had a strange playing arrangement. Since 1932 they had played their home games in two different parks—League Park, an unusual concrete marvel when it was built in 1910, and Municipal Stadium. The much larger stadium was generally reserved for Sunday and holiday games.

This dichotomy symbolized Cleveland baseball. A charter member of the American League, Cleveland began play in 1901. But originally Cleveland was a National League city. It was an N.L. Cleveland team that brought Cy Young to the big leagues. And in its final season it produced the worst record in the National's history.

Cleveland's first baseball year was 1879. The manager-pitcher, Jim McCormick, was also a 20-game winnner—and a 40-game loser. His team eventually dropped out, but another club was created in 1888. Young joined the team in 1890, beginning his 511-victory career with a 13-12 record. The club became a power in the 1890s, though, with Young a consistent 30-game winner—36 in 1892, 32 in 1893, 35-10 in 1895. Jess Burkett captured the batting titles in 1895 and 1896 with averages of .423 and .410.

But the team's owners raped their own franchise—and the city. They had also acquired control of the St. Louis franchise. Suddenly they started shifting Cleveland's stars to St. Louis. In 1899 the manager, Young, and Burkett all wound up in St. Louis. The remainder of the club—its informal nickname was the Spiders—struggled through a farcical season. They lost 134 games, winning only 20. In that woeful campaign, the Spiders suffered through losing streaks of 24, 16, and 14 games.

It got so bad that no one in Cleveland wanted to see them play. So no one did. From mid-August to the end of the season, the team left home and played every game on the road. The National League dropped the Spiders.

While the Indians never performed so badly, they hadn't won, either. A 1920 pennant was, in fact, the only first-place finish the Indians could boast in their history. A second-place finish in 1940 had been their highest since 1926. Now, with Veeck interested, the Indians had the great Bob Feller, of course, and a manager-shortstop in Lou Boudreau.

"When you stop and think about him," says Rudie Schaffer, "Bill was like a kid with a new toy, and once the novelty of the toy wears off, he looks for another toy. That was Bill Veeck. Success came to him so easily with the Indians that he thought he could do it any place. When he felt that he had accomplished just about anything you could do in Cleveland—setting all-time attendance records, winning a world's championship—he had to set out for new worlds to conquer."

First, though, Veeck had to see if this was a team that would interest him. When he arrived in Cleveland he took a cab. As usual, he got into the front seat with the driver. Veeck always seemed embarrassed to be sitting in the back seat. He asked the driver when the Indians' next game was. The cabbie didn't know. Bad promotion, thought Veeck. He was to repeat that anecdote many times.

Veeck went to Cleveland in secrecy so no one would know he was negotiating for the club. He registered at hotels as "Mr. Edwards" or "Mr. Lewis." He went to ball games. He even attended the United States Open golf tournament nearby. But he tried to be careful. His limp—he wore a cast—made him an easy target. Finally he acquired a host of investors, including the meat-packing names of Armour and Swift and the show-biz name of Bob Hope, who lived in Cleveland.

This was not an ideal situation to step into, but Veeck became convinced that Cleveland fans would back a winning team. He noted that with remarkably poor publicity and public relations, the team virtually was breaking even. He discovered, though, that if you were a fan you couldn't even call the ball club. The team's offices were at old League

Park. If you wanted to call the team for any information, you could not get past the stadium operator. The team was merely a tenant. League Park's concession stands, rest rooms, clubhouses, and seating were in poor shape.

Yet, it was typical of Veeck that he saw something in all of this that interested him. After all, hadn't he revived the moribund Brewers? That was in the minor leagues, though. This was the big time. It took him until late June 1946, but finally he got the financing he needed and took over the Indians. It was five years to the day since his purchase of the Brewers.

Spud Goldstein helped Veeck get the money for the Indians, a deal that required about $2.2 million and another large group of investors. Goldstein remembers it with fondness:

"In 1945 my brother was producing a picture called *The Egg and I*. Fred MacMurray and Claudette Colbert. At Universal. Bill had a ranch in Tucson, and they claim that he went out of town to buy a ball club, and he kept going until he wound up in Cleveland.

"Bob Hope had lived in Cleveland and about $200,000 was left for people who lived in Cleveland, so Bob Hope had about one-eighth of the $200,000. About 15 or 20 percent of the total cost belonged to Bill.

"I had gotten together with him because he needed venture capital, and I figured that was the end of it. But Bill called me one day and asked if I could get some Indian costumes. He was putting the band in a tepee behind the center-field fence. Anyway, after this I was ready to leave to go to Hollywood, and he said, 'Why don't you stick around?' I got intrigued with the whole thing. I liked it better than pictures. I started out as the public relations director for about a month. I'm the only public relations director who never gave out a story. Why did Bill Veeck need a public relations director? So then I became traveling secretary."

At the age of thirty-two Bill Veeck became a major-league owner. In Cleveland they described him as an ex-Kenyon halfback. He promised to reinstitute ladies' day and to find a radio station to broadcast the games. No one had wanted to in 1945. He said someone would be able to answer the fans' phone calls and that cab drivers would know when the team was playing. He also took a swipe at the baseball Establishment. "Baseball generally has been too grim, too serious," said Veeck on taking over. "It should be fun, and I hope to make it fun for everyone around here."

Veeck also imparted his philosophy of the game: "There are two ways of going about this business. One, you can budget your expenditures over a season based on past attendance and probable receipts. That's percentage baseball and I don't believe in it. I can't say it too strongly that I am opposed to that type of operation. The other way is to get more people in your park, increase your receipts, and spend more money for players and salaries. That's what I hope to do."

There also was Veeck speaking on owners vs. players: "I believe in a closer relationship between the club owner and player. I don't understand why an owner considers it lèse-majesté to go to dinner with one of his players. That's part of the old, stuffy tradition," said Veeck, who wore a sports shirt at the conference announcing the multimillion-dollar deal.

Then he went to the ball game and, reflecting on all the secrecy that had marked the negotiations, said, "I don't have to hide any longer." He was in the stands, out in front of everybody, to stay. And that very day, his Indians, who trailed the first-place Boston Red Sox by 17 games, promptly defeated them with a home run in the bottom of the eighth inning.

Bob Fishel was the unlikely partner-in-puff for Bill Veeck. With Fishel as his reluctant, but fascinated, observer, Bill Veeck began a legendary attack on some of America's most highly held values: doctor's orders, abstinence, a good night's sleep. In short, Veeck destroyed moderation. He enjoyed charades. So why not pick up in the early evening, catch a plane to New York, pop into Skitch Henderson's, stay up all night playing charades, and then catch the first flight back in the morning?

Did someone say something about Cleveland not being a party town? Veeck invented his own party. Wherever he went the shadows lengthened. He had a talent for bringing out the impish side in people, a side they didn't know they had, or if they were aware of it, tried to suppress. But that was hardly possible when he was around.

"I was a tremendous baseball fan, living in Cleveland," recounts Fishel. "I was with an advertising agency and I had just come out of the service in the spring of '46. I had been with this agency a long time, and when I came back they decided to give me small accounts. They gave me three— the Cleveland *Plain-Dealer*, a shirt company, and the third was the Yellow Cab company, a taxi-cab monopoly in Cleveland.

"Yellow Cab was run by racketeers, a very interesting company. But it was going to start a football team known as the Cleveland Browns. Because I had the Yellow Cab account I automatically had the Cleveland Browns account. And I was in Paul Brown's office before they even played a game. In June of 1946, a Saturday—we worked on Saturday—and my office called all excited that Bill Veeck had just called.

"Bill Veeck's name was in the headlines every day. In Cleveland they don't even run baseball on the seventh sports page now, which can drive a club out of there. I thought somebody was pulling my leg. I called the number he left, and Bill Veeck was in Lakeside Hospital, having surgery on his leg. This was before it was amputated. He said he wanted to see me right away because he wanted to run advertising in the next day's paper. I said this is Saturday, it's too late for Sunday's paper. But I went out there anyway."

Fishel found Veeck in bed, but doing business. "The theme of what he wanted was to give the Indians back to the fans. Bill offered all the radio stations in Cleveland—this was before TV, which was just coming—free rights to the games. Anything they sold was theirs. Great idea. So in the season we had as many as four different stations broadcasting our games, where the year before we didn't have one. That year, as many as six or seven stations broadcast the games.

"He took over June 22, 1946, the day he called me into the hospital. Paul Brown never forgave me. He knew baseball came first with me, but baseball never came first with Paul Brown.

"Bill and I couldn't have been two more different people. I'm somewhat introverted. He's totally extroverted. Different people, but we got along fabulously, right from the beginning."

The Browns had four full-time office employees. The ticket manager was Edna Jamieson, and Veeck had asked her about public relations and she said the club didn't have a public relations man and that the only one she knew in the advertising business who came to the games was Bob Fishel. That is how Veeck found Fishel, who was to give Edna Jamieson a Christmas present in thanks every year for the rest of her life.

"We had all kinds of experiences together," Fishel continues, his face glowing. "Some of them I was for, some I was against. One of the greatest promotions he ever had was for Kenny Keltner, a good ballplayer who had a lot of good years at third base. He's still a candidate for the Hall of Fame. He's the one who made the great plays that stopped DiMaggio's streak in '41. Fans wrote in letters about that night. Then a fan wrote a letter to Whitey Lewis, a good sportswriter then, a great guy, womanizer, used to play Monday-night poker games. Whitey came with the letter to Bill. This fellow wrote in and said, 'Here I am a GI, like thousands of other GI's, and you have a day and you're giving this guy a car and gifts to ballplayers who makes ten times as much as I do.' Keltner was making $35,000, which in those days was a lot of money. It was signed, 'Your fan, Joe Earley.'

"Bill looked at it and said, 'Greatest thing I ever saw. We'll have a Joe Earley Night for Mr. Average Fan.' And it was spectacular."

They still talk about it in Cleveland. Joe Earley Night. The night the fan was honored. "It was spectacular. It was great," says Fishel. "They brought in a 1922 or 1923 car that could hardly move anymore. That was going to be the car they were giving him. But they really gave him a nice car after that. They gave him some other junk—a hundred pounds of ice, four chickens. Then they brought out a trailer and it had a bonfire on it. They didn't say anything, but I knew what the bonfire was for. Toward the end of the program, Bill announced that now we're calling on the vice president of the Cleveland Trust Company, and Bill says, 'Mr. Earley, a GI just out of service, has a mortgage on his house, and we're going to burn the mortgage.' A great thing. Everybody was sympathetic to that because everybody had a mortgage. So they lit the bonfire and the vice president of the bank burned the mortgage. It was a tremendous thing. They did all kinds of things like that.

"And twenty-five years later, I think the Yankees were playing in Cleveland, they tried to recreate that day. Bill Veeck was there. Even I was there. And it flopped. Fans didn't relate to it. He had a lot of other promotions that were great. On Saturday he had Ladies' Days, which are now illegal, and he gave away boutonnieres, Hawaiian orchids, when they were rare, and silk stockings, when they were totally rare."

Now, many people have tried to live high and to do well at the same time. The thing about Veeck—and what has helped keep his remarkable exploits fresh and constantly retold—is that he succeeded doing both. Sportswriters—and, I suppose, fans—will love you for being an oddball, a shaker, or a rogue. But after a while they will get to you, wear you down, expose your flaws—unless you produce. And even producing doesn't guarantee tranquility (see: Williams, Ted, and Maris, Roger). Still, America's heroes had a longer shelf life in Veeck's time. We would not be so quick to take potshots at their clay feet. Let someone get to the top today, though, and that person becomes as scrutinized as if he covered up the Watergate break-in.

Not so with Veeck. Perhaps part of it was because he not only delivered, but he was part of an era when excesses were beloved by newspaper reporters. They had been known to keep late hours, belt down a few, drag on a couple dozen cigarettes a day. This was not too long after *The Front Page*, remember. Hecht and MacArthur and the legendary reporter lived in black-and-white on movie screens—the reporter forever rushing into a phone booth, tilting back his fedora, and shouting, "Sweetheart, get me the desk."

Reporters in Bill Veeck's time drank not only with one another, but with the people they covered. Veeck kept up that crowd-pleasing habit until the end. He refined the art at Max Gruber's. If the fun life in Paris in the 1920s revolved around the salons, then Cleveland society, the underworld, the sporting fraternity and the fun-seekers revolved around Gruber's nightclub after World War II. Forty years later, Max Gruber has no trouble remembering how he and Veeck had met:

"In 1946, Bill Veeck came to Cleveland, anonymously, and checked into a hotel. Apparently some Chicago lawyers told him to get in contact with me. I had the reputation—and I'm not bragging—of a trial lawyer. I also owned with my brother a large restaurant of 450 seats patterned after the '21' Club. It was very expensive and we tried to be exclusive. It was the place to go.

"Anyway, I met the burrhead. He was a very fashionable guy. He was negotiating with a friend of mine who owned the Cleveland Indians, so that's how I met Bill Veeck. My initial impression of him was that he was a bright guy, very clever, very public relations oriented. At my restaurant he picked up a lot of big checks. He was the last of the big spenders. I went over to him and said, 'You're the last of the big spenders. Are you trying to take the town by storm? Where did you learn this?'

"He said, 'My father was a sportswriter,' and I said, 'You got it from Dad, huh?' My impression was he was very likable, very public oriented. I had the feeling that he would get far in Cleveland."

Soon, Veeck and Gruber presided over the Jolly Set. Their exploits were chronicled almost daily in the newspapers. What the Jolly Set said and did became a sort of Great Lakes Algonquin Round Table, merely missing a Dorothy Parker or two.

"The Jolly Set was a group of people hell-bent for fun," recalls Gruber. "It was spearheaded by a fellow named Winsor French, a gossip columnist, and a group of sportswriters who patronized the restaurant. It ranged from a fight promoter named Larry Atkins, to Larry Hanna, the richest man in Cleveland, to the reporters—but of course Veeck really made it. He romanced the reporters, set up the Wigwam Room [the reporters' dining room at the stadium] and sold them tickets. There was a newspaper artist and he'd run a cartoon once a week, sometimes on Page One, of the conversation of the Jolly Set."

Late at night, very late, Gruber recalled, Veeck would reminisce about his father. "He adored his father. Every time he got a little too much of that beer or wine in him he always told some kind of story about his father. I recall once we had a conversation and I asked him how did your Dad ever get into baseball. He said his father was criticizing the Chicago Cubs so damn much that one day Wrigley says to him, 'If you can do any better, you run the club.' That's the way he told me. His father trained him in public relations. I asked him where he learned all that crap, and he said his father. The rich and the poor, the famous, bookmakers, his father trained him."

Although Gruber stayed open late for Veeck and his cronies, at the end of the evening everybody went home—everybody except Bill Veeck.

"I personally think that the hours he kept...he'd go out in the early morning instead of going home. He'd go to a truck stop and talk baseball with truck drivers and give them some free tickets. I think he was trying— and I'm just guessing—that he had this problem with his leg. He'd have it cut off a little every once in a while. I think he had a fear of death. I think that's why he kept these hours that no man could hardly keep up with. This is just my guess. But he was very strong. He could play doubles in tennis. You could see him with the wooden leg. You could go up to the gym with him, very strong."

The amputation of the right foot took place in November of 1946. Was it only the war wound that caused it? Was it the fall from the dormitory ledge at Kenyon College?

His son Peter believes it might have been aggravated by the fact that as a child Veeck had the bone disease osteomyelitis. One of the symptoms is infection, causing a continual problem with pus in the affected area.

Veeck was hospitalized in late October 1946 with an infection. Antibiotics didn't help. "Right now, the doctors are trying to get the infection confined to the foot," he said in a bedside interview. "I'm so full of penicillin that if you were to wring me out, you'd have enough for a dispensary."

At that point Veeck had undergone surgery ten times attempting to save the foot. Indeed, he had been hospitalized three times alone since buying the Indians in June. As a result, he attended games in a cast much of the time. He hauled himself into Gruber's for an evening of fun. He seemed never to miss a step.

On the eve of the surgery he said, in a manner described as "airily," that he had told the surgeons to "go ahead and now it's their ball. When a nurse comes in here and starts brushing me up, I'll know it's getting on for that time. There's only one thing I'm sure about. That's the two and a half years I wasted trying to make this thing work when I could have been learning to use an artificial foot."

Yet, he told the surgeons that he planned to attend baseball's winter meetings in Los Angeles in a month. And that he would go through spring training in 1947 on crutches.

To many people, Veeck's excesses were part of his charm. If they saw them as weakness or as a search for...what?—escape? release? merely fun?...his friends kept it to themselves.

"I can't figure out any other reason other than he had a fear of death," says Gruber. "Why go to a truck stop at three in the morning with twenty other truck drivers and just talk? And sit there for a long time, sometimes for two hours. That led me to the belief that he didn't want to go to bed. I know this—that when he did go home, he'd put on a record, he'd soak himself in that damn bathtub for a couple of hours and smoke cigarettes instead of going to bed. All I can say about him is he was very brilliant. Whether it was an act or not, people loved him."

But Veeck also understood baseball. And he helped transform the Indians from a collection of good ballplayers who were lacking in big hitters and good fielding. In Bob Feller, they had baseball's most acclaimed pitcher, just returned from the war and on his way to the season of the year: a record 348 strikeouts, a majors-leading 26 victories, as well as the leader in games started (42), games completed (36), innings pitched, and shutouts.

On a team that won only 68 games, he captured 38 percent of their victories. And one of them was a 1-0 no-hitter over the Yankees in New York.

Feller respects Veeck, but also believes there was a measure of luck in some of the deals he created to help make the Indians contenders. Feller is an outspoken Hall of Famer who does not bite his tongue. That opinionated trait has not always made him admired. Still, ego and all, he knows baseball and not only talks it all the time as the Indians' principal speaker at banquets, but he still pitches in charity games in his sixties. His fingers are remarkably thick and wide, as if a giant's hand were grafted onto a normal body. Those fingers gripped a baseball and enabled him to become the fastest hurler of his time, if not all time.

"Bill was the luckiest guy in the world when he came here," contends Feller. "He bought the ball club, which was going nowhere, then he made the trade for Gordon, which was real good. But see, Allie Reynolds became a great pitcher after he traded him."

In 1946, with almost half a season gone when he arrived, Veeck could do little with the team but make some patchwork adjustments. Reynolds was an 11-15 pitcher for the Indians that season, and he was already thirty-one years old. Joe Gordon, meanwhile, batted only .210 for the Yankees in 1946. He, too, was thirty-one. Veeck made a deal after that season that transformed both clubs, with Gordon coming to Cleveland, where he joined Boudreau in a peerless double-play combination, while Reynolds became a great clutch pitcher for the Yankees.

"I had a contract when Veeck bought the ball club that was based on attendance and performance," Feller recalls. "I got a nickel a head on everybody we drew over 500,000. We never dreamed of drawing over 900,000 even if we won the pennant. Well, we came far from winning the pennant. We finished sixth, but we drew 1.1 million fans and I got about $25,000 more than I had anticipated. Of course if I was getting fifty cents a head like Reggie Jackson did, instead of getting $25,000, I'd be getting $250,000."

Was Feller discouraged playing in a city that never won a pennant?

"I didn't have that feeling. We had some good ball clubs. In fact in 1940 we lost by one game when we got beat 1-0 when I lost a 2-hitter."

That season the Indians audaciously presented a petition to the team's owners to fire Manager Ossie Vitt. But with the Indians in a pennant race, there weren't going to be any changes. The Tigers, paced by Hank Greenberg, who led the league with 41 homers and 150 runs batted in, captured the pennant.

"There was a more personal relationship among players," says Feller. "There was more roots, more loyalty between the players and the club owners and the players and the fans. You see, I think the agents have taken the players away from the clubs. They want to divide and conquer. They want to keep the players from being friends with the general managers and owners. It's the old army game of divide and conquer.

"I think they've done a great job for the players, but they didn't invent the pension plan. I know who invented the pension plan. It was Happy Chandler, Lee MacPhail, and Dixie Walker, and Johnny Murphy. It was 1946 and they wanted to give the guys amnesty who jumped to come back from Mexico. That's where it started, and why. Chandler still lives in Versailles, Kentucky, but they pronounce it Versales. Those ridge-runners in Kentucky don't pronounce it ver-sigh. That's a city in France."

Veeck would like the way Kentuckians pronounced it. He didn't like things smacking of sophistication. He extended that to stuffed shirts, as well.

"Well, that was probably because he didn't want to wear a tie," suggests Feller. "Of course if they helped him buy a ball club or something like that.... I don't think Bill really cared too much for that, but I think he liked to do that for publicity, and baseball fans, particularly, are from all walks of life, a lot of blue-collar workers. I think that was his trademark. If he wore a necktie and shirt and coat like everybody else, he wouldn't have gotten the attention. Bill was very media-conscious. Bill knew very well where his bread was buttered. I think a lot of that was done for a purpose."

Veeck also had, in Feller, a pitcher who delivered. He delivered a very fast fastball as well. "The Army tested me in Washington, D.C., after the war. The speed at home plate was 98.6 miles an hour and when I released the ball it was 117.2 and they figured the average speed of the ball—and I have movies of it, both sound and silent—and they figured the average speed—which of course I couldn't continue for a whole ball game—was 107.9. Maybe I could sustain 104 miles an hour."

Is that comparable to anyone?

"The only guy who could throw as hard as I was Walter Johnson. And he didn't have a curveball."

A lot of people were unhappy in 1947 when Bill Veeck attempted to follow Branch Rickey by bringing in a black player. And among the most unhappy were owners of black ball teams when they learned that Mrs. Effie Manley, the owner of the Newark Eagles, had done business with Bill Veeck. She had sold him her star infielder, twenty-three-year-old Larry Doby. Going to the big leagues? That was great for freedom, agreed the other Negro League owners. But when the black ballplayer entered the mainstream of the American Pastime, the end of the Negro Leagues was certain.

But it was in the air. In 1946, Rickey had put Jackie Robinson into the Dodgers' top farm team, in Montreal, and Robinson had starred, in that one season becoming the most prominent ballplayer in the minors. So in 1947 it was apparent that there would be other moves besides Robinson's. That season was one of the more intriguing in baseball history, with enough drama besides the pioneering black ballplayers.

Before the season, Larry MacPhail, one of the Yankees' owners, lured Coach Charlie Dressen from the Dodgers. That infuriated Leo Durocher, the combative Dodgers' manager, who then accused MacPhail of entertaining gamblers in Havana, where the Yankees and Dodgers played an exhibition. Durocher made his complaints in a column under his name that was ghostwritten in the *Brooklyn Eagle*.

MacPhail, of course, denied he had any connections to gamblers and complained to Commissioner Chandler. The commissioner agreed and suspended Durocher for the entire 1947 season and also fined the Dodgers and Yankees $2,000 apiece for "public feuding."

Larry Doby was performing with the Newark Eagles in July when the deal was finished for $10,000—plus another $10,000 if he made the Indians. Doby was batting .430 in the first half of the season for the Eagles, who played near his hometown of Paterson, New Jersey.

Over the years he had often faced big-league pitching. It was a curious fact of American baseball life that Negro and white ballplayers often played against one another, but not for anything that counted.

After the 1946 season, Doby was playing winter ball in Puerto Rico, and his team faced the Yankees in a three-game series. He smacked a pair of singles against Allie Reynolds and got a double against Frank (Spec) Shea.

Now, with the Eagles as batting star, leading the league with 14 home runs, 16 doubles, and 51 runs-batted-in, he got a call on July 3 from Mrs. Manley. "She told me Cleveland had purchased my contract," he recalled, "and wanted to know if I wanted to go."

Of course he said yes. Doby had prepared for this moment for ten years, since that day as a newly arrived kid on the block from Camden, South Carolina, he put on his first baseball uniform. It was for a Negro team called the Smart Sets.

At Eastside High School Doby became one of the state's finest players and made the all-New Jersey squad as a first baseman in his junior year, when he batted .559. The next year he batted more than .400 and was an all-state second baseman. Then he received a basketball scholarship to Long Island University, but instead entered the Navy. Against such major-league hurlers as Virgil (Fire) Trucks and Schoolboy Rowe—who played for the powerful Great Lakes Naval Training Base team—he batted .342. As soon as the war ended, he joined the Eagles. One of the Indians' scouts, Bill Killefer, saw him and described him to Veeck as "a great ballplayer."

Today, in this era of watch-your-language, when semantics becomes philosophy, it is interesting to look back to see how Veeck regarded Doby. Veeck used the word "boy," a common term for blacks in his time. Veeck also was aware that many white ballplayers, and fans, wondered what would happen if Doby and the other blacks made it. Would this start an influx of black ballplayers—to the exclusion of whites?

"I wanted to get the available Negro boys while the grabbing was good. Why wait? Within ten years Negro ballplayers will be in regular service with big-league teams."

Yet, Veeck also told the New York newspaper columnist Dan Daniel, "I'm forced to reveal that our scouts say there aren't six of that color who are qualified [for the big leagues]. Not six in the entire country. Now that the Negro ballplayer finds the major-league door open to him, there doubtless will be an improvement in Negro material. There will be a great incentive. But at this time there is no prospect of a Negro influx into the majors. Very emphatically, there is no racial problem in our business."

Veeck also told *The Sporting News*, "Robinson and Doby may do for the colored boys in baseball what Joe Louis did for them in boxing. Something of that sort undoubtedly will happen in baseball, but at present there's no possibility that Negro players will be arriving in wholesale numbers in the majors."

Certainly Veeck was aware of the quality of black ballplayers around the United States, especially in the Negro Leagues, with which he was so familiar. Yet, he downplayed the possibility of a mass Negro migration. Obviously he was attempting to avoid a racist backlash against the few blacks who finally did make it to the big time.

Doby's last game as a Negro League ballplayer was July 4, 1947. His wife and mother were in the stands for his final appearance. The game, in Newark, New Jersey, saw him lash a home run and single. He was presented with a traveling kit by the Newark Eagles. A local sports club gave him $50.

Louis Jones, a black public relations assistant Veeck had hired shortly before the deal, phoned Doby to make arrangements for him to join the club in Chicago. "Do you want to fly, or go by train?" Jones asked.

"If it's all the same to you, I'd rather go by train," Doby replied. "You see, this is a big opportunity for me and I don't want to miss it."

Doby didn't wait long for his major league debut. The next day, July 5, he suited up in Chicago. There wasn't a spot in the infield for him, though. Boudreau manned short, and Gordon anchored second. The first baseman was Eddie Robinson, who had been the International League's most valuable player the year before and was a top Indians' prospect.

So Doby started the game on the bench, where he was joined by two other blacks wearing civilian clothes. In the warm-ups, observers noted, he looked tense. Doby had similar problems on his team that Robinson suffered with the Dodgers, where several ballplayers announced they were opposed to the experiment.

Veeck had signed Doby to a contract in the White Sox offices just before game time, then told him, "Go down to the clubhouse and meet Lou Boudreau. And remember—a baseball player is judged on one basis only, what he does with a bat and a glove."

This matter-of-fact approach to the game and this almost offhand approach to an historical precedent helped make it easy for most of the Indians. If they were the first team in the American League—and only the second in baseball—to play alongside a black ballplayer, it was no big deal to Veeck. His approach to the occasion helped keep a calm atmosphere. This was not the time for wild promotions and attention-grabbing statements.

Finally, in the seventh inning, Doby was called by Boudreau to pinch-hit for Bryan Stephens, a Cleveland hurler. Earl Harrist, a right-hander, was pitching for the White Sox. If history were headline-oriented, Doby would have performed a dramatic feat. Instead, he struck out swinging, his final lunge spinning him nearly 180 degrees as he wound up facing the catcher.

In the ninth inning, with Doby back on the bench, Umpire Bill Summers called time and walked to the steps of the dugout. He asked Boudreau about the two black men in civilian clothes. Baseball rules forbid anyone who is not in uniform from sitting on the bench unless he is a member of the team, such as Manager Connie Mack of the Athletics, who sat wearing a straw boater and high collar. Boudreau explained their role.

When the game ended, the strangers—plainclothes Chicago policemen—followed Doby across the field to the locker room. As Ed McAuley of the Cleveland *News* saw it the next day, "The precaution turned out to be unnecessary. Chicago's colored fans obviously are happy and excited about the turn of events, but they realize that any large demonstrations at this time only would embarrass their hero; possibly would make it difficult for him to concentrate on his objective—staying in the big time."

The next day, in a surprising move, Boudreau inserted Doby as a starter for Robinson—who the day before had hit two homers when Doby was striking out. Boudreau immediately was criticized for the move, especially after Doby went only 1-for-5, scratching out an infield hit. His hardest-hit ball was a foul down the left-field line. He struck out twice, swinging. He handled eight chances in the field. Doby was playing only after Veeck told Boudreau to put the rookie in.

Larry Doby's debut in some ways was more difficult than Jackie Robinson's with the Brooklyn Dodgers. In 1947 the American League was the elite league, the Establishment, home of the Yankees and the Red Sox. The American League rarely lost all-star games or World Series. It was the league of DiMaggio and Williams, the league that had produced Babe Ruth and Ty Cobb. And it was less ready for a Negro ballplayer than the National League was.

Doby's struggles were monumental, and overlooked. He was to Robinson what the second person to solo the Atlantic was to Lindbergh. But the accomplishment was as real.

If Branch Rickey was the strong guiding arm that Robinson leaned on, Veeck was the less sure-footed guide for Doby. For Veeck commanded none of the admiration and respect among his American League peers that Rickey enjoyed in the National League.

"As I understand it, Mr. Veeck and Mr. Rickey got together and decided it would be nice to have a representative in the American League, and they chose me."

The first time Doby met Veeck was the day Doby was going to play for the Indians. "I said, 'Mr. Veeck...' and he said, 'Call me Bill,' and from that day until he passed away I was Lawrence to him and he was Bill to me," recalls Doby.

Doby now is director of community relations for the New Jersey Nets basketball team, who play in the Meadowlands, not far from the streets of Paterson where Doby played stickball. But that July day in Chicago, Doby was a pioneer, given a set of commandments from Veeck.

"He made it very comfortable for me," says Doby. "He sat and talked with me and told me things, you know a list of things you could and couldn't do—and most things on the list were things you could not do."

Doby, being black, could not have arguments with players. If someone said something to him, he had to walk away. He was not allowed to argue with the umpires. "Other players could do it. I guess it was a different set of rules for me. The thing was, if you want to be successful in this business, first of all you have to play. But if you played, then you had to abide by these rules, because if you didn't, you were going to be out."

In the accounts of the time, reporters noted how smoothly his entrance was, how easily he fit into the team. The reality was something different.

"Welcome? I couldn't live with the team," says Doby.

After Veeck sent him downstairs to meet his new teammates, and after Boudreau had held a team meeting to...well, warn...the players about Doby's arrival, Doby was not exactly mobbed. He walked into the clubhouse and found that Boudreau had the players lined up in front of their lockers.

"Joe Gordon, Larry Doby," said Boudreau to Gordon, who took Doby's offered hand and shook it. But Doby went to the next locker, was introduced, stuck out his hand—and there was no hand to take it. That snub was repeated throughout much of the locker room.

"I don't know why people say I was accepted," says Doby. "People didn't write it. They wrote about Jackie Robinson, but the same thing happened in the American League. This wasn't supposed to happen. This is America. I slid into second base, guys spit tobacco juice on me. Nobody wrote that and of course it never bothered me. I always figured Robinson was the first one, should get the publicity."

According to Doby, though, "mine was worse than Robinson. This is a society with great egos. The American League was the top of baseball, while the National League was like a bush league, really."

So Doby remembers the bench jockeys yelling, "You're not supposed to be in this league. You're supposed to be in that bush league with that other nigger." According to Doby, the insults came from the Yankees, from Boston, from Detroit—from all of them. Even coaches and some managers.

"Joe Gordon was a very fine man and was a person who showed some courtesy when I first joined the ball club. As a matter of fact, he was the only guy I warmed up with the first couple of days."

Veeck was unable to prevent the slurs and the slights, but he and Doby did talk from time to time. Still, Doby realized there was little Veeck could do. Yet, even though Veeck had given Doby the list of don't's, Doby never saw them as actually emanating from Veeck.

"One of those 'don't-do' things was don't fight. If you do, black people will come out of the stands. That's a lot of bunk, but they had you psyched that way. I had Bill to guide me. If you're a pioneer in an historic-type thing, you're gonna suffer. But you look down the line and see you're in a situation that could be very, very big in the future. Martin Luther King made a big thing by turning the other cheek. But we had done it earlier, on a smaller scale. But if we hadn't done it, you probably wouldn't have the Mays and Aarons and Banks and Newcombes."

Doby was aware that Veeck had to take a certain stance in regard to the possible influx of black players. Thus, when Veeck went on record denying there were many black players likely to come up after Doby, that really was so much eyewash.

"Bill Veeck was a very intelligent man. A genius," says Doby. "He had to deal with the masses. A great romancer. He knew how to romance people, and that statement was a romance-type statement. We'd talk a lot, but we tried to avoid talking about that crap."

The "crap" included being knocked down, but not simply with a brush-back pitch. With Doby, the fast ball would be thrown behind him. Still, he looked at it as a duel between the pitcher and himself, and, as he says, "the point is if you get up off the ground and finally hit the baseball, you've won the contest."

Doby remains bitter about the things that happened to him as a player and after his career ended. He still recalls, for example, his very first start. It was to be as the Indians' first baseman.

"Eddie Robinson was supposed to loan me his glove, and he wouldn't. I didn't have a first-baseman's glove because I was a second baseman. Joe Gordon or someone talked him into letting me use the glove. That season I never played but one full game—that second game of the doubleheader in Chicago."

Doby played some games in the infield, but never starting, only finishing when the game was out of hand or the Indians had a huge lead. Finally, toward the end of the '47 season, Bill McKechnie, one of the coaches, took Doby aside. "He told me that Joe Gordon is the second baseman and he's probably going to be the second baseman, and that I should try to see if I could play the outfield. He told me to buy a book on how to play the outfield, read it in the winter, and then in spring training I'd go to the outfield."

Doby bought his book and became an outfielder. They originally tried him in right field in 1948, then switched him to center.

"I had begun to get a little relationship with Bob Lemon and Jim Hegan, in addition to Gordon, but of course it wasn't social. The restaurants they went to I couldn't get in."

In 1948, Doby batted .301. In only 439 at-bats he scored 83 runs, swatted 14 homers, and drove in 66 runs while scoring 83. He was to play with the Indians until 1955, then play two seasons with the White Sox before returning to Cleveland in 1958. He went to Detroit the next season, and wound up his career with the White Sox in '59 after Veeck acquired the team.

"When I left baseball I got a job as a scout and I got another job in

Paterson. Bill left baseball and of course I lost the job scouting. I tried for eight years to get back into baseball."

Finally Doby returned when the Montreal Expos franchise was created and he joined the team as a scout. Then he became a hitting coach. And then he heard that the Indians were talking about hiring a black manager. The first.

So he joined the Indians as a coach in 1974, hoping that he might become the first black manager in major-league history. Instead Frank Robinson got that job.

Doby and Veeck eventually worked together again in 1976, after Veeck bought the White Sox for the second time. And in 1978 Doby got his chance. Veeck named him manager. Doby, the second black player in the majors, became the second black ever to manage.

He replaced Bob Lemon in mid-season, and the club had a mediocre finish, winning 37 of 87 games. Bill Veeck had to fire Doby. But it was not, you understand, Veeck's doing.

"I think the most sad part of his life and my life was when he had to tell me that he was relieving me and taking my job. But I understood because no one could tell me that he himself would do that, if he had the authority to say who's going to be the manager. But I knew he was getting pressure from other people and I knew that it was not his doing.

"He called me into his office and said, 'Hey, I got to make a change, and we're not going to discuss it. You understand because you've been with me a long time and you know the circumstances as to how this thing, the political part of this thing, is. But,' he says, 'we can't sit here and talk about it because I'm gonna cry and you're gonna cry.' I got up and left. That was it."

Doby's eyes mist over when he reminisces about Veeck and the impact the owner had upon the player. "The greatest humanitarian that I have ever known. Those who have not had the opportunity to know him really missed a great person. I feel sorry for them. If my father had lived— my father died when I was eight years old—I would have hoped my father would have been like Bill. You see, the man wasn't a hypocrite. He didn't have one set of values in the church and another outside the church. The man was straight. The man was for people."

Boudreau, meanwhile, had an unusual relationship with Veeck, who made no secret of the fact that he didn't want Boudreau to manage his team.

"He thought that I was a hunch manager," Boudreau explains. "He felt that after doing this for three or four years, I should give up managing. In fact, during the '47 season he made a trade with the St. Louis Browns for Vern Stephens and a pitcher for me. The story was leaked out, and the fans went in an uproar. Bill put a ballot in the Cleveland *Plain-Dealer* and the *News* and had the fans vote. I defeated him 4-1."

Yet, their relationship was sustained for more than forty years. Boudreau eventually became the Cubs' announcer, and he often spotted Veeck in later years sitting in his beloved bleachers.

"When he bought the club, he moved the training camp to Tucson, Arizona, not far from his ranch, the Lazy Vee Ranch," recalls Boudreau. "That was 1947, when we also moved to the stadium from League Park. He had a beautiful ranch, settled in the atmosphere of the desert. He had many horses on the ranch. We'd take rides into the mountains for steak fries. But the roads were terrible and we had some drive back in the morning to get to the ballpark. The coaches would stay at his place. His wife, Eleanor, was a very nice person, very personable. She'd associate with everybody."

Before the season began, Veeck made a key deal—Reynolds for Gordon. "One of the greatest trades he ever made was Allie Reynolds for Joe Gordon. He gave up a great 20-game pitcher, but Bill knew he needed someone to play alongside of me. I agreed with the deal because we were getting someone who could play every day."

Veeck did not bring many people into his confidence, though, and Boudreau wasn't even aware of the Doby deal until it happened. "I received a call from Bill Veeck and he told me he signed this ballplayer from New Jersey, and he was quite a ballplayer and could help us out. He could play the infield or the outfield and he could run and he could throw. And he asked me to play him.

"I asked him, 'Where do you want me to play him?' and he said, 'That's up to you.' I couldn't remove Joe Gordon so the man I removed was Eddie Robinson. The club was very, very quiet. I held a meeting to introduce Larry to everybody. Of course, it was a surprise. I gave a short speech, maybe not so short because it was a history-making event. I introduced Larry and he was very, very calm. He went to his locker, very quiet. I remember after he struck out he went to the bench and sat down at the end of the bench. And Gordon went over to him and tried to build up his spirits.

"Of course Robinson felt bad about being taken out of the game and one of my coaches also talked to him so he shouldn't take it so hard. After a few games, I put Doby in center field and I decided that was the spot for him.

"We had Hal Peck in the outfield then. He was a favorite of Bill Veeck's. He traded him away on several occasions and got him back. He thought he was his lucky charm.

"Center field turned out to be Doby's spot. He became a fine defensive outfielder and started to swing the bat better."

Did you feel like a pioneer then?

"Definitely. It opened up the game for a lot of great ballplayers. But in training camp and the season it was very difficult to find places to eat. Spud Goldstein, our traveling secretary, had a tough job. There were hotels that wouldn't accept Larry. There were restaurants that wouldn't accept Larry. We had to find outstanding individuals in towns that would house Larry for us and also find hotels. He went through a very difficult life that first year, no doubt about it. He was the only black player on the club until Satchel Paige came along the next year."

The '47 Indians did not win a pennant, but they were getting better, improved to six games over .500 and moved up to fourth place. The combination of Gordon and Boudreau immediately clicked and Gordon had an outstanding season, collecting 29 home runs to lead the team while batting .272.

The move from League Park to the larger stadium was complete. The Indians still needed pitching, though. Feller turned in another 20-game season, and Bob Lemon, after an erratic career in which it could not be determined whether he was a pitcher or an outfielder, posted an 11-5 mark. A youngster from the farm named Gene Bearden came up late in the year to pitch only one inning. Hal Peck, the man with three toes on one foot, stole three bases while batting .293 as a platooned player.

That year Veeck also hit his stride in Cleveland, firming the legend. It wasn't merely the promotions he fathered, although those alone secured his baseball niche. He had orchids flown from Hawaii and he gave away stockings. Before the words "day-care" became a part of the American lexicon, he created a nursery costing more than $20,000 so that mothers could come to see the Indians and leave their children with trained people who cared. It didn't help him make any money but it helped secure the image he wanted—the Indians were the people's team.

This doesn't mean that he was completely altruistic. He could be sly in some of his deals. Take Johnny Berardino, for instance.

Berardino these days is best known as a star of *General Hospital*. But in the 1940s he was a struggling, though versatile, infielder.

"I was giving up my baseball career in 1947," says Berardino. "I had been traded from the St. Louis Browns to the Washington Senators over the winter. I felt, my goodness, I'm going from a seventh-place team to an eighth-place team. And I was working in a movie at the time. I decided at that point I'd just quit baseball and continue with my movie career. Bill Veeck changed my mind for me. He doubled my salary, and gave me a bonus clause based on attendance.

"He insured my face for a million dollars. He wanted to give me a movie contract at Universal. You know, all that was part of the deal. So it seemed too good a thing to turn down.... As it turned out, it was a mistake to take Bill's offer because I spent five years as a utility player. The Indians already had their infield set. They had Ken Keltner, Joe Gordon, Lou Boudreau, and Eddie Robinson.

"I didn't know it at the time, but I learned about a year later that Bill had really wanted me because he was afraid Detroit would come after me. They were lacking a second baseman. [In fact, Detroit used five players at second base that season.] He didn't want them strengthened, of course. I ended up playing all four positions in the Cleveland infield. I played second, short, third and first. I was the only infielder they had the whole season, which gave them eight outfielders and a lot of pinch hitters. I think it hurt my movie career. Instead, I was just playing utility baseball."

Still, Berardino had a longer career than most, but because he was so oriented to a life outside of baseball, he measures success in the game by how far he came in it. Veeck, though, was able to get a gimmick out of Berardino—the million-dollar insurance policy with Lloyd's of London. Hollywood had its million-dollar insurance policy with Betty Grable's legs, and now Veeck had his.

Fishel calls some of Veeck's promotions opportunistic—even those that seemed altruistic, geared solely for a charitable purpose. "He took advantage of circumstances that developed," says Fishel. He recalls that even the Don Black charity night in 1948 was one of those events.

Black, a pitcher, was batting in a Monday makeup game against the Yankees. The game provided an extra "gate" for Veeck since the game originally was the second of a doubleheader played the day before. But after the teams played the first game, the second was rained out. The next night, while Black was at bat, he suddenly slumped to the ground with a cerebral hemorrhage.

"Bill immediately announced he was going to hold a Don Black charity night and that all tickets sold from this day on would go to Don Black. Bill booked it for a game against the Red Sox—and turned it into a night game.

"The Red Sox didn't want to play at night because they were fighting us for the pennant, and if it was at night, that meant Feller would pitch against them, and they didn't want him in a night game. But Veeck made such a big deal about the fact it was a benefit that how could the Red Sox say no to it? Feller pitched that night and beat them."

An interesting footnote to the Don Black situation is provided by Schaffer. Asked whether Veeck was surreptitious in deals, whether he tried to pawn off damaged goods, Schaffer replies, "No, if anything, Bill was always on the other end of these things. He had a passion for taking somebody that had a problem, whether it was a drinking problem or a family problem or some physical problem and he tried to resurrect these people. He would seek these people out from other clubs—and as it happens he'd get a bargain rate on the guy. But he had a fascination of trying to rehabilitate people.

"A fellow by the name of Don Black was one of them. He was an alcoholic. There was an earlier one at Milwaukee called Vallie Eaves, an American Indian. He was an alcoholic, and Bill brought him along. But after Bill left Milwaukee, Eaves didn't get the same kind of attention and he went sour again. Bill had experience with people like that because Hack Wilson was with the Cubs when Bill was there.

"Bill always was for the little guy. In his days of better health—I'm going back to Milwaukee and Cleveland—he'd move around the ballpark and sit in the stands and chat with the fans, and move around an inning later."

Veeck also threw a day for Lefty Weisman, the club's trainer. Weisman had been a fixture on the team since the 1920s and was part of that majority known as the "little people" whom Veeck forever seemed to be helping.

"Tris Speaker had brought Lefty in years before," recalled Fishel. "Lefty was practically an illiterate. Speaker was supposed to be anti-Semitic, but Speaker was nice to Lefty and he was nice to me. Anyway, Veeck got a wheelbarrow filled with silver dollars. He must have collected about $7,000, and that was quite a bit back then. Then Lefty tried to push the wheelbarrow and of course he couldn't. It was quite a promotion."

When Veeck got rolling, surprises abounded. His father was credited with having Ladies' Days in Chicago on a regular basis in the 1920s to lure customers to a game against a mediocre opponent. But Bill Veeck made every Saturday in Cleveland Ladies' Day. They were invited free, paying only a small service charge. Usually, they were accompanied by a man who paid the full general admission.

One Saturday found the Indians in the middle of a three-game series against the Yankees. Since women didn't need tickets, there was no sizable advance sale, but Veeck usually could estimate the size of the crowd. This time he was fooled.

"We drew about 70,000 people the night before," Fishel recalls, "and we thought we'd draw about 15,000 or 20,000 people on Saturday. I was looking forward to the game. I had my own box seats, which I paid for. They weren't prepared when 40,000 women suddenly showed up and Bill said, 'I need everybody to help.' I wasn't a member of a union, but I went into a booth to help out. First time in my life I was ever in the booth. I sold general admission tickets. I think they were $1.10 apiece, and I sold several hundred tickets. At the end of the day I was seven tickets short. So I was $7.70 short and I had to pay for that. I didn't see the game, and I never got my $7.70 back. I didn't let Bill forget that."

The good times rolled off the field too. It wasn't only life in the Jolly Set at Gruber's that marked the Veeck era in Cleveland.

Schaffer recalls the time Veeck brought his cronies to New York, where Elsa Maxwell arranged a party at Le Pavillon. It was an unusual group—the Indians' coaches, the manager, front-office people, while Miss Maxwell's society friends were on the other side of the room.

After the party, Salvador Dali said to Veeck, "I don't understand this baseball you talk about." And Veeck replied, "Well, that makes us even, pal, because I sure don't understand those paintings of yours."

That is a charming story and indicates, once again, the Veeck style—his common-man touch, his gentle tweaking of sophistication. It is highly unlikely Veeck didn't comprehend Dali. Veeck's daughter Marya is an artist in Chicago.

If Veeck traveled without a tie, it also seemed he traveled without a watch. "I'd be in bed," recalls Schaffer, "and I'd get a call at 2:30 in the morning and he said, 'I want to play charades,' and I said, 'Bill, it's 2:30 in the morning,' and he said, 'I'll be right up.' We're half asleep and we'd play and then after twenty, thirty minutes he'd say, 'You're no fun,' and he would leave."

Veeck even took a fling at acting in Cleveland. For fun, he portrayed Sheridan Whiteside in *The Man Who Came to Dinner*.

It was a part brilliantly created by Monty Woolley, and Veeck knew there would be comparisons. "I'm just a country boy," said Veeck, waiting in the star's dressing room on opening night. "I'm just going to be myself."

In one respect, the role was tailor-made. It requires Whiteside to per form in a wheelchair. By then, Veeck's right leg had been amputated below the knee.

The play ran for a week at the Hanna Theater, and the drama critic for the Plain-Dealer, W. Ward Marsh, noted that Veeck hardly was the man for the role. "Veeck played Veeck all evening," Marsh wrote. "And the role filled with brimstone and sulphur was read by a man who too obviously has his house by the side of the road and is forever a friend of man...."

That lost leg not only resulted in his acting debut, it allowed him to throw a party celebrating the arrival of his wooden leg. When he learned in 1946 that he would lose the leg—he had insisted on abusing it by disdaining doctors' orders—he waited eagerly for the wooden replacement. When it arrived, he tossed himself several parties, hiring bands and dancing late into the night.

Veeck did his running around in Cleveland virtually as a bachelor. "His first wife stayed in Arizona. She claimed she had an allergy, but they never got along," says Feller. "Even back in the fall of 1946 they had all kinds of problems."

Look over the newspaper clippings of William L. (Bill) Veeck, Jr., through the years, and it seems that every sixth item is about his visit to a hospital: He needed further surgery (actually, removal) on the leg, or he had difficulty on the left leg, or he suffered vision problems, or was partly deaf in one ear, or he battled emphysema, was stricken with lung cancer, or suffered terrible headaches brought on by coughing spells that nothing seemed to ease. If while speaking to someone he suddenly went into a coughing fit, he would say something like "Suffering is overrated."

Dick Schaap, the television personality and co-author of such books as *Instant Replay*, is not easily surprised. But his eyes still widen when he recounts his first meeting with Veeck. Schaap was the editor of *Sport* magazine at the time, and asked Veeck to do a piece on ways to improve baseball.

Schaap met Veeck at the airport in New York, and they got into a car for the drive to the city. Suddenly Veeck pulled an ice pick out of a pocket and plunged it into his right leg.

"I just sat there with my mouth open," recalled Schaap. "I didn't know what to think. I didn't know that he had a wooden leg. It was some introduction."

How about Al Rosen's first meeting with Veeck? Unable to use his right leg, Veeck drove a car by bending down and pressing the accelerator with his right hand. Rosen, the Indians' great slugger of the time, had this startling introduction to Veeck:

"In 1947, I had completed my season in Oklahoma, which was in the double-A Texas League, and I was recalled by the Indians," says Rosen. "I got a message that, instead of flying from Oklahoma City to New York, where the Indians were playing, I was to fly via Chicago. I flew in and got off the plane at six o'clock in the morning—and Bill Veeck was there to meet me.

"Now, you've got to understand the impact on a young kid. This is the first time and the owner and general manager of the ball club took the time to meet me. He took me out in his car.

"At that time he didn't have a wooden leg, but wherever we drove to, he used his hand on the accelerator. He'd bend down to accelerate when he started out. It was a fascinating event in my life. At breakfast that morning he handed me a check for a thousand dollars. I had never seen a thousand dollars before in my life. That was my first introduction to Bill Veeck. He then took me back to the plane. I got back on and went to New York to join the Indians. It's always been prominent in my memory."

Over the years Rosen remained enamored of Veeck. And even when Rosen in 1977 became the president of the New York Yankees, of all people, the special bond remained. "There was always a feeling about him that he was one of the guys. When he was in Cleveland he used to actually go out...he'd meet guys coming off the 4 A.M. shifts and have a beer with them. Those stories were legendary. At the same time he could go to the swankiest restaurant and rub elbows with the so-called in crowd. He could transcend any level of society."

Their relationship, Rosen contends, remained strong even in the two years Rosen was with the Yankees. "His tweaking the Yankees really was designed to tweak Steinbrenner. Bill, while he could involve himself with the Establishment, and talk very easily with them, delighted in being anti-Establishment. He was a man for all people."

Rosen, too, was aware of the special place the Cubs always held for Veeck. "It's like it was for anybody who's ever succeeded, but still has another mile to go," explains Rosen. "It didn't work out for him."

If the Cubs remained that unattained goal, Veeck wouldn't let on. Through his years with the Indians he threw himself into their lives and the lives of all they touched. He would go anywhere, talk to anyone. Just invite him.

One of his owners, Bob Hope, remembers how completely Veeck did his job. Hope still lived in Cleveland at the time, although he spent much of the year in Hollywood making movies and doing his radio show. "I enjoyed him very much because he was a personable guy," recounts Hope. "I was from Cleveland, you know, and my attorney got me interested in the Indians and I bought a good chunk of them and I made two capital gains with Bill. I knew him and I loved him because he was such a promoter. I just loved him because he'd get the job done one way or another. Cleveland isn't an easy town to move, and he moved them, I'll tell you that.

"I was not involved directly in the team. I was traveling quite a bit then. I got in because of a civic thing. My attorney, Joe Klein, was very civic-minded. But Bill was a great personality. He'd go to any luncheon, he'd go to Canton, Ohio, just to talk about the Cleveland Indians, which I admired him for. I did see him many times at dinners and things, and I loved him."

Chapter 4

In Cleveland, Veeck was living the life of a bachelor. He was known for his exploits with women as well as his all-night prowling. A part of Veeck's life was about to end, a part that he rarely spoke of and about which most people never bothered asking. That was his first family, the ones he left behind in Arizona. He and Eleanor Raymond had three children: William Louis Veeck, III, Peter, and Ellen.

Over the years, in his writings and in interviews, Veeck glossed over those children—"It was as if we didn't exist," his daughter Ellen said. Veeck, the humanitarian, the generous, outgoing, affable, innovative impresario, virtually forgot about the children from his first marriage. Twenty years passed between meetings with his sons, and many years went by between visits with his daughter.

But his first family speaks easily about themselves, as if with Veeck's death a window has opened on their lives, and the two surviving children were able to talk about Veeck. His ex-wife, though, while willing to recall her own fascinating past, preferred not to speak about Veeck. "Let the public remember him the way they want," said Eleanor Veeck, almost gratuitously. So their relationship, and what led to their break-up, has to be seen through the eyes of their children. That is not the best way. But it offers insights into their own beliefs and fantasies about the two, and Bill Veeck the man.

Ellen Maggs (she is married to Charles Maggs and has three children) lives in Phoenix. She is anxious to analyze her relationships. She wants to be a sculptor. Her primary business is creating party balloons—balloon bouquets. She was born in 1943, the third of his three children with Eleanor, and was six years old when they divorced in 1949.

In trying to recall him, Ellen says, "He wasn't home much, so I don't remember him. I don't know much about him except what I've read in the newspapers." But it turns out she has some very strong feelings about him, and may even know him better than she realizes.

Did he see her at all?

"Yeah, when I was eighteen he sent me roses on Valentine's Day. And then he invited me back to his estate. I met his family."

She then recalls there was an earlier meeting. "He had difficulty with intimate relationships. I was in the hospital when I was ten years old. I had broken my arm, and he came into the room and said, 'Hi, I'm your dad. How are you?' And I smiled, and then he went and spent the rest of the time kibbitzing with the nurses and the doctors because he was this wonderful, important person. So you see, he just wasn't capable...he probably didn't know what to say, when you see your child that you haven't seen in ten years. A man really has nothing in common with that kid."

According to Ellen, Veeck was capable of being close only with Mary Frances, "and I think the world of her. They were just right for each other, and my mother and he were not. My mother was raised in a family where the wife was put on a pedestal and she was taken care of. When my grandmother died, my mother's mother, she must have been eighty-nine, and she still was a little child. And so my mother expected to be treated like a little princess. And my father was a child-hearted person himself. So he wasn't capable of treating her the way she expected him to treat her. They were compatriots, where what she wanted was a daddy. Their relationship never could work."

In a stream of consciousness, Ellen offered many reasons for the marriage's failure as well as her own views of Veeck. She suggests, for example, "My father's brother was killed nine years before my father was born. And I think my father felt he could never measure up to that dead sibling." With bitterness, she describes her father's personality:

"On the outside he was charming and it worked. I don't understand why my mother stayed with him so long. All the time they were divorced he paid us $250 and he lived magnificently. He gave her a lump sum when he sold the Indians, but the agreement was he was supposed to pay her a certain amount a month. We lived in poverty. He had a very wealthy life-style. My mother said he sent her one check for $250. He was supposed to pay a thousand dollars a month. He had six kids and another wife to support. How could he afford to?"

According to Ellen, "My mother came out of that marriage a broken woman, as far as I'm concerned. I grew up with a dead woman because emotionally she was so withdrawn. She withdrew into herself, so I feel as if I've been raised as an orphan." As a child, she recalls, there was much hatred and bitterness directed against Veeck. "There were so many things that I was not allowed to talk about as a child."

Ellen knew that Veeck converted to Catholicism in order to marry Mary Frances, and Ellen also knew that her mother despised the Catholic Church. Bill Veeck once told her that his father-in-law "was crazy about him." But according to Ellen, "My grandmother had nothing good to say about him." And when Ellen's grandfather died, Bill Veeck sent her flowers. Her grandmother—his mother-in-law—told her to put the flowers in the bedroom, out of sight.

In the years before Bill Veeck's death, Ellen actually established a firmer relationship with Mary Frances. "I saw him, but mainly my relationship was with Mary Frances. She's a very wonderful person and I think it's very lucky that she and my father were married because I think they complemented each other wonderfully."

Once, Ellen recalls, she asked her father if he "stepped out" on Mary Frances. He replied that if he ever did, she would take the shirt off his back. And he laughed.

Ellen's sculpting has to do with what she describes as "relationships, needless to say from my past." She was currently working on an ambitious piece. It was of a sculptor chiseling a child. The chisel was right at the child's nose.

"On the right elbow hang these masks—extreme anger and extreme joy and extreme anguish. And I'm going to have something written that the child isn't a slate for an adult to do anything with that he wishes."

Bill Veeck's firstborn was named William Louis Veeck, III. He was born in 1937 and died of cancer in January 1985—a year before his father died.

Bill Veeck, III, was known as Will. He was graduated from M.I.T. and spent the last twenty years of his life on the island of Kauai, in Hawaii, where he taught mathematics at a community college. Almost twenty years went by between meetings with his father.

"He didn't know his father that well," recalls Will's widow, Bernice, a social worker. "By the time he was thirty, say, it was difficult for him to think of going to see his father. He finally met his dad when he was forty. Will flew to Chicago to see him. I think he might have seen his father a few times after the divorce, but he hadn't seen him since he graduated from college."

Their reunion took place in the late 1970s. And it filled Bernice with bittersweet thoughts. "I thought Bill Veeck was a fascinating person," she explains. "It was sad because my first thought was, here he had a wonderful father and didn't have a chance to know him. Bill was a warm, loving person, and if he had only kept in touch with his children... We always got calls from people—'Oh, did you hear about your father? Your father is on the news.' After a while it became irritating because here you have a man who is so well known and yet you don't know him. Other people probably knew him much more than his own children did."

Ironically, when Will finally was reunited with his father, it was for a brief period. "It wasn't until my husband was taken ill that they really became close," recalls Bernice. "All of a sudden, for the first time in his life he felt as if his father was interested in him. Six months after my husband got cancer, Bill Veeck discovered that he had cancer."

And did Bernice know why Bill Veeck never contacted Will in the early years?

"When they were young, he didn't see that much of his father anyway, especially when his father was into baseball. His father was away quite a bit. So, after the divorce, it wasn't that traumatic. I think that when my husband became ill he looked back on his life and felt that, you know, not having a father, and having to be the responsible son, that... he felt that might have had something to do with his illness.

"The main problem with the marriage was that Bill was gone a lot. I think that basically they were two different people. He lived in the fast lane. He was the playboy of Chicago at that time. Will was brought up more in Arizona than Chicago. I've heard him talk about Chicago, though—how they struggled in the winter without their dad. They had a rough time."

Bernice also recalls the role Mary Frances played in the unusual relationship between the families. "I just finished reading the article about Bill Veeck in the *Reader's Digest* [written by Hank Greenberg]. There was no mention about his first family. But his second wife always kept up with the family. She kept in touch, ever since we were married. She'd always remember our birthdays, our anniversaries, our children's birthdays. So maybe Bill Veeck just wasn't the type to be in touch with, you know."

He also apparently put some of the onus for his estrangement on his first wife.

"Well, I think he said he tried to see them but he couldn't," says Bernice. "He said a couple of years ago he tried to, but their mother wouldn't let him."

Will Veeck was not a flamboyant sort and had no interest in baseball. He liked to swim and play tennis. But according to his widow, "He was active in soccer. He helped organize soccer on Kauai, and they renamed a tournament in memory of him. It's called the Will Veeck Cup."

Peter Veeck, Bill and Eleanor Veeck's second child, doesn't take many things seriously. He lives in Bonham, Texas. Is that outside of Dallas?

"It's outside of just about everything," he replies.

Peter Veeck has a wink in his voice. He has an antipathy toward celebrities and he enjoys speaking metaphorically about his father. There is an edge to Peter's tone, though. Like his brother and sister, he had more contact with his father through magazine and newspaper articles than in person. People forever were clipping out stories about Bill Veeck and mailing them to Will, or Ellen, or Peter, or Eleanor. At the least, the children grew up with mixed signals about their father.

Everyone else in America seemed to know where Bill Veeck was. But he was virtually a stranger during his children's preteen and teenage years. While friends and relations phoned them excitedly, or sent along stories whenever Bill Veeck's name appeared, or he was seen on television, their mother and grandmother let his children know he was not the universally acclaimed figure everyone else seemed to have adopted.

Peter, born in 1941, had scant memories of his father before the divorce—Peter recalls having a race with him once, and he can remember Bill cutting the stock off a rifle for Will. "And I think there's one other memory there if I dig around enough. I saw him very little." That was part of the Veeck children's childhood—a father out there, somewhere, but rarely at home.

Peter Veeck recalls that his mother's father—a wealthy plumbing manufacturer, producing quality fixtures for Sears—was family-oriented. "He had the capability of making a whole lot of money," explains Peter, talking of his grandfather. "But that meant he would have to keep himself away from the family. Or, he could keep the family, and he made the determination to make a modest amount and maintain his family ties. So

my mother came out of this background of family and family relationships."

But after her marriage to Bill Veeck, she found her own marriage
vastly different from her upbringing. Her husband's business kept him
away from home. Very quickly, she and her children led separate lives
from Veeck's.

"You had Milwaukee, and my family was kept in West Bend, while
Bill and the team lived in Milwaukee," says Peter. "You get the house in
West Bend, and you look at what this house is going to be—after you take
the log cabin and you chink between the logs, and you fix it all up and
everything else, it's going to be a fabulous house. But for a couple of years
you live in it with snow sifting across the floor, the pipes all freezing, and
you have to plow the roads to get to town and stuff like this. We were
always separated from him," continues Peter. "After the divorce, and until the time I was twenty-three years old, I met him twice. Our paths just
never crossed.

"After the divorce there was a certain amount of bitterness there. I
think things were compounded because of the goldfish-bowl effect, and
because of the marriage into Catholicism, and because of the way the
whole thing came about—there was an announcement in the newspaper
that he was getting married, and that was before he was even divorced. At
least that's what I've been told."

Peter Veeck attended Arizona State University for a few years, then
joined the Air National Guard because they promised to teach him to fly.
He learned, and became a pilot for Braniff.

But he avoided baseball and shunned team sports, and had a quirky
attitude about the famous. Even today he says that if he were sitting next
to Ronald Reagan, he wouldn't recognize him.

Peter, though, has analyzed the aura and the attraction of Bill Veeck.
The son comes to the conclusion that his father was the sort who would
not accept responsibility for his actions. It is an interesting theory, borne
out in his firing of Larry Doby as the White Sox manager in 1978, when
Veeck blames "politics." Doby, who owed so much to Bill Veeck and still
regards him so highly, still doesn't pin the dismissal on Veeck, who was
the team's president.

Bill Veeck also said that he tried to have contact with his children
from the first marriage, but that his ex-wife stood in the way. Other battles Veeck lost because, he contended, he was struggling upstream against
the powerful Yankees, or an unfeeling baseball commissioner, or Philistine-
like opponents who did not have his common-good approach to the game.

And the thing is, there was some truth in what Veeck said. He often fought the good fight and often was struck down by lesser people.

In any event, these are some of the ways Peter saw him:

- "He was a logical person. He was honest. A little bit blind, perhaps. I don't think he ever did anything that was wrong. If anything went wrong, it was probably somebody else's fault. He was an egotist and he spent most of his life on an ego trip."

- "His life was dedicated to his public. I think he differentiated to a certain extent between his family and his public, but I'm not really sure how much. I don't think he had a lot from either one. There was a lot on the surface."

- "He was an excellent promoter. He was a very intelligent man, very knowledgeable, but most promoters are good at promoting. They usually have somebody else going along picking up the strings, tying everything together. With Bill's operations, I feel that Rudie Schaffer did this. I think Mary Frances did too."

- "He operated twenty-four hours a day, 365 days a year, with a little time off for sleeping. Every so often he would have to take a vacation, so most of his projects went for a period of time and there was a recuperation, or a rest period. Now, whether that's for tax laws or health reasons or it's just for getting something going, spending all your time on it, then you need a break."

- "Bill never had a lot of money to put into a team. He fronted for a lot of people. Most of his income came from the operation—the gate. So he had to take a team that was down in the dumps, the cellar. He had to develop attendance, get a good gate. He had to bring the income in, and he had to appreciate the value so that after four years he could sell it, take the profits and be in position where he could get another team going."

Interestingly, Peter and his sister both claim that in many ways they are like their father, but in ways they have difficulty describing. "I haven't worn a tie since I left Braniff," says Peter. "I figure your father goes through all this effort to do without a tie, so I really ought to help him out in some way or another." And he chuckles.

Mrs. Eleanor Veeck, Bill's first wife, lives in Scottsdale, Arizona.

"You know," she told me, "you really don't have to have much of me in a book connected with Bill Veeck. It's been so many, many years. I was divorced in 1949, and we had no contact; neither did the children. We've all kept still through the years and just as soon keep still."

But she is willing to talk about her upbringing and her circus days: "I grew up with Bill Veeck. We went to school together in Hinsdale. We were in the same class."

But her obsession was the circus: "We went to Florida in the winter, and of course the circus winter quarters were in Sarasota, and that was probably where I got the circus bug. I loved the circus. When I look back now, I can't believe I ever did it."

She was nineteen years old when she joined the circus, and needed her father's written permission. This he granted after having an agreement with her: He would allow her to join the circus if she attended college for a year. She spent two semesters at the University of Nebraska, "marking time."

In his writings Veeck described her as an elephant trainer and as a daring young lady who rode a horse bareback through a ring of fire.

"I wasn't a trainer," she says. "I just worked elephants that were already trained." She also did some bareback riding, but nothing so dramatic as Veeck painted.

In an old *Billboard* weekly from 1935, there is a brief article about Eleanor Raymond appearing in Ring Number One, having recuperated from her ankle injury. She often told her children that she met Bill Veeck as a result of that injury. Sidelined, she had time to date him. She spent a total of two years with the circus. Will was born within two years of their marriage.

Speaking of her children, she says, "I'm very proud of them. I think I was very lucky."

You did it on your own?

"Well, that's for sure."

And she really doesn't want to say anything more about Bill?

"He was public property and they think a lot of him. He's gone now. Let the public keep their image."

Chapter 5

The work, the speech-making, the wheeling-dealing that marked Veeck's arrival in Cleveland paid off with the championship season of 1948, one of the most remarkable in baseball history.

It took shape during the World Series of 1946, which Veeck, of course, attended merely as a spectator. He knew that Larry MacPhail, the Yankees' president, and Joe Gordon, the New Yorkers' second baseman, were battling.

MacPhail's Yankees had finished third, 17 games behind the pennant-winning Boston Red Sox, and MacPhail now started to shop around. He needed pitching help. His 20-game winner, Spud Chandler, was already thirty-eight years old. MacPhail asked Joe DiMaggio which Cleveland pitcher he thought was the toughest. DiMaggio replied, "Reynolds."

Veeck recounted this anecdote in a 1949 article for *The Saturday Evening Post*:

"Gordon was the best second baseman in the business. I made up my mind to get him. MacPhail opened the subject of a trade. 'I need pitching help,' he confessed. 'I like your man Embree, but Joe DiMaggio touted me off him. He told me to get Allie Reynolds. What'll you take for him?'

"I pretended to think it over. Then, 'I might take Snuffy Stirnweiss,' I said.

"I was merely obeying the first rule of baseball trading—the rule that you must never, never approach a prospective deal directly. MacPhail had violated it by laying his cards on the table. I didn't want Stirnweiss and didn't believe MacPhail would trade him.

"Larry recoiled at the mention of Stirnweiss. 'Nothing doing,' he said. 'How about Gordon?'"

So Gordon became an Indian and Reynolds became a Yankee, where he also was to become the best clutch pitcher in baseball.

Gordon, though, was brilliant with Cleveland. His arrival marked the first major trade in the big leagues for Veeck, who explained his approach to the game:

"I'm not the kind of fellow who can sit around for three, four, or five years waiting for the kids to get the experience they need to become top-flight big leaguers. I want the best team I can get every year. That's why I traded for Joe Gordon and that's why I'll take any other so-called veteran whom I think can help us."

MacPhail subsequently wanted to make another deal with Veeck after Veeck told him that he was pitching-poor, having traded Reynolds. Veeck pointed out that, while MacPhail seemed to have a promising catcher in Yogi Berra, the Yankees still needed a backup catcher. Veeck proposed Sherman Lollar, along with an infielder named Ray Mack, if MacPhail sent two pitchers from the Yankees' reserve list: Allen Gettel and Frank Shea.

MacPhail was willing to part with Gettel, but balked at Shea. Instead, MacPhail offered Veeck a list of fifteen available pitchers.

"Choose one," MacPhail told him.

Veeck excused himself from the room. He telephoned his old friend Casey Stengel, who was managing Oakland of the Pacific Coast League. Stengel and Veeck had joined forces once before, at Milwaukee. Stengel had been his manager there. Now Veeck was asking Stengel for advice. Veeck wondered about one of the pitchers on the list, Gene Bearden, who was playing at Oakland.

"What do you want me to do—throw in Christy Mathewson?" said Stengel. "Grab the guy before MacPhail recovers his sanity."

So Veeck returned and told MacPhail that Bearden was acceptable. But there was something else Veeck wanted. "Tell you what," said Veeck. "Throw in Hal Peck and it's a deal."

Peck, the three-toed outfielder, had wound up with the Yankees, but was bothered with a serious arm injury. The Yankees had little use for him. But Gettel won 11 games for the Indians in 1947, including a one-hitter. Peck suddenly was forced to become a regular after the right field-er, Hank Edwards, suffered a shoulder injury. Peck responded by batting .293, 14 points above his career average. Bearden, meanwhile, was sent to the minors for seasoning. But he came up in 1948.

Ironically, that year started with the manager that Veeck didn't want—Boudreau. When word got out that Veeck wanted to trade him, people collared Veeck on the streets and drove his office staff crazy with letters. Veeck was an easy man to spot walking along the street with his one-legged shuffle, and invariably passing cab drivers or truckers or pedestrians would shout at him to keep Boudreau.

It was apparent that 1948 would be a special year for the Indians. On Opening Day—an event that baseball people capitalize as if it were a national holiday—they set a season's-opener record of 73,163 fans. Feller shut out the Browns on two hits, and the Tribe went on to win six straight games.

This was a year that became etched in children's memories if they followed the Indians. It was to be a part of them forever, defining a special region of their childhood.

The Indians drew 2,620,627 fans, by far the greatest number of people ever to see an athletic team play in this country. They broke the Yankees' mark by almost 400,000. Cleveland's record, though, was set in a city with one of the smallest population centers in baseball and stood for more than thirty years. And in actual attendance, it probably remains the baseball record. In those days, season's-ticket sales didn't account for a significant number of fans. But today those figures are computed in attendance—whether or not the season ticket-holder actually shows up.

No one had seen anything like the impact the team had on its city. By late May the first television broadcasts of Indians' home games were beaming the team to those who had sets, and still fans turned out—82,781, a record for a regular-season crowd in a doubleheader against the A's; 65,797, the most ever to see a night game, for a tilt against the Yankees on the second anniversary of Veeck's presidency; 73,484 as Boudreau, injured, hit a pinch single to help beat the Yankees twice.

Veeck was now joined in the front office by Hank Greenberg, the prodigious slugger who finished his career with the Pirates in 1947. Veeck at first was interested in putting Greenberg in an Indian uniform for 1948. In 1947, at the age of thirty-six, Greenberg had smacked 25 home runs for the Pirates, although aided by something called Greenberg Gardens—in essence, a friendly left-field fence. Veeck, of course, knew about constructing these fences. Indeed, one might even say he had invented the movable fence. When Ralph Kiner joined the Pirates that left-field area became known as Kiner's Corner.

Veeck described Greenberg's position with the Indians as "unique in baseball history." For Greenberg, who did not become a player, nevertheless became a coach—as well as a stockholder and vice president of the team. Greenberg was to move with Veeck into other baseball ventures, a distinctly odd couple of sports. Greenberg was aloof and argumentative. Yet, almost forty years later Greenberg was to describe Veeck as "my best friend."

The two had met at the 1947 World Series. Greenberg had just been released by the Pirates and was attempting to get into the business end of baseball. He had accumulated a considerable amount of income. Still, Veeck explained later, Greenberg had not much experience in operating a ball club. So they worked out a deal. Veeck induced a number of his stockholders to sell part of their holdings to Greenberg. He wound up with $100,000 worth. Veeck agreed to make Greenberg vice president "and to teach him what I knew about the baseball business in return for certain services from him."

Greenberg also served as a batting coach, and one of his projects was the free-swinging power hitter Pat Seerey. But Seerey struck out eight times in 23 at-bats before he was unloaded with Gettel to the White Sox in a trade for Bob Kennedy. Seerey wound up as the league leader in strikeouts while Kennedy became a .300 hitter.

Meanwhile, Greenberg gave Veeck a cachet he had not otherwise enjoyed. Greenberg not only was a respected slugger, and future Hall of Fame player, he was married to a society woman, the daughter of the owner of Gimbel's department store.

"As an executive, he was invaluable," Veeck explained in *The Saturday Evening Post* in 1949. "He joined me on the mashed-potato circuit. In meetings he was respected and liked by executives of other clubs. That last factor is important to me because my fellow club owners haven't exactly lavished their affection on me. I believe I have offended their sense of dignity. They have, many of them, intensified my dislike for stuffed-shirtism. I hope I have made them uncomfortable by demonstrating that a little extra hustle pays off in the front office as well as on the ball field. Nevertheless, it is necessary that we have a representative in the league councils who doesn't raise the blood pressure of our fellow magnates whenever he opens his mouth. That's where Greenberg fits in."

But Veeck was doing his own dealing in 1948 despite the imposing presence in the front office and on the field of the six-foot, four-inch, 210-pound Greenberg.

Thirteen days after Veeck acquired Bob Kennedy, Veeck parted with $100,000 and a pitcher named Pat Kennedy to get the Browns' Sad Sam Zoldak, who had only a 2-4 record on the terrible Browns. But he also had blown up against Manager Zack Taylor, who fined him $200 for "insubordination." Zoldak had gone into a tirade after being relieved in a game against the Philadelphia Athletics. Obviously another wounded player (pride, in this case) just waiting to be revived by Veeck. Zoldak posted a 9-6 record with the Indians down the stretch.

Veeck, of course, could not stay away from controversy and the outrageous. And so, into a mad pennant race with the Yankees and Red Sox at mid-season, Veeck suddenly signed Leroy (Satchel) Paige. Official baseball was outraged. The fans loved it.

"Veeck has gone too far in his quest for publicity," said J. G. Taylor Spink, the publisher of the baseball bible, *The Sporting News*. Why, said Spink, there are some reports that Paige is fifty years old. "To sign a hurler at Paige's age is to demean the standards of baseball," contended Spink. He also said there was the "suspicion that if Satchel were white, he would not have drawn a second thought from Veeck."

But Veeck and Boudreau had personally worked out Paige before signing him. Boudreau batted against him—while Veeck, on his artifical leg, shagged fly balls.

Officially, Leroy Robert Paige was forty years old and, at the least, a legend. Veeck used to see him pitch in the 1930s, when Paige's black teams frequently traveled to Chicago—and practically anyplace else that had a baseball diamond.

He was a gangly creature with a shuffling gait, moving slowly. He was nearly six-four, but weighed only 175 pounds. He had a peculiar sort of wisdom: "Don't look back; something might be gaining on you," he advised.

These were part of his posted rules for staying young:

1. Avoid fried meats, which angry up the blood.
2. If your stomach disputes you, lie down and pacify it with cool thoughts.
3. Keep the juices flowing by jangling around gently as you move.
4. Go very light on the vices such as carrying on in society. The social rumble ain't restful.
5. Avoid running at all times.

6.   Don't look back; something might be gaining on you.

But he was no old fool. Bob Feller knew him and respected him. Feller, an inveterate barnstormer, had pitched many times against Paige.

Truth or fiction? Who knew? Paige supposedly had pitched in the 1920s. One of his former teammates on the Kansas City Monarchs, John (Buck) O'Neil, who later scouted for the Cubs, recalls this incident from 1942, which O'Neil described to *Reader's Digest* as "the greatest of his feats":

The Kansas City Monarchs (Satchel's team) were playing the Washington Homestead Greys in the Negro League World Series. The Greys had Josh Gibson, acclaimed as the league's Babe Ruth, and perhaps even a greater slugger than Ruth.

Satchel led his team into the ninth inning with a 3-2 lead. He struck out the first two batters, then yielded a triple. He called O'Neil, his first baseman, to the mound. "I'm going to walk the next two to pitch to Josh," he announced to O'Neil. He did, and then Gibson stepped up. Paige shouted to the feared slugger, "Hey, remember when we were with the Pittsburgh Crawfords, and you said you were the best batter in the world, and I said I was the best pitcher, and one day we were going to meet?"

"Yeah, Satchel."

"Well, this is it."

Three strikes later, Satchel strode off the mound, the winner.

By the time he reached the major leagues, Paige estimated he had appeared in 2,500 games and won 2,000. He once pitched twenty-nine consecutive days when playing for a white semipro team in Bismarck, North Dakota. It was there, he claimed, that the Sioux Indians taught him to make a special snake-oil preparation to rub on his pitching arm.

The man was made to order for Veeck, who signed Paige on his forty-second birthday, July 7. Paige promptly announced he really was only thirty-nine.

Veeck was almost defensive in making Paige a big-leaguer. Veeck explained that he had tried to make a deal by the June 15 trading deadline but couldn't get together with another team.

Paige admitted he no longer was the overpowering pitcher he had been, say, in 1934, when he defeated Dizzy Dean by 1-0 in a 13-inning exhibition duel. Paige explained he no longer could overpower the hitters, and instead now could "out-cute" them. His pitching weapons included a knuckleball, a hesitation pitch, a screwball, and several slow curves.

Two days after he was signed, and put in the bull pen, he made his major-league debut, the first black pitcher in the American League. It came against the Browns in Cleveland Stadium, in relief of Bob Lemon.

It was a 400-foot walk from the bull pen in right field to the mound, and Paige made the most of it while the crowd of 34,780 stood and whistled. With each shuffle the cheering grew louder and the mob of photographers got bigger, and finally nine of them surged onto the field and took the pitcher's mound. Umpire Bill McGowan didn't even shoo away the photographers and allowed them to snap their pictures while Paige was winding up.

He unveiled a windmill delivery, his right arm revolving until he finally was ready to throw a pitch. Sometimes he wound up his arm with six revolutions, sometimes two. The classic pitcher is supposed to throw every pitch with the same motion so the batter can't guess what's coming. Instead, Paige tossed one sidearm, one overhand, one underhand.

He tossed his hesitation pitch—a remarkable delivery in which his arm came over his head without the ball being released. It seemed he was ready to go into his follow-through when all of a sudden the ball appeared and headed toward the plate. Manager Zack Taylor of the Browns protested that the pitch was illegal, but McGowan said no.

Chuck Stevens, the Browns' first baseman, was the first batter Paige faced, and Stevens singled. Paige then retired the next three batters. The same situation arose in the next inning, and Paige again got three outs after a lead-off hit.

Five nights later the Indians attracted 64,877 fans for an exhibition game against the Brooklyn Dodgers. Paige arrived in the seventh inning, relieving Don Black, who had given two runs in the sixth to tie the game at 3-all. This time Paige displayed his corkscrew windup. He looked like a man about to tunnel into the ground with his right arm. But on 12 pitches he struck out the side. First, he struck out Gil Hodges on four pitches. Then he set down Erv Palica on three curveballs. Finally, he fanned Tommy Brown on five pitches. In the eighth inning, Paige mowed down three batters.

One night later, with the Paige momentum building along with a first-place Indians team, 20,000 fans were turned away. They missed seeing Paige's first big-league victory. He earned it in the second game of a doubleheader. He relieved Lemon in the sixth, and held the A's to three hits the rest of the way.

When he wasn't pitching, good ole Satchel—a nickname he acquired as a seven-year-old working at a train depot, where he outfitted himself with a harness contraption that permitted him to carry four satchels at a time—continued to have fun with his age. He offered $500 to anyone who could prove he pitched before 1927. Actually, it probably was Veeck who put him up to that deal. Someone found an article from a 1926 Memphis newspaper that listed a "Satchel" hurling for the Chattanooga Black Lookouts. Paige was confronted with the article.

"I musta slept a year somewhere," he said.

The Paige legend grew so quickly that a remarkable event occurred on August 13—Paige's first start. It came against the White Sox in Chicago. The moribund Sox were in last place, so far out of the pennant race that the Chicago *Tribune* ran an editorial suggesting the team be sold because it was an embarrassment to a great city.

But that night Paige created one of the worst traffic jams in the history of Comiskey Park. A crowd of 51,013 shoehorned its way in, while police estimated another 15,000 were turned away. Sixty minutes before game time, the police threw up their hands and allowed drivers to double-park just to ease the traffic. Ticket-holders showed up as late as the third inning. Just before game time, the crowd pressure at one entrance was so intense that the gate collapsed. Hundreds of fans entered without tickets. It was the largest nighttime crowd in Chicago history, and the Sox high for the year.

To add to the circus atmosphere, the umpires didn't have their uniforms—they had been shipped to Cleveland. So Art Passarella, behind home plate, wore brown trousers and a blue coat. Ed Rommel, at third, sported a powder-blue suit loaned by the White Sox manager, Ted Lyons. All the umpires wore White Sox caps. But that didn't mean they were partial. For the cap was emblazoned with a "C," which, they explained, stands for Cleveland as well as Chicago.

In addition, Passarella's ball-and-strike indicator was mixed in with his Cleveland-bound clothing. So he kept count on his fingers.

What better setting for Paige? He hurled a shutout, which merely set the stage for his next appearance. One week later the Indians were home and the White Sox were the opponents. A record night-game crowd of 78,382 turned out.

This time Paige tossed a three-hit shutout and the Indians tied an American League mark with their fourth straight shutout as he followed Lemon, Bearden, and Zoldak with a blanking.

No sooner did the game end then Veeck, mindful of the criticism he had received a month earlier, tossed off a telegram to *The Sporting News's* Spink:

"PAIGE PITCHING—NO RUNS, THREE HITS. HE
DEFINITELY IS IN LINE FOR SPORTING NEWS'
'ROOKIE OF YEAR' AWARD. REGARDS."

Veeck made the telegram public, and that distressed *The Sporting News*. So in the same edition and on the same page that printed Veeck's telegram the following week, *The Sporting News* retaliated with two boxes and a column denigrating Paige's accomplishments.

One box was headlined "Three of Five Paige Wins Over 2nd Division Teams," and went on to explain that, even though he had a 5-1 record after his first 14 appearances, two of his decisions came against the last-place White Sox. Further, he had pitched only 17 of 49 1/3 innings against first-division clubs. And these contending teams "combed Satch for 16 hits."

Another story pointed out that Dom DiMaggio of the Red Sox homered against Paige over the left-field wall in Boston and eventually Paige was knocked out of the game. As if to rebut Paige's accomplishments—and Veeck's telegram—Spink wrote he could not express "any admiration for the present-day standard of major-league ball that makes such a showing possible." This is the sort of reaction that makes logical men angry—and probably gave a gifted thinker like Veeck even more reason to gnash his teeth against the Establishment.

The day after Paige's shutout, the Indians started a four-game losing streak. It knocked them out of first place as the Red Sox took over, helped by a victory over Paige, who was pitching with only three days' rest. The slide continued until Paige faced the Senators on August 30, with the Indians two games out. He halted Washington. It was to be his final victory of the season, a 6-1 rookie year.

Meanwhile, there was a pennant to be won. Their slump had pushed them to 4 1/2 games behind the Red Sox on the eve of Labor Day. A week later Black suffered his collapse in a game against the Browns and was taken unconscious to the hospital. Nine days later Feller defeated the Red Sox on Don Black Night to propel the Indians back into a first-place tie. And six days later Joe Earley Night attracted 60,405 fans as the Indians toppled the White Sox.

The pennant, though, seemed almost assured the day before the regular season was to end. On Saturday, Bearden, the rookie, earned his nineteenth victory and shut out the Tigers to clinch at least a tie for the Indians. Meanwhile, the Red Sox were eliminating the Yankees.

The Indians needed either a victory on the closing day or a Red Sox loss. They got neither. For Hal Newhouser of the Tigers halted Feller and the Indians while the Red Sox again defeated the Yankees. That set up the first playoff in American League history—one game to decide the pennant. Several days earlier the Red Sox had won the toss of the coin for the home-field advantage, and so the play-off game would be held at Fenway Park on Monday.

That presented Boudreau with a tremendous problem. His pitcher, Lemon, overworked during the stretch drive, had hurled Friday. He led the league with 294 innings pitched. Bearden had pitched Saturday, Feller had lost Sunday.

At a team meeting after Sunday's game, Boudreau told the players he had his pitcher in mind. But first he asked if there were any suggestions. Gordon told him the players would go along with anyone he picked.

"My choice is Bearden," said Boudreau.

He warned his players, though, not to mention that to anyone, especialy the reporters. He wanted Bearden to get a night's sleep on the train heading for Boston. Everyone assumed Lemon would be the pitcher. The play-off would be a battle of right-handers—Lemon versus Denny Galehouse.

Left-handers and Fenway Park didn't get along well. That short wall in left field had driven southpaws to the showers consistently. Yet, fifteen minutes before game time, the Red Sox were surprised to learn that Bearden, a left-handed rookie, would start with one day's rest.

That game, though, also climaxed Boudreau's spectacular season. He put his team in front in the first inning with a home run, then led a rally in the fourth by singling. In the sixth he belted another homer and later added a single for a 4-4 day. Bearden coasted to an 8-3 victory.

In Veeck's third season as owner—and not even three full ones at that—the Indians had won their first pennant in twenty-eight years. Boudreau wound up batting .355, with 18 homers and 107 runs batted in. He was soon voted the league's most valuable player over Ted Williams, who had captured the batting championship.

"Cleveland won the pennant," conceded Veeck, "the day I was forced to keep Lou Boudreau."

There still was a World Series to play. The Indians didn't have to go far. It was against the Boston Braves and opened in Boston.

The Indians were Destiny's Tots for one more week. They lost the opening game by 1-0 to Johnny Sain as Feller came the closest he ever would to winning a World Series contest. Feller had a no-hitter for four innings, and a one-hitter into the eighth. With men on first and second, Feller wheeled and threw to Boudreau in a pickoff play that the pair had perfected at second base. But Umpire Bill Stewart called Phil Masi safe. Tommy Holmes soon singled Masi home for the game's only run.

There were no days off between games when the teams shifted cities. The Indians won four of the next five as Bearden saved the final game for Lemon. The Indians were world champions. They celebrated like baseball champions too.

On the overnight train ride back to Cleveland, recalls Johnny Berardino, "Bill had gotten some cases of champagne on board and everybody was swizzling it down and I had champagne poured on top of me." Berardino then got on top of a table and started to recite Hamlet. "To be, or not to be..." he started, only to be stopped by champagne streams directed at his face.

The next morning crowds estimated at almost half a million lined the Euclid Avenue route from Cleveland Terminal to University Circle to welcome the world champions. Alvin Silverman, writing in the *Plain-Dealer*, described it as a victory for the city. This was the National Pastime, America's game, and in the heartland of the United States. Veeck's team seemed to speak for what was good in the country.

"Each nationality and racial group in a great metropolitan center had someone on the Cleveland baseball club who was the embodiment of his own ideals and aspirations and dreams," said Silverman, getting warmed up. "Each [fan at the parade] felt that he, personally, had contributed to the victory. Each sensed that the men in the automobiles were not merely winning ballplayers but Americans who had succeeded in the favorite American way, the hard way."

It was a glorious, golden moment for everyone in Cleveland. Everyone, that is, except Veeck. He recalled in his autobiography, written fourteen years later, that he went to his empty apartment and thought of his son, "who was something less than proud of me." He also thought of his failed marriage. At that moment of triumph, said Veeck, "I had never been more lonely in my life."

Chapter 6

Veeck devised interesting ways to beat the blues. He outflew them. Or, at least, he tried to.

In the early days of Milwaukee and Cleveland he had local hangouts to run to. Fame and notoriety increased his horizons. Veeck now was a nationally recognized figure. Through his connection with Bob Hope he met Bing Crosby, and through Bing Crosby he became friendly with Skitch Henderson and then Frank Sinatra.

Veeck wound up a regular in New York's Copacabana nightclub—perhaps the only commuter from Cleveland the place ever had. The show-place club was more noted as a hangout for the delicious Broadway characters that out-Runyoned Damon Runyon, where ringside tables went only to the best bookmakers.

But Veeck was fascinated by the place and embarked on a year-long commute that saw him take a late-night plane from Cleveland to New York, taxi in from La Guardia airport to the Copa, spend the early hours there and at a Midtown restaurant, and then catch a flight back to Cleveland.

It was a time he flirted with leaving baseball. After all, what could Bill Veeck do after a World Series triumph? Show business was an interesting frontier and, the way Bill Veeck ran the National Pastime, the fields were not so different after all.

Henderson had not yet received the national renown he was to enjoy after joining Steve Allen, which helped launch a major career as a conductor and pianist. He was trying to find himself in music and needed someone to goad him. Veeck was the man. The pair established a strong bond—Henderson looked up to Veeck and eagerly followed his advice on career choices, while Veeck jumped easily into the show-business waters that surrounded Henderson and his life.

Speak to Henderson today, and he still thinks of Veeck as one of the most important people in his life. "I was conducting the Lucky Strike show, called *Light Up Time,* with Sinatra," says Henderson. "We were doing what was called 'doubling,' playing the Copacabana, which was the place to go in those days. And Bill was there—I mean, almost every night.

"At that time he felt he should be in show-business management, which I don't think has ever been touched on. I don't think people realized he wanted to leave baseball. He was very observant of everything we did and literally was always there at the last show. He and I became personal friends as well as, in a strange way, show-business friends."

Veeck already was exploring the crossover possibilities between baseball and show business, not to mention theatrics. He told Henderson how wonderful it would be if he could have an orchestra playing in the ballparks during games. Henderson suggested a symphony orchestra ("Did you know he used the Cleveland Symphony once? I think they played 'William Tell,' you know, to be safe.").

As usual, Veeck was complaining about the state of baseball. Individualism was gone. It wasn't like the old days, especially the old days with the Cubs. Those were characters then, those were real people. And the owners, they really cared about baseball.

"He thought baseball was going down the drain at the time. I followed baseball but he was the first one I ever heard talk about showboats. He explained to me about them, what they did, why he liked them, and I really was a ball fan. And I tried to learn baseball from him, but he didn't want to talk about it. He wanted to talk about show business, and I remember many nights sitting at the Copa with our trivia games, talking with him. We used to play charades all the time, go in my dressing room with Frank and some other people."

This was a turning point in the lives of the three—Veeck, Sinatra, Henderson: Veeck, separated by design from his family, getting antsy about staying in Cleveland; Sinatra, his career suffering because of vocal-cord damage as well as several well-reported tiffs and some allegations from right-wingers about his politics; Henderson, unsure about his status in the music business.

"Bill wasn't afraid to speak his mind, which wasn't the most popular concept at that time," says Henderson. "That was a bad time for Sinatra, but Veeck was one of the people who was totally warm and understanding. He wasn't a gossip. He was one of the men I met in the sports business who was an enigma to me because he was so totally outgoing and knowledgeable, but never obnoxiously knowledgeable.

"I can tell you, it was a bad time for Frank. The next year it was the bottom of the ladder. Veeck felt that we were all dummies in our careers. I had gotten out of the Air Force and I was just starting to realize that maybe I had a chance to do something. He felt that the people who handled us—and I really shouldn't use the word—were all just flesh peddlers. They had no interest in people. He was incredible. He could sit down and talk to you and look right through you. The only other person that affected me as much was Crosby. In my life, I'm talking. And I've been with a lot of heavyweights.

"Veeck helped me psychologically, which is a hard thing to admit. He just said to me, 'Get off your ass, don't let anybody push you around. What you can do, you can do, and nobody can take it away from you.' And he made that speech to me. It was like he was talking to a first baseman."

As Henderson continued to reminisce about Veeck, the musician grew more and more wistful and recalled the many sides Veeck presented. Veeck showed himself to be a good, even fascinated, listener, a trait so many others vividly remember. Veeck also displayed his enjoyment of hanging out with characters on the fringe of the law—if not downright crooked.

"You know, he was a music fan. He drank his music like he drank in everything else. He was an engulfer of aesthetics. If people were square with him, he was fair and square with them. I wasn't too happy in those days because Frank—and I loved him—was very tough to work with. Strange that Veeck filled an almost fatherly niche in my life at that point.

"He was a commuter before it was popular to be a commuter. He would stay till five o'clock in the morning and then he'd go back to Cleveland because in those days we did a 1 A.M. show. It was a different time. We did a first show at 10 P.M., but on Saturdays we did three shows and by the time we sat down and talked it was late. Then we'd go to one of the midtown restaurants, a hangout, the late-night place to go and talk."

Between shows, though, they met backstage at the Copa, where they played games. "He was wild at charades, and a hell of a competitor," remembers Henderson.

Despite the social gabbing and drinking milieu, Veeck was never seen with a woman, although a longtime associate claims it was a reason he went to New York so often.

"He was always alone. I never saw him with anybody, male or female," says Henderson. Veeck would sit at ringside, or sometimes join newly found acquaintances. Henderson remembers Veeck's cigarettes: "He was quite healthy at the time, but an absolute smokestack.

"He was not a Broadwayite. I think that's important. He was not a Stage Deli guy. He didn't go to Dempsey's. He was funny that way. He was a snob in a way. He had his idea of who was successful or was going to be successful in the business, and those were the people he affiliated himself with. But he could also be very taciturn. He wasn't too crazy about Fat Jack Leonard [an insult comedian, years before Don Rickles], for one. He was strange. He was an enigma."

Indeed.

Veeck's liberalism also shone through in what were the stirrings of the McCarthy era. In his fight for the black ballplayer, in his thoughts on the plight of the blacks in general, he made himself clear, which Henderson still remembers. And of Veeck's fondness for those beyond the law? Perhaps in some way he saw these people as anti-Establishment figures, tilting at authority. That was a stance not unknown to Veeck.

"The trips to New York were like a separate block of his life. We used to talk about it, how he would show up and he was accepted. You know, at that time the upper level of, shall we say, Brooklyn, sat at the Copa. And he was in a strange way accepted by them, but in a detached way. He had no truck with them."

You mean mobsters? Bookies?

"Really, if there is such a thing, Mafioso types. And it was funny that they would accept him. But he lived with us."

And the effect he had on you?

"There are very few people in my life, and Bing is Number One, but Veeck, very much, put a stamp on my forehead that never went away, and I watched his life all the time. It really warmed me to be able to think about him. There's really no one to talk to about those days, unless you talk to sports guys, and their concept of him is totally different. I didn't drink, and he always used to say, 'Stay that way, stay that way.' I mean, he really was incredible—strong, strength and warmth, which is an incredible combination. What a story his life would make. Robert Redford. That's what he looked like to me. He was glamour without exuding glamour. And that's rare."

And did your paths cross after that period?

"I would go out of the way to try and come by and say hello, and he would either be brusque—which was his manner—or he would totally engulf you and want you to give up your life for two days and go someplace. Occasionally, I would feel as if I was in the way."

The first blending of baseball and theatre for Veeck probably occurred a year after he had arrived in Cleveland. He installed an incredibly double-jointed, rubber-faced ex-pitcher named Max Patkin as one of his "coaches." He teamed him with Jackie Price, best described as a comic infielder. Their job? To make the fans laugh in a pre-game show.

Now, baseball had enjoyed a rich tradition of comics, with Al Schacht renowned as the Clown Prince of Baseball. But Schacht's shticks were part of a pre-game exhibition.

Patkin actually became a coach for the Indians. For a few innings a game he would take over at first base. He would bend himself into outrageous contortions and he would make fun of the umpires. One day, he went too far.

In Cleveland one afternoon, the Indians were playing the Red Sox. Cal Hubbard, the former football Giants' lineman, was umpiring behind the plate. Hubbard called a strike on Les Fleming. Patkin, coaching at first, signified the ball was high by drawing his hand across his throat. But that is also the "choke" sign—in other words, a charge that the umpire, intimidated by the other team, blew the call. When the Cleveland fans saw the gesture, they laughed and applauded.

Hubbard choke? The six-foot, two-inch, 250-pound Hubbard—a charter member of the Pro Football Hall of Fame—was furious. He tore off his mask and immediately thumbed Patkin out of the game.

That night Veeck protested to Will Harridge, president of the American League. Harridge ordered Patkin reinstated for the next game. Patkin became known as the Indians' tenth man. Had he remained in baseball, Harridge probably would have had to make a hard decision on the man's future.

Steve O'Neill, the Tigers' manager, was the first to complain to the umpires about Patkin's "coaching" tactics. "The guy is wonderful," O'Neill conceded, "but how can you play ball when you hear the fans laugh and you know that everyone in the park is watching Patkin?"

Patkin sort of sneaked up on people. Often, he might have been coaching at first for an inning or two before the fans even noticed. But Patkin, double-jointed, soon changed that.

He was six-three and weighed 175. Fans might notice the runner at first taking a lead. Suddenly Patkin would stretch the upper half of his body forward, parallel to the field. Slowly he would continue to lean until his chin scraped the ground. By then everyone in the ballpark—including the opposing pitcher—was keeping an eye on the clown and not on the runner. As he leaned forward, he pretended he was stealing the catcher's sign to the pitcher.

This approach to the venerable game in one close contest did not amuse the Yankees' manager, Bill Dickey. He threatened to pull his team off the field if Patkin didn't stop clowning.

Patkin might have been a comedian on the field, but off it he was a nervous wreck. He had a bad stomach and could eat only once a day. He slept only four hours a night, and used to smoke several packs of cigarettes daily. "I work under a great handicap," he liked to say. "I have no talent."

Finally he went too far, even for Veeck's Indians. On a team train trip Price terrified several women passengers by pulling his pet snakes out of a basket. "What are we running—a circus or a ball club?" Boudreau asked Veeck. Patkin was shipped to the minors.

But he was to be reunited with Veeck over the next twenty-eight years. When Veeck bought the St. Louis Browns in 1951, Patkin made several appearances. And in 1976, after Veeck took over the White Sox, he hired Patkin as first-base coach for a series against Oakland. Patkin, who never made it to the majors as a pitcher, found he had a longer career in uniform than almost any pitcher who ever lived.

Veeck's friends knew that his marriage to Eleanor was virtually over. So he made no secret of his dating. Later, he said that divorce proceedings already were under way in 1949 when he met Mary Frances Ackerman, a woman of many talents who was to become his second wife and bear six children. She was a publicist for the Ice Capades, a graduate in drama of Carnegie Tech. She was twenty-eight years old, witty, attractive, and eligible.

"Bill was a Protestant and he met Mary Frances on a joke," recalls Bob Fishel. "Somebody in the hockey business that he knew introduced them. Mary Frances was a very proper lady, very beautiful lady. Very religious lady. Catholic—and I guess nobody touched her.

"I guess this was the gag by the guy who introduced them. Bill was all-conquering, and he wouldn't be able to connect with her. But that wasn't the case at all. He fell in love with her and he wound up marrying her. But the only way she'd marry him was in the Church, and he was non-Catholic and already had three children." Veeck and his first wife had been married in the Episcopal Church.

According to Fishel, Muddy Ruel—Veeck's former coach and a lawyer—put the complicated plans together that first led to Veeck's religious conversion and then marriage. "Bill went and studied Catholicism. Nobody saw him for three or four months. He went to Chicago, and that's all he did was study Catholicism."

In looking back over her meeting Veeck, she once said, "I had a wonderful job and I was not dying to meet men." But she agreed to be introduced to him at a dinner party in August of 1949. That was six months after an Associated Press brief noted that Mrs. Bill Veeck had filed for divorce in Tucson. So it appears that his first children have grown up under a misconception about the timing of his second marriage—his first wife already was seeking a divorce before he met the woman who was to become his second wife.

"A friend was pretty persistent in wanting to introduce me to Bill," recalled Mary Frances. "One argument the friend used was that Bill Veeck's genius for promotion would provide some new ideas for the ice show."

What she knew about Bill Veeck she didn't like. For his antics and his celebrated team had made it hard for her to break into newspapers with stories about an ice show. Still, they met at the friend's for dinner.

"We argued," she recalled. "Afterwards he wanted to drive me to my hotel. We stopped for hamburgers in a greasy spoon. He floored me by asking for a date the next night—just at the moment when I was telling myself I wasn't ever going to see this fellow again.

"A week later he asked me to marry him. A week after that we were engaged."

At their wedding—in a cathedral with nuptial mass—he surprised her family when he turned up without a tie. Her mother took it in stride, though, and said, "Well, I guess they'll be just as married whether he wears a tie or not."

Mary Frances once claimed that when she was thirteen, and watching a game in her home town of Pittsburgh, she was distressed when fans booed a ballplayer. She never became a fan as a result.

But she stepped easily and quickly into a new role—owner's wife. Indeed, she defined it. Wherever baseball took them, the Veecks were known as Bill and Mary Frances. She was not simply Mrs. Veeck, or Mary Frances Veeck, but Mary Frances. She established her own identity. Even today there are many baseball people who believe she was behind—or helped to create—many of his deals and promotions. Wherever she went she had a radio or television show, often in collaboration with Bill.

At the time they met he was about to begin another major-league change—getting rid of the Indians. Then again, Bill Veeck was always getting rid of things just when it appeared he was most interested.

Winning is hard. Winning again is harder. The special magic that Veeck had brought to the Indians translated itself into a world championship.

But things change. With the title came the end of a cinematic-like happening. Reality set in for Veeck and his ballplayers. Suddenly everyone demanded more money. Suddenly Veeck found himself looking once again for a new challenge. Suddenly his marriage really was over. He needed to raise the money to bring it to a financial close as well.

The 1949 season saw the Indians attract more than 2.2 million fans. But Bearden suffered a sore arm and Boudreau could not repeat his spectacular 1948 campaign. The Yankees, meanwhile, had Casey Stengel as their new manager, and he kept discovering subs to bring in and play like all-stars. The Indians had a decent season, but finished third.

It was the start of the Stengel era—dynasty, more accurately—with the Yankees. Under Stengel through twelve seasons, the only team other than the Yankees to finish first in the American League were teams that Veeck was associated with or had a hand in building—the 1954 Indians and the 1959 White Sox. In fact, from 1947 to 1964 only the Indians and White Sox interrupted the Yankee marches to first place.

The 1949 campaign marked Veeck's fourth season in Cleveland. Rumors surfaced early that he was interested in selling the team, but he always denied the stories.

His friends, and Veeck, always contended that the reason he finally did sell was to be able to pay a divorce settlement that was to include a trust fund for his three children. There is another aspect to that sale, though, that has been rumored but that many of his closest friends have never even heard of. And that is that he was involved in a serious auto accident in Arizona at just about that time and needed cash for an out-of-court settlement, since his insurance could not cover the damages claimed by the other people in the accident.

Bob Feller has heard this story, and so has Pete Veeck. Few others have, though. Either way, Bill Veeck still needed money. His longtime associate, Marsh Samuel—who grew up with Veeck in Illinois and worked with him at Cleveland and then in the public relations business—recalls that time:

"His wife stayed in Arizona the whole time he was in Cleveland. They were totally estranged, so he wanted to make financial provisions for her that nobody could argue about and that involved selling the ball club."

Veeck dealt with the ubiquitous Jacobs Brothers. They were probably the most far-reaching concessionaires in sports. They sold most of the hot dogs at ballparks and race tracks. They also made money by underwriting teams—advancing food and cash. They also had undergone many Federal investigations into alleged mobster ties.

"One of the Jacobs Brothers offered to help Bill," recalls Samuel, "but Bill wanted a clean break with the Indians. I think that Bill thought that with his record, he wouldn't have any trouble buying another team. He sold out and he did provide for Eleanor and the kids very generously, keeping nothing for himself, really. He had made a lot of money with the ball club." How much money Veeck provided in the divorce settlement has been a sore point for his first family ever since.

Veeck claimed in his autobiography that after the sale of the Indians he received a check for $1 million—"the end product of the $1 I had started out with in Milwaukee."

Then, he said, the tax bite cut 25 percent off his million. Presumably, that left him with $750,000. And here is the questionable part: "In addition to turning over half of what was left to Eleanor, I also bought the ranch... from her." In other words, he purportedly gave Eleanor $375,000 and, for an additional amount, bought the ranch.

But a divorce settlement signed on October 29, 1949, in Tucson, and filed with the Arizona Superior Court, paints a different picture. In that document Bill Veeck agreed to pay 25 percent of his future compensation to Eleanor Veeck "as long as she lives." The legal papers noted that Veeck's earning capacity was unpredictable, and so it stipulated he pay at the rate of $1,000 a month.

He also agreed to a lump-sum payment of $100,000 to his wife—and he received the ranch. He also placed $125,000 in a trust fund for the children's expenses. That translates to a $225,000 outlay, far from the figure he mentioned.

There was another point. He promised to give half his property at his death to his wife. Yet, in 1962 he drew up a will that specifically made Mary Frances his sole beneficiary. In addition, two years later he added a codicil that if his children from the second marriage survived Mary Frances at his death, they would divide the money—nothing was earmarked for his first family. That will was filed in Chicago on January 13, 1986, eleven days after his death.

Samuel, who wound up working for the Yankees in marketing, and then became an official of their Fort Lauderdale farm, recalls that there were unfulfilled Veeck ideas when he left the Indians.

"He had a list at all times of possible ideas. One of the things he wanted to do was to change the all-star voting and put a traveling Hall of Fame on the road, get a corporate sponsor and use Rogers Hornsby. He was looking for a girl baseball player. Of course that never materialized. He had the idea to bring a midget to the plate in Cleveland, but we had a winning team, so you don't do things like that."

One of the strangest promotions Veeck ever unveiled, though, took place that final year in Cleveland. He literally buried the pennant they had won the year before.

The Indians trailed the Yankees and Red Sox for most of the season. Finally, when the Indians were eliminated from the race, Veeck decided to mark the demise with mock solemnity. After all, baseball was only a game, wasn't it?

He staged a funeral. The procession moved in funeral time to center field. There the world championship pennant was buried.

"If you look in the 1950 Baseball Guide you'll see a huge picture of it," recalls Bob Fishel. "I'm in it, if you look in the back. Most people wore high hats and white gloves and they had a big hearse. It was terrific, but I don't think you make fun of a funeral. It was one of the promotions I didn't like. But it was terrific anyway."

Bob Feller still looks back at that with dismay. "It was the only thing I ever disagreed with Bill about," says Feller.

Finally, late in 1949, and shortly after Veeck met Mary Frances Ackerman, Veeck sold the Indians for $2.2 million. It was a difficult time to work the sale, for Veeck was also living in Chicago. The way Bob Fishel recalls those days, Veeck was there learning Catholicism. He also was juggling his finances and the Indians.

"The only way she'd marry him was in the Church," says Fishel. "Muddy Ruel was one of his coaches. He was an assistant to Commissioner Happy Chandler and Ruel was also a lawyer. He told Bill the only way he could convert was to study. Ruel had connections in Chicago."

Veeck also found a buyer for the team, an insurance executive named Ellis Ryan. While the deal was brewing, Veeck summoned Samuel to Chicago to help him answer the phones and deflect questions from the press. And the deal got more complicated when two different business-men were quoted as saying they had been led to believe Veeck would sell to them. One of the Indians' shareholders was even to sue Veeck, charging bad faith.

Publicly, Veeck never mentioned the divorce settlement as a reason for the sale. Nor did he ever suggest there was an automobile accident. He had given many hints during the '49 season that he would sell. He needed a challenge, he explained. "I have to have a challenge. That's why I've been playing tennis every afternoon. One-legged men aren't sup-posed to play tennis. I have to prove that I can do it."

Chapter 7

The wedding announcement carried a Santa Fe, New Mexico, dateline from April 29, 1950. It said simply that thirty-six-year-old Bill Veeck had married twenty-nine-year-old Mary Frances Ackerman of Oklahoma City.

Obviously, his studies, his desire, and the disposition of his first family had made him acceptable to the Roman Catholic hierarchy. There were ways to make him acceptable.

"I always thought if you were divorced you couldn't remarry in the church," says Peter Veeck now, with that tart tone that marks his statements about his father.

Bill Veeck, who had married his first wife in an Episcopal ceremony, apparently was enthusiastic in his conversion studies, at least the way Marsh Samuel remembered. "Bill had a very inquiring mind. When he got into it, he was extremely interested. He questioned, but not to the point he couldn't accept it. It was a challenge, and he met it just like he met all the other challenges."

He wouldn't have to wait long for his next baseball challenge. Not much more than a year. Deals abounded. Even while he had owned the Indians, the head of Miller's beer in Milwaukee asked Veeck to take over the St. Louis Browns, a continually troubled franchise, and move it to Milwaukee. And soon after Veeck actually sold the Indians, he started getting even more queries. He also told people he was interested in the New York Giants.

Milwaukee was joined by Los Angeles, Queens, New York, and Baltimore. Various business and civic groups called Veeck and told him how ripe their area was for major-league ball. Wouldn't he consider buying a team and moving it to their place? Eventually all those cities did, in fact, get major-league franchises—the Dodgers leaving Brooklyn for Los Angeles, the Browns leaving St. Louis for Baltimore, and the Mets being created so they could fill the void left in New York when the Dodgers and Giants left.

Two months after he sold the Indians, and three months before his marriage, he was in Minneapolis to be fitted for an artificial leg. He was not interested in buying a team, he said. "Just call me a wanderer, a drifter, a vagabond." He added, though, "If I should change my mind, it wouldn't make any difference whether it happened to be a major- or minor-league club, Dubuque or Detroit, just so it presented a challenge."

Shortly after his marriage, he spent a week in a Tucson hospital, where a section of bone was removed from his shoulder. Physicians said the procedure was to ease irritation in the shoulder joint.

Undaunted, Veeck pursued the Browns' situation. Why? anyone might ask. Anyone, that is, who didn't know Veeck and his penchant for the troubled team.

This is how bad the Browns were: In their 1950 training camp they hired a hypnotist and metaphysician named David Tracy. His aim? To halt what he called the Browns' defeatism complex. And quite a history of failure it was. The team had joined the American League in 1902 and won only one pennant—in the war year of 1944. The year before they had finished sixth. The year after, they finished third. After winning that single pennant—by one game over Detroit—they bowed in the World Series to their city rivals, the Cardinals. After the war, they failed to get out of the second division.

Tracy suggested that positive thoughts—mingled with some posthypnotic suggestions—could rid the Browns of their losers' shackles. His degree of doctor of metaphysics had come from the Divine College of Metaphysics in Los Angeles.

Meanwhile, the Browns' owner, Bill DeWitt, was busy selling as many players as possible. The Browns hardly had a chance to do well. If there was a good player on the team, he eventually knew he would be traded to another club. The Browns were a terrible drawing card. They shared Sportsman's Park with the Cardinals, but routinely drew fewer than half the number of Cards fans. Indeed, in the Depression year of 1935, the Browns drew the smallest season's attendance in league history—80,972. Veeck's Indians drew that in one game.

The Browns had nearly moved to Los Angeles, a shift that could have changed their fortunes. In December 1941, at the annual winter baseball meetings, the Browns' owner, Donald I. Barnes, actually completed arrangements to transfer the club to Los Angeles. Barnes had even arranged with Jack Frye, president of Trans World Airlines, to fly two ballplayers on each of the twenty-one daily flights from Chicago to Los Angeles when the Browns played in the East. The reason? To avoid the loss of an entire team in the event of an air crash.

But the meetings coincided with December 7, 1941—and the attack on Pearl Harbor effectively ended any plans the league had to shift franchises. So the Browns wound up staying in St. Louis. Now, with the war over and the unexpected league title years behind them, the Browns were doing business as usual—bad business.

Baseball, like politics, makes strange bedfellows if it is mutually helpful. And this time, the Yankees needed Veeck.

Del Webb, a Yankee co-owner, was pleased that his powerful club was the best drawing card in baseball. The sport has always rewarded a good drawing card by giving the visiting team 25 cents for every seat sold. The Yankees generally attracted two million fans on the road. But no one turned out at St. Louis. A trip there brought the Yankees barely enough money to pay for the visit.

In June 1950, Webb planted the idea with Veeck of acquiring the Browns and keeping them in St. Louis. Webb might not have liked the way Veeck did things, but he knew Veeck could increase attendance.

An associate of Webb's had once been a minor-league owner. He knew a former owner of the Browns who held a note on the team for $700,000. Webb was anxious to help his friend and got him together with Veeck. Soon other St. Louis businessmen who wanted to keep the team there joined forces with Veeck. He was even able to buy 100 shares of stock from a famed opera singer of the time, Helen Traubel.

"Bill Veeck is the man to get the team out of the cellar and turn it into a pennant winner," she explained in selling her shares to him. She urged other stockholders to do the same.

With the usual roomful of investors (officially, sixteen), Veeck got together about $2 million and bought control of the Browns on July 5, 1951. They were 23 1/2 games out of first place, and it was raining. In fact, he called off the game the Browns were supposed to play that night—against the Indians.

Just twenty-four hours earlier, before he had officially taken over, he went to their doubleheader against the Indians and circulated among the fans in the bleachers and in the box seats. "I wanted to know what the fans would do to improve the Browns," he explained. "They didn't pull any punches. I was amazed over the shrewdness of those fans out in the bleachers. They're swell people and I value the tips they gave me."

It was a longer day than he bargained for. The second game carried into the fifteenth inning and was not over until 9:15 P.M. He had arrived at the park at ten in the morning.

Among his first announcements the next day, when he took over, were: He was eyeing a Japanese pitcher in Honolulu, was thinking of reviving Satchel Paige, and hoped to bring back Max Patkin to coach at first base.

All these pronouncements made Ed McAuley wistful. McAuley was a writer with the Cleveland *News*.

"Close association with Bill Veeck is like a ride on a runaway express train," wrote McAuley. "You wouldn't trade your memories for a fortune—but a fortune couldn't persuade you to climb aboard again. Still, it would be fun, on this fifth anniversary of Veeck's purchase of the Indians, to sit back in a corner of his office in St. Louis and watch the wheels start whirling."

Veeck tried to calm jittery Browns' fans (yes, some admitted they were) by emphasizing that he did not come in to move the team someplace else: "I've made an iron-clad statement of fact that the Browns will remain in St. Louis. I reaffirm that statement emphatically."

He had to do something, though. His new boys had won only 21 of 70 games—and 10 of those victories had been hurled by one pitcher, Ned Garver.

The club needed help every place, but most of all it needed a hitter. The team had no black ballplayers. It had brought up two, Hank Thompson and Willard Brown, late in the 1947 season. Both were soon gone, however, and since then the Browns had not hired one black.

That was hardly surprising, given the times. St. Louis was the southernmost city in baseball. If the South had a major-league team to root for at all, it was in St. Louis, the Browns or Cardinals. Even the Yankees and Red Sox had not hired a black ballplayer by 1951.

When Jackie Robinson came up for the 1947 season, players on only one team in the National League voted to rebel, to refuse to appear on the same field against him—the Cardinals. That uprising was stopped by Commissioner Chandler.

While addressing the need for black ballplayers—even "Japs," anyone to help his club—Veeck also spoke of Frank Saucier, who was the mystery man of St. Louis. He was a Bunyonesque character who preferred working at an oil job in Oklahoma rather than sign a Brownies' contract for what he had considered low pay and a meager bonus.

The Browns had counted on him for 1951. The year before, he had batted .343 for San Antonio in the Texas League. Once he refused to sign, though, DeWitt simply placed him on the suspended list. In those days of virtual serfdom, players were not free to look for their best deal. He would play for the Browns or for no one. The longer Saucier stayed away, and the worse the Browns became, the more the legend of Saucier grew. Why, when he joined the club, things would begin happening, said the fans, He was the missing ingredient for victory.

Veeck quickly moved, and within a few days of taking over the team, he signed Saucier. It was a symbol of a positive attitude, but it didn't help the club. For Saucier was to produce only one hit in his major-league career. In fact, after his 14 at-bats in 1951, he went into military service and never appeared in the big leagues again. His career batting average was .071.

Saucier, though, was to become noted for one at-bat he never took. And the boss needed to take the fans' minds off this terrible team.

The only time a midget had batted in a big-league game was in a fictional work by Ring Lardner called "You Could Look It Up." The story took place in St. Louis. A midget named Pearl du Monville was sent to bat with two out in the ninth inning and the bases filled, the tying run on third.

Pearl's orders were to get a base on balls and force in a run, but after throwing three balls, the pitcher eased one up with an underhand lob, so soft and tempting that the midget swung. He grounded out, ending the game.

Veeck was to claim he had never read the story until after he had arranged for life to imitate art. For he hired a midget and put him in— sacrilege of sacrileges—a major-league baseball game.

If for nothing else, Veeck was to become a part of baseball lore for that single, tongue-in-cheek act—one might even say it was blown out of proportion. Yet, it put into perspective Veeck's approach to the grand old game and it annealed his detractors and the defenders of tradition. This time, they huffed, Bill Veeck had gone too far. For he unveiled the midget at a fiftieth birthday celebration of the American League.

Shortly after he saw a few Brownies' games, Veeck realized drastic action was needed. One day, driving with the radio announcer, Buddy Blattner, he said, "If only we could get the leadoff batter on base."

Bob Broeg, the longtime St. Louis *Post-Dispatch* columnist and sports editor, recalls what happened next: "You know, he tipped me off about the midget, which as a newspaperman I appreciated. The night before we were having a drink and he told me what he was going to do. The reason I was there was interesting. Normally, I covered the Cardinals. The *Post-Dispatch* was one of the few papers in the country then that paid its own way when it covered a team on the road. The other papers, the clubs would pick up their tabs. So periodically, when times got tough at the *Post-Dispatch*, we simply wouldn't travel with the team. So I was home this series with the Browns."

Veeck had signed a twenty-six-year-old theatrical midget from Chicago named Eddie Gaedel to a one-game contract for $100. Gaedel weighed 65 pounds and stood three feet seven inches tall.

The boss told as few people as possible about his outrageous plan. He didn't even mail the contract to the American League president, Will Harridge, until the day before he planned to use Gaedel. Naturally, Veeck informed Manager Zack Taylor, whose days were numbered anyway. Taylor was not about to dispute Veeck, upon whose kindness he had become dependent. When Veeck had taken over control of the team he had announced he was considering four different managers for the job, and the incumbent Taylor wasn't one of them.

Veeck was going to use Gaedel on Sunday, August 19—a festive day. Between games of the doubleheader against the Tigers, the Browns would stage a golden anniversary salute to the American League. Why, Commissioner Happy Chandler himself was coming to the park for the festivities.

There were things Gaedel had to know, first of all. He was a wise guy, brash, and also something of a troublemaker. Veeck's plan was to put Gaedel up to bat and, if he got lucky, would not only create a sensation but would also walk. Pitchers, after all, were hardly accustomed to throwing such low strikes.

"I've got a man up in the stands with a high-powered rifle," Veeck told the midget, "and if you swing at any pitch, he'll fire."

First, they had to find a proper Browns uniform for Mr. Gaedel. Enter nine-year-old Bill DeWitt, Jr. His father had remained with the club in an advisory role after selling the team. "I was the only one other than the players who had an official Browns uniform because when they ordered the uniforms, I had gotten one too," recalls Bill, Jr., now president of a financial company in Cincinnati.

"My father and Bill Veeck told me they were doing this midget promotion, and they had signed a midget and that I had the only uniform that would be able to fit him. Actually, I had the number 6 on my uniform because Bobby Dillinger had been the third baseman and he had been one of my favorite players.

"Anyway, they took my uniform and said they were going to change the 6 to 1/8. That was going to be Eddie Gaedel's number. I've still got the uniform with the number on it."

The uniform was a bit floppy on the little guy. Before game time he suddenly became so nervous that he was unable to tie his own shoes, and Manager Taylor had to fix the laces.

A crowd of more than 20,000 showed up, including 18,369 paying customers—the Browns' largest attendance in four years. They didn't know what would happen, for Veeck rarely announced outrageous promotions in advance.

After the Browns, of course, lost the opening game, there was a fine between-games show: Max Patkin jitterbugged, a four-piece band of Browns players (including Satchel Paige) performed, there was a parade of old-fashioned cars, and at first base a hand-balancer balanced, trampoline artists leaped at second base, a juggler worked third base—and then came the birthday cake on the pitcher's mound.

Out popped Gaedel, wearing Number 1/8, and the crowd howled. Everyone soon was whisked off the field for the start of the second game of the doubleheader. Things would be back to normal.

The Browns' leadoff batter was Saucier, their erstwhile savior. Suddenly the field announcer, Bernie Ebert, droned over the loudspeaker, "For the Browns, number 1/8, Eddie Gaedel, batting for Saucier."

And there was Gaedel coming out of the dugout to go to home plate. He limbered up by swinging a small bat.

Umpire Ed Hurley at home plate crooked a finger at Zack Taylor—who trotted out with the "legal" evidence. It was a contract signed by Gaedel, along with a carbon copy of a telegram Veeck had mailed to league headquarters that added Gaedel to the Browns' roster. Red Rolfe, the Tigers' manager, complained to Hurley, but, reluctantly, the umpire motioned Gaedel to the plate.

Bob Cain was the pitcher. Bob Swift was the Tigers' catcher. Now, they had to figure out how to pitch to Gaedel.

Cain figured that if he tossed the ball underhanded he would have a better chance of throwing a strike. But Swift reminded him that "submarine" pitches were illegal. The little guy would have to be faced *mano a mano*.

At first, Swift wanted to sit on the ground so he could provide a lower target for Cain. But Hurley wouldn't hear of it. So Swift went to his knees. Even that action didn't help. Cain walked Gaedel on four (high) pitches. Gaedel, beaming, ran to first. He didn't stay there long. Jim Delsing, a pinch runner, came in for Gaedel.

The midget gave Delsing a patronizing pat on the rump, as if to say, "Well, I did my job, now you do yours." The crowd cheered as Gaedel went back to the dugout.

The memories have never left Cain. In fact, Gaedel was to become a significant part of the very religious Cain's life. He accepted his role in the historic moment with good humor. Still, he would like to be recalled as a pitcher who was involved in some other interesting events as well.

"I come up with the White Sox in the latter half of 1949," he recalls. "In 1950 I got my first major-league start. It was against the Yankees and I beat them, 15-0, which I think is still a record for the worst beating in their home park. And that's when they had a real good ball club. I went ahead and beat the Yankees four times that year. I pitched, as I remember, about eight times against them. The Sox would work it out so I'd always start against them. In the spring of '51 I was traded to Detroit, and I was with Detroit when that incident with the midget happened."

It takes no prodding to make Cain remember. It is still vivid.

"First of all, we thought it was a joke until Ed Hurley demanded to see a contract. And Zack Taylor comes out just as Hurley is walking to the dugout and Taylor pulls a contract out of his hip pocket. Hurley's neck was getting red. And he comes back and he says, 'Play ball.'

"Bob Swift, in order to go along with the joke, or whatever it was supposed to be at the time, he laid down and put his head on one hand and held his glove up for a target, and Hurley made him get up into a regular catcher's position. Ed Hurley had a short fuse, and he was a real good umpire. He was one that you wouldn't want to cross up."

Now, how to pitch to Gaedel?

"We talked it over and tried to get a ball down low enough for him because he only had, I'd guess, an inch, inch and a half strike zone because him being three foot seven. And then he put his feet wide apart like Joe DiMaggio, and then crouched over, he didn't have much of a strike zone. But I think the pitches that I threw would have been close to a strike on an ordinary man. I was trying to throw fast balls.

"At first I was laughing, but after I walked him and then turned around and walked the next batter, things weren't so funny then. We won the ball game, 6-2."

But that wasn't the last that Cain had to do with Gaedel. Nor was it the last that baseball had to do with Gaedel, although the American League president, Will Harridge, wished it had been.

Harridge tried mightily to expunge Gaedel, to make him a nonperson. So if you have the 1952 Baseball Guide and look up the official American League batting records for 1951, you will not find a line for Edward Carl (Eddie) Gaedel. Yet, the base on balls is included in Cain's record and Delsing is credited with a pinch-running appearance.

Gaedel was all right with Commissioner Chandler, though. "I saw the midget. I saw the little fella bat," says Chandler. "It was all right with me. They had to have nine fellows on the field. I was amused. Old Harridge didn't find it out until it was too late to stop it, and of course the owners complained to Harridge and he stopped it."

Cain was more than merely a footnote to history. His future was to be tied in with Veeck and, to an unusual degree, with Gaedel.

As soon as Gaedel ran off the field, he quickly changed clothes. He had another appearance to make someplace else. But Bob Broeg, the *Post-Dispatch* reporter, needed him for a story, so he dashed down to the locker room to find Gaedel, sporting a natty yellow shirt, ready to leave.

"You little son of a bitch," said Broeg, "I've got to talk to you." So Broeg picked up Gaedel and placed him on a desk and interviewed him.

"For a minute," Gaedel told him, "I felt like Babe Ruth."

Broeg told Gaedel, "You're now what I wished I'd become."

"What's that?" asked Gaedel.

"A former big-leaguer."

Gaedel, a White Sox fan, returned home and said, "I never thought I'd live to see the day I'd be a major-leaguer."

Veeck, meanwhile, felt vindicated. He sensed that this was going to give his critics fits and that they might finally believe they would have enough on him to disgrace him. He was disappointed afterward only in the fact that, following Gaedel's walk, the Brownies loaded the bases and failed to score.

"I wanted to prove that this was a practical idea too," said Veeck. "...a practical idea too." In other words, all his other wonderfully eccentric schemes had been nothing but practical ideas. This, then, was merely another one.

Two days after his first at-bat, Gaedel said he expected to be called on again. This time it would be with the bases loaded. The Veeck magic was working on him, as it did for so many others. The incident wasn't over simply because it ended. For those associated with Veeck, those things never died.

"They would walk me sure as the world and force in a run—that run might win," said Gaedel, savoring the fantasy. Now he was warming up.

"Two guys I'd like to face on the mound are Bob Feller and Dizzy Trout. Any young fellow dreams of being a big-leaguer—and that's what I consider myself. I've got a Browns uniform with number 1/8 on the back, a glove, and a contract. I've spent all my life in Chicago and never played ball, but I've always wanted to. I made up for it by becoming a red-hot fan."

The midget expected to be called on when the Browns faced the White Sox in a month in Chicago. That wasn't to be, though. Harridge barred all midgets from baseball—even retroactively.

Veeck immediately wrote back to Harridge, "Fine. Let's establish what is a midget in fact. Is it three feet six inches? Eddie's height? Is it four feet six? If it's five feet six, that's great. We can get rid of Rizzuto."

Years later Veeck was to reflect, "You know, if I'd had any courage, and we used eight other fellows like Eddie, we might have won a game or so. We'd have run around and around and around and might never have finished the game."

Frank Lane, the general manager of the White Sox, welcomed any attempt by Veeck to use the midget at Comiskey Park. "As far as pitching to the midget—well, I don't know. But there is a strike zone and it seems to me that the way some umpires have been calling 'em, it's the same as having a midget at the plate anyway."

Within a week the midget was arrested in Cincinnati for being drunk and abusing a policeman.

Ten years later, on June 18, 1961, Gaedel died. Police reports were sketchy. An inquest ruled he died of natural causes. An autopsy revealed that bruises on his body "were probably suffered in a fall." He was found dead in his bed at the Chicago home where he lived with his mother. Three days later there was a funeral and services. One of the floral tributes was sent by Bill Veeck. Bob Cain was the only person from baseball who attended the funeral.

"The funeral was in Chicago," says Cain. "We drove up from Cleveland. I hadn't seen him since I pitched against him, but after the funeral we met his mother. We sent Christmas cards to Helen Gaedel, his mother, until just a few years ago. We sent her a card and never heard anything more from her."

What made Cain attend the funeral?

"We kind of felt it was part of baseball history, and we knew there'd never be another midget in baseball, so we felt we were more or less kind of obligated to go. There wasn't too many people at the funeral at all. There was mostly his family. It was a small funeral. His mother was a very nice person. We explained to her who we were. We got very friendly with her.

"She explained to us that he fell into the wrong crowd up there in Chicago. He was out drinking very heavily. On this particular night he came home, a gang had gotten hold of him and had beaten him very, very badly. He came home and during his sleep, his mother called the doctor and the doctor examined him and the doctor told him he was just drunk, and never mind, he'll just sleep it off.

"But something happened during the night that, I don't know, about four o'clock in the morning his mother heard a noise, and foam was coming out of his mouth. He passed away right then and there. She always told us that it was murder."

Cain never saw Gaedel again after the pair faced each other, but Cain and Veeck soon were reunited.

After the '51 season Cain had a contract squabble with the Tigers. Who else would be interested in acquiring this unhappy ballplayer other than Veeck?

"I was traded to St. Louis, and Bill Veeck said at the time he insisted I be put in with that trade. Four of us went from Detroit and five from St. Louis. So I played for Bill Veeck two years, '52 and '53. I never discussed the midget with him. But I do remember a lot of things that happened as a result of that trade.

"In 1951, Bob Feller had pitched his third no-hitter against me. I lost that game, 2-1. It was just a year later, when I was with St. Louis, Bob Feller and I each pitched a one-hitter and I beat him in that game, 1-0, so I kind of evened things up with him a little bit."

Cain wound up the 1952 season as the winningest pitcher on the Browns—along with forty-five-year-old Satchel Paige. Each posted a 12-10 mark, remarkable considering that the team finished 26 games under .500.

"At the end of the '53 season the team went to Baltimore and I was traded to the Philadelphia Athletics," recalls Cain. "In the spring training of 1954, I came up with calcium on my wrist. After that I was sent down to Ottawa. I played some more trying to get that out of the wrist, but it didn't do any good. So I finally quit baseball altogether in '56."

Yet, Veeck was a part of his baseball life as much as the midget.

"You know about the Browns uniform? Bill Veeck would give the wives an authentic St. Louis Browns uniform if they had children. We just happened to be the last. My wife gave birth to our daughter, the last baby born in St. Louis. So we've got the last Browns uniform ever issued, the complete uniform, socks, even a miniature bat.

"Veeck was one of the greatest guys I ever played for. He treated ballplayers as human beings. He didn't like the idea of babying the ballplayers, but he would go out of his way to help them. I had trouble when I got traded to him. He called me on the phone, on St. Valentine's Day, and said, 'I understand you're having contract trouble with Detroit,' and I told him that's why I hadn't signed. He asked me what I wanted and I told him and he said, 'All right, come in and sign the contract.' It was just that simple with him."

Cain, who made Gaedel's funeral, was unable to make Veeck's.

"We would have gone to Bill's funeral, but we were in Palm Beach, Florida, with my daughter. Mary Frances is my daughter's godmother. We were undecided what to name my daughter, and Mary Frances said she'd be the godmother under one condition—if she could name her. She said my wife's name is Judy and my name's Bob so we'll call her Judybob. That's how we named her."

Cain remains a religious man who says he never was insulted over the fact that he was the man whom fate—and Veeck—decreed to become part of a perennial trivia question: Who was the pitcher who pitched to the midget?

"I feel enough happened to me without pitching to the midget," explains Cain. "Beating the Yankees, 15-0, in my first major-league start, and then pitching the one-hitter against Feller. I had a lot of real good games that could have gone either way. I had a lot of good experiences in baseball."

Veeck was not going to let the baseball world off easy now that he had unveiled a midget. Standing pat was not his style. Why, the day before Gaedel took the plate Veeck had even tried another stunt, but that failed to work.

The day before, the Brownies were en route to trouncing the Tigers, 20-9. He rigged a fire gong in the dugout for use when a relief pitcher was about to be called in. Relievers have been known as "firemen," presumably because they arrive to put out the fire, or uprising, by the other team.

The pitching coach, Johnny Tobin, went to the mound to relieve the Browns' starter, Fred Sanford. Tobin, a former fire chief, had a long string attached to the gong. He stood on top of the mound and yanked the string. Nothing happened. The gong malfunctioned.

Undaunted, Veeck not only created the midget, but five days later he produced Grandstand Managers Day.

Harridge was ready for this one. He had decreed that it wasn't enough for Veeck—or anyone—to send a contract to his office and show an umpire a copy of it. Now, the team needed to have the contract approved. And Harridge wasn't about to approve much of anything by Bill Veeck this week.

On Tuesday the Browns mailed out 1,100 Grandstand Managers cards. These cards would entitle each card carrier to a "NO" or "YES" sign for Friday night's game against the Athletics, in which fans would vote for plays by holding up their signs. And on Thursday Veeck would announce the names of two guest managers drawn from the names of those who had applied for their cards. Each manager would be on the field, one on third, one on first. The lucky winners were named Charles E. Hughes and Clark Mize. Veeck signed them and put them in uniform.

But Harridge ruled the stunt out on the grounds that the contracts had not been approved by his office.

Still, Manager Taylor sat in a rocking chair in a box seat near the dugout. He took off his jacket, and was outfitted in a fedora, shirt, and tie, and he puffed a pipe and leisurely read a newspaper

Eighty-nine-year-old Connie Mack was also in the stands, and he even held up a "YES" card. Mack had retired after the 1950 season as the Athletics' manager following a fifty-year career as their leader.

Berardino was in the dugout asking the fans questions on giant cards: "Bunt?" or "Steal?" or even, after a close call by the umpire, "Protest to Umpire?"

Throughout the first inning "YES" and "NO" signs bobbed in the stands like seaborne corks as Berardino asked questions of the fans. Their responses were noted by someone in the stands with a walkie-talkie who relayed the information to the dugout. Of course by the time the answer came back, it often was too late to argue with the umpire. And when you tell everyone in the place you are going to steal a base—well, the runner doesn't have much luck.

The Brownies, though, survived the A's three-run first inning—after the fans turned down a query on whether Ned Garver should be replaced as the starter. The Browns tied the game in their half of the first and went on to win, 5-3, for Garver's fifteenth victory.

Veeck made sure his ex-managers were rewarded anyway. He gave

Hughes and Mize trophies that read "The Best Coaches Ever Banned From the Coaching Lines."

Veeck knew that the Browns needed more than a pair of fans to coach on the baselines. Attendance averaged barely 6,000 people a game. And why should there be any more people than that? The '51 Browns finished 46 games out of first place. They were gone from the pennant race well before mid-season. The only interest the club could generate—apart from Veeck's handiwork—was in Garver. No pitcher for a last-place club ever had won 20 games. But Garver did. He finished with a truly spectacular 20-12 record. No other pitcher on the club won as many as seven games. Garver started 30 times, more than anyone else in the league except for the top hurlers on the Yankees and Indians. But Garver also led the league in complete games with 24. Once he was in the game, he just never came out for a pinch hitter. Only two Brownies—neither of them regulars— could match his .305 batting average.

To bring some interest—to bring something—to his team, Veeck hired a pair of quirky oddballs: Dizzy Dean and Rogers Hornsby. Hornsby would manage the club and Dean would tell the world about it as the radio announcer.

Both were former Cardinal heroes. Hornsby had starred for them in the World War I years and the 1920s. When he turned to managing, he found he could spur his players for a time—and then lose their respect and desire. In fact, Bill Veeck, Sr., fired Hornsby as the Cubs' manager in 1932—on a day the Cubs were in first place.

That same season young Dizzy Dean came up to the Cards, won 18 games, and began a stretch of marvelous pitching that made him the league's dominant hurler of the thirties. As an announcer, he not only was colorful, he also confused his listeners.

His syntax and his grammar outraged educators, and they kept hounding him wherever he worked. Players didn't slide—they "slud." A batter had an "unorsodock" stance. For some reason the Yankees had hired him in 1951 after he was fired in St. Louis for having called the Brownies "a bunch of humpty-dumpties." He lasted only a year in New York after the Yankees' management, sensitive to the team's image, discovered that Dean's cornball musings and freewheeling grammar just wasn't...well, Yankee...enough for them.

When berated about his syntax, Dean replied, "What, don't them fellers in Washington get enough already? They want to tax sin too?" Or he reminded fans as he signed off, "Don't forget to miss tomorrow's game."

They even made a movie about his life, with Dan Dailey. "I didn't think I'd ever get $50,000 just for living," he said after signing the contract.

The Hornsby signing was made out of desperation. In personality, temperament, philosophy, he and Veeck were no match—even opposites. One thing they had in common was that they bounced around.

Everywhere that Hornsby had been there was a blow up that cost him his job, from the Cardinals in 1926, to the Giants the next year, to the Cubs in '32, and the Browns in '37. Indeed, that last firing appeared to have forever washed out Hornsby from baseball.

Soon after Veeck hired him, the irascible Hornsby proclaimed, in describing his checkered work history, "Any time anybody thought the ball club wasn't going good or wanted to fire me, they blamed it on my betting on horses. But get this straight—I never made any agreement with anybody giving them control over my private life. I don't drink and I don't smoke, and I never did anything to hurt baseball and I never will. But if I want to entertain myself and risk my own money, that's my business."

There was talk that baseball had "blackballed" the Hall of Famer who had a career batting average of .358 and once had hit .424 in a season. Hornsby bounced around from 1937 to 1952—he operated baseball schools, he went to the Mexican League, he ran a baseball clinic. Finally he caught on as a manager in the minor leagues.

When Veeck tapped him to return to the big time, Hornsby did it on condition that the circuses stop. "There ain't going to be any clowns on the ball club anymore, and Bill ain't going to tell me how I'll lead my private life," said Hornsby. He signed a three-year contract.

Veeck tried to upgrade the playing talent. As usual they included the slightly off-center. There was a talented rookie center fielder, Jim Rivera. He was a twenty-nine-year-old from the Bronx, and if people wondered why it had taken so long for him to make it to the big leagues, the answer was—he had been in prison.

The new shortstop was to be Marty Marion, who had been the Cards' shortstop from 1940 to 1950, then their manager in 1951. He had been fired. The catcher was a rookie, Clint Courtney, who had been kept in the minors by the Yankees because they had Yogi Berra.

In spring training at Burbank, California, the barrel-shaped Hornsby prowled the field holding a fungo bat, as if he were a drill instructor with a swagger stick. He clamped down on smoking during workouts and he outlawed beer in the clubhouse.

Hornsby knew he was able to work with only a certain kind of player—

especially if that player knew him. So when he and Veeck discussed players the Browns might trade, Hornsby told him, "Do anything you want with anybody who was with the Browns last year, but leave my guys alone."

These were the players who had performed for Hornsby in the minors—including Rivera, who had been the Pacific Coast League's batting champion in 1951, and Courtney, the aggressive catcher who had played for Hornsby with Beaumont of the Texas League. Eventually, Veeck was to close a deal to bring Cain, Bearden, and Dick Kryhoski to the Browns from Detroit and, eventually, Garver wound up in Detroit.

In Hornsby's managerial career he had prodded two teams to first place, although he finished the season with only one of them. As a batter, he produced a five-year stretch with the Cards in the 1920s when his average was more than .400, including consecutive years over that figure. He consistently led the National League in most hits, most runs batted in, most doubles, triples, and homers. The trouble was, no one who played for him could ever approach anything he did. And when he managed, no one could ever tell him what to do.

He believed that the reason Bill Veeck, Sr., fired him in 1932, with the Cubs in first place, was because of a minor incident in one game. Hornsby, the thirty-six-year-old player-manager, needed a pinch hitter. Rather than bat himself, he sent in a young outfielder named Frank Demaree. Hornsby believed that players needed to be put into clutch situations. Demaree failed at the plate.

Later, Veeck, Sr., complained to Hornsby and suggested that Hornsby should have batted. Hornsby shot back that he was the manager and if Veeck didn't like it...well, get someone else. Hornsby was soon fired. Now, with Bill Veeck, Jr.'s Browns, he thought it might be different. Veeck had told him he would not interfere.

Hornsby lasted exactly 50 games with the Browns. They posted a 22–28 record when Veeck finally dumped him—not because the team was losing, but because it was coming apart with complaining.

Hornsby always maintained that Veeck orchestrated his demise and even made a show-business joke about his dismissal. Veeck contended that the players ultimately chased him.

The day after Veeck fired Hornsby, Veeck made newspapers all over America. He held a huge loving cup on which was inscribed, from presumably grateful Brownies players, "To Bill Veeck for the Greatest Play Since the Emancipation Proclamation."

In other words, firing Hornsby had freed the players and, to show their gratitude, they were presenting the cup to Veeck. It was an outrageous, unheard-of gesture and the picture received tremendous circulation. Hornsby claimed he received phone calls and messages from players who assured him they had nothing to do with the trophy. Hornsby quickly suggested to reporters that the trophy was a phony, that Veeck himself had bought it and had it presented to him. That story wounded Veeck, who always insisted that the cup idea originated with the players, including Garver and Bearden.

In any event, Hornsby was out after a third of the season. But not for long. He returned to managing shortly—the Reds hired him and he spent the final third of the 1952 campaign in Cincinnati and got that undistinguished team to play better than .500 ball. He was fired midway through the 1953 season.

When Veeck wasn't worried about Hornsby and his players in '52, though, he was worried about making ends meet.

Bob Broeg of the *Post-Dispatch* believes that Veeck had wanted to move the Browns all along. It wasn't that moving a team was unheard-of. There always were rumors. It just simply wasn't done. No major-league franchise had been created or moved since 1903. Veeck was to admit, though, that he began thinking by the middle of 1952 that one day he would have to move his franchise. The Cardinals were being sold, and he feared he would not be able to compete against the new owners—the Anheuser-Busch beer company. Not everyone believes that Veeck always was sincere in his attempts to keep the Browns in St. Louis. Some contend he took over struggling franchises in order to move the clubs as quickly as possible to a city that would offer...oh, the moon and the stars. That would immediately enhance his franchise's value to considerably more than he had paid for it.

"The one thing about Bill that always bothered me was the move—I don't buy that business about Busch moving in and forcing him. I think he would have moved anyway." The speaker was Broeg, who, though retired, still ranks as an expert about the city's sports operations.

The Cardinals' owner was the hidebound Fred Saigh. It was a source of frustration and denigration that his team—a team, after all, that won pennants and drew a million fans—was nothing more than a tenant of Veeck's Browns in Sportsman's Park. And a second-class tenant at that.

Newspaper accounts of the Veeck era there are replete with Veeck's anti-Saigh digs:

- Did the contract call for a painting of the stadium? Of course it did. But it didn't say what color. So Veeck painted the park a pleasant shade of brown. That made Saigh see red.

- To give fans a sense of Browns history—a somewhat thankless task—Veeck hung pictures of old Brownies players. The pictures stayed put when the Cards were using the park, though. In anger, Saigh directed that the pictures be covered over with Cardinals banners.

- Veeck kept the private owner's box off-limits to the Cards' brass when their team was playing. Saigh never could entertain his friends in the manner that befitted a Cardinal official. When Anheuser-Busch took over, that private box became a source of amusement to Veeck and his friends. They would read the directives issued by "Gussie" Busch that detailed when underlings might use that box ("If I am not there by the third inning, then the first vice president may use it").

Saigh was so aggrieved after the 1952 season that he brought formal complaints about Veeck's barbs and slaps to Ford Frick, the commissioner of baseball who had succeeded Happy Chandler.

Saigh claimed, for example, that Veeck "tampered" with Harry (the Cat) Brecheen, an aging left-hander who had been a 20-game winner with the Cards and was a true St. Louis fixture. In baseball, "tampering" was a serious offense since it struck at the heart of team loyalty and the so-called sanctity of contracts. A player could be considered "tampered" with, for example, if a rival owner met him at a cocktail party and said, "Gee, I'd love to have you pitching for us."

In a sense, Saigh asked that Frick put a permanent restraining order on Veeck, who was gobbling up ex-Cardinals greats by the carload—in '52, when Hornsby didn't work out, Veeck simply replaced him with another ex-Card, Marty Marion. Veeck now had Brecheen, lifted from the Cards on a technicality. It seemed that every time the Cardinals wanted to make a move on the waiver wire, Veeck was there to pull the player off it. Waivers were simply a way of allowing a club to move a player off its roster to the minor leagues. Technically, the player had to be exposed to "waivers"—that is, allow other teams the option of taking him before he could be reassigned. Veeck took that to mean literally what the rule said—that he could take a player for the listed waiver price. The thing was, everyone he took was a Cardinal.

"Saigh is convinced Wild Bill has no intention of promoting such players to the Browns, but just claims them for the hell of it," contended Gayle Talbot in the *Post-Dispatch*.

Yet, some observers saw this whole situation as potentially leading not to the loss of the Browns—but the Cards. This was the reasoning as the winter meetings loomed following the 1952 season:

The Cards' lease on the park had seven more years to run, and Saigh was unable to build himself a new stadium. So if Veeck planned to be in St. Louis for the long haul, Saigh would have to continue to operate at a disadvantage. For under the lease at the time, the Cards paid only $35,000 a year in rent to the Browns. They'd get that their first full house. But if Veeck could last out the seven years, he simply could refuse to renew the Cardinals' lease. Then they would have to move.

The lease also called for the Cards to pay half of any park improvements. That included painting. Even to this menial job Veeck brought his own brand of Peck's Bad Boy. He painted the whole place brown. One could not find a daub of Cardinal red anyplace. And the Cards had to pay. While he was at it, Veeck also installed a series of giant murals of former St. Louis heroes along the walls beneath the stands. The heroes happened to be former Brownies.

Veeck, though, wanted to move the team to Baltimore, to Florida, to Los Angeles, to Milwaukee. Anyplace where there was no other team and wanted him. And everyplace he tried to go, the American League owners stood in his way—especially the Yankees, who were able to rally support against him, support he often thought he had but that evaporated behind closed-door caucuses.

In one meeting before the 1953 season, he tried to get a bigger slice of the television pie for visiting teams—a change in rules which, of course, would help his Brownies, who were a terrible drawing card.

Veeck proposed that visiting teams be reimbursed if their games were televised by the home team. In a sense he was promoting share-the-wealth, equal distribution of revenue.

That tenet became the backbone of the National Football League, with its Green Bay Packers, for example, receiving as much TV revenue as the New York Giants even though the New Yorkers played in a market ten times as large.

Unfortunately for Veeck, he had tried to implement his theory in a bitter 1952 clash with the Yankees. He had forbidden them televising any games with the Browns in Yankee Stadium unless his team got a cut of the receipts. The Yankees retaliated by canceling night games with the

Browns and rescheduling them as day affairs—a move guaranteed to cost Veeck money since the Browns were the worst drawing card in baseball, and day games attracted fewer fans than night games. He relented.

Baseball wouldn't hear of his ideas. As usual, he was forced to abandon his best ones.

The American League rules required two "no" votes to block any rule from being voted in. Veeck had believed he had an ally in Frank Lane, the White Sox general manager. Meanwhile, Saigh was arguing for the same thing in the National League—which required only one vote to stop any rules change. Saigh won a concession from the Chicago Cubs, who agreed to give the Cardinals a share of the television receipts when they played in Wrigley Field.

No one, though, wanted to give the Browns anything. Perhaps more explicitly, no one wanted to do anything for Veeck.

Veeck was to claim the Browns' fate was sealed when the giant brewery, Anheuser-Busch, bought the Cardinals in February 1953. And there is reason to believe he was right. With that purchase there no longer was a one-man owner who had to worry about what to do when his lease expired and he didn't have to worry about paying enough money to keep his players. A megacompany now owned the Cards.

August A. (Augie) Busch, Jr., not only ran the brewery, he was now running the Cards. And he was not about to move them. He even spurned a $4 million offer from Milwaukee to shift his club there. Instead, he was remaining in St. Louis, where his brewery could enjoy a symbiotic relationship with the team. And if the team happened to lose money, why, the brewery would simply underwrite the piddling amount.

The ownership shift was completed while Veeck was at the height of his own dealings with other cities—especially with Milwaukee. In fact, the Chicago *Tribune* reported that the deal was virtually closed soon after Busch turned down Milwaukee. Veeck, of course, denied as "absolutely untrue" the reports and added, the Browns had "no plans to go any place."

But it was generally accepted that the Boston Braves' owner, Lou Perini—who owned the giant construction company—had his eye on Milwaukee, where he already owned an American Association team. And to keep out Veeck, he set an outrageously high price on the minor-league club, which Veeck would have to buy out before moving there. Finally, in March of 1953, the Greater Milwaukee Committee said that its plans to bring in a major-league team were "dead," at least for the season.

Veeck was getting desperate. In 1951 the Browns drew 293,790 fans. In Veeck's first full season running the team, 1952, they attracted 518,796.

But they needed 850,000 fans just to break even. That was an unlikely figure in a two-baseball-team town the size of St. Louis, where the Cardinals were a proven winner and had such gate attractions as Stan Musial and Enos Slaughter.

An associate of Veeck's was quoted as saying, "We'd have to win a pennant to draw 850,000 fans here, but I'm afraid that if the club faltered, and drew only 500,000 or so again, we'd all lose our shirts."

Perini, though, turned down a $500,000 bid to reimburse him if he moved his American Association team to another city. The city of Milwaukee, meanwhile, had a brand-new stadium sitting there and waiting for a team to fill it.

Veeck realized it would not be his Browns, so he hurriedly turned to Baltimore only weeks before the 1953 season was to open. He also constructed a deal with the new Cardinals' owners to buy Sportsman's Park from him for about $800,000 if he moved his team. Baltimore had a 40,000-seat park named Babe Ruth Stadium—it already had 7,000 more seats than Sportsman's Park and could be expanded.

The frenzied dealing involving the two cities—Milwaukee and Baltimore—was more than a touch ironic. For the last franchises that ever left cities had come from just those two—Milwaukee's team left to become the St. Louis Browns in 1902, while the Baltimore team switched in 1903 for New York, where they were known as the Highlanders, better known since as the Yankees.

During the frantic talks going on in mid-March, the president of the National League, Warren Giles, announced that "this is a bad time to move franchises. It is not healthy." He explained that television deals had been set, travel arrangements made, schedules agreed on, tickets sold. That same day a story appeared in St. Louis suggesting that the Browns might move that very day to Baltimore.

Both reports were untrue. But another one was: that Perini was going to move the Braves to Milwaukee. If the Browns were doing poorly at the gate with their half million fans, consider how the Braves had deteriorated in Boston—they had attracted fewer than 300,000 people.

Four days later Veeck tried to sell the Browns. He was angered and shocked that at a league meeting the owners officially turned down his request to move to Baltimore. The shift had been considered such a shoo-in that the league's publicity director had even tried to work with the schedule-maker to see what impact it would have. The Browns were the league's westernmost team, and if they moved to Baltimore there would now be five Eastern teams almost touching—Washington, Baltimore, Philadelphia, New York, and Boston.

Behind closed doors the other owners screamed at Veeck and berated him. One called it "the most chaotic situation in baseball history"—all the fault of Veeck's carpetbagging.

When Veeck left the meeting he charged that the Yankees had led the break against him: "I've been the victim of duplicity... by lying club owners. The vote against me was silly or malicious, and I prefer to regard it as malicious," he said.

Meanwhile, Harridge and Frick said they had been overwhelmed by a flood of letters from fans in St. Louis asking them to keep the Browns there. These letters, said Harridge, apparently evoked sympathetic responses from the other owners. Could it be that these owners believed it would hurt the psyches of the good people of St. Louis to lose a baseball team?

If so, then they showed more attention to the fans there than their own mayor did. It never became a rousing cry from the heart the way it did in years to come, when the leaving of a team became synonymous with the breakdown of some of the great American cities.

But there was another reason that the owners forced Veeck to remain. It wasn't simply that few of them liked him or trusted him. They were afraid of being sued by the International League, which already had a franchise in Baltimore. The president of the league, Frank Shaughnesy, described a move into his territory as "piracy." And piracy meant court action.

"There's been a double cross somewhere," charged Acting Mayor Arthur B. Price of Baltimore after he learned of the vote against moving to his city.

The decision to stay forced a hastily prepared statement from the American League. It ended with "In view of the increased attendance at Browns games last year and the urgent requests from St. Louis fans..., the American League looks forward to increased support for the Browns in St. Louis in 1953."

Veeck didn't believe a word of it. He offered to sell his 80 percent of the Browns for $2.4 million. When he bought the club in the middle of 1951, he had paid about $1.5 million.

As the *Post-Dispatch* reported, "The Browns at present have outstanding notes and indebtedness of an undetermined amount, presumably little working capital and little prospect of getting any because Veeck's associates, mostly Chicago businessmen, have pulled their purse strings."

Veeck contended he had lost $400,000 operating the Browns, although he admitted that the figure included $200,000 in cash he had dished out for players. He carried them on his books as a cash outlay with no value. He explained, somewhat ingenuously, that they're not worth anything until you sell them.

This 1953 season, he explained, was going to herald the boom of television in baseball. And he was in the wrong city to get any benefit out of the new entertainment. "The threat of Anheuser-Busch televising their games is more than we can bear," he added. For the Browns not only failed to get a TV sponsor, they probably now would be victimized by the fact that the Cards did have one and would televise their games back to St. Louis—when the Browns were playing.

"Things have changed," he explained. "Television has had a tremendous impact on baseball. I sincerely believe that except for New York and Chicago, the one-club setup in cities is inevitable."

Defending himself for trying to leave St. Louis, he said, "I didn't want to give it up, but felt I couldn't take another financial beating this season."

The 1952 campaign had been a season of disappointments for him even though the Browns did double their attendance. But they had started from such a small base that even a 100 percent improvement in ticket sales left them far short of breaking even.

His first disappointment came on opening day, when, despite his efforts to ballyhoo the team, his boys could attract only 12,000 fans. He was to explain many years later to another ornery owner, Charlie Finley, that St. Louis was just too tough a town for him.

"They say you shouldn't ballyhoo a funeral, Charlie," said Veeck. "But I tried to ballyhoo one in St. Louis."

He did it with a minimum of working capital. The following excerpt is from a letter written to Robert Miller, a New York advertising man, who had suggested that Veeck might want to consider erecting a roof for Sportsman's Park—it would work like the top of a convertible car, raised when there's rain, taken down when it's clear.

The letter was written early in Veeck's first season of 1951. He didn't get around to answering it until the middle of October. That was three months after he took over the club—and he still used the old stationery that had William O. DeWitt listed as president. Indeed, Veeck's name appeared only at the bottom of his signed letter. There apparently was no money for frivolities such as an up-to-date letterhead.

In the letter Veeck said, "I obtained figures for a similar plan while I was in Chicago back in 1940. The cost was in excess of $1,800,000 and by now would probably be more than double that figure. Many other people have come up with similar proposals and some of them have even submitted architect's drawings, but nothing practical has ever been developed along this line." Of course what he didn't add was that he had no money to try to keep up with the park's continual deterioration let alone make any radical changes.

Finally, before the 1953 season began, he bowed to the pressure of money and the pressure exerted by the city of St. Louis's buildings inspectors, who wanted the park fixed up. He sold the place to Busch.

Busch had walked through the old park after he bought the team and was disgusted with its condition. The central seating section had been built in 1909. Busch immediately announced, "I'd rather have my team play in Forest Park"—a public park.

Because the Cards now were owned by a brewery, Busch envisioned his company besieged with lawsuits by people who might be hurt in the ancient park. But Veeck could not make the repairs to Busch's satisfaction.

Busch then made Veeck an offer that hardly endeared the brewery to St. Louis fans—he would give Veeck $800,000 for the park, and $1.1 million if Veeck also left town. Veeck took the $800,000. In time, he also got the additional $300,000.

By now it was obvious he would be a lame-duck owner in St. Louis. Or was it? The sale of the park was actually a good thing for Brownies fans, Veeck claimed soon after the deal.

"It only eases the load on us," he explained. "It amounts to this—it was a matter of selling the park or selling players and the park was a luxury that we did not feel we could afford."

Veeck was more interested in talking up his Browns. They were going to be a good club, he said. And of that pitching staff that seemed to wither in spring training, why, he claimed, they would straighten out once it got cooler. The staff included Paige, Cain, and a pair of young hurlers who would make a name for themselves on the Yankees: Bob Turley and Don Larsen.

Asked what attendance he needed to keep the club in town, he replied, "Just a respectable attendance. Somewhere around 750,000."

The place the fans would be coming to now was renamed Busch Stadium. Something else about it was different too. Veeck had moved his family out. When he bought the team he decided to live in Sportsman's Park. So he converted the old Browns business offices into an apartment, and he brought his wife and burgeoning family inside. There they entertained before and after games.

Mary Frances Veeck always spoke of that apartment as an adventure in living, as if, say, they had moved into an old barn in the country and fixed it over. As simple as that. But it really was something more. "We remodeled the offices into a ten-room apartment," she once explained. "A home in the ballpark."

The morning routine began at six o'clock with Veeck having breakfast. That consisted of, she said, "coffee, papers, and telephone." Veeck and the telephone coexisted as if joined at the chin. People who have met him recall his constant companion: a notepad listing telephone calls he had to make first thing in the morning.

When Roger Angell of *The New Yorker* found Veeck years later in the Wrigley Field bleachers, Veeck had a notepad-toting secretary with him. People would amble over to Veeck and she would look in the pad and say, "7:20," and Veeck would tell the visitor, "Call me at 7:20 tomorrow morning."

In St. Louis, Veeck's early-morning calls were finished by 8 A.M. Then Manager Marion and his coaches joined the Veecks for breakfast.

"So did the fellows from the front office," said Mary Frances. "It was the same at noon, except that generally Bill wasn't there. He was off making a speech. At lunch they often platooned me. A new group would swarm in just as the first wave was finishing the dessert."

The apartment became the Browns' hub, the meeting place of choice for writers, coaches, players' wives. "We played a full night schedule, and that made dinner hectic," Mary Frances recalled. "If we had a rare day game, a few always would drop in for dinner, but the crowds were greatest before night games.

"Following a night game, the fellows and wives got together in the Brown Jug, the club's refreshment center. There were always some waiting to go up to the apartment after the Jug was closed. So that meant fixing up a late snack for them. These sessions could last all night.

"There were times when some who had been at dinner were on hand and helping us with the breakfast eggs. It was fun, although I believe had I known what was in store before I married Bill, I would have pulled the trigger.

"That didn't stop with the baseball season. It went on practically the whole year. We didn't have night games during the winter, of course. Instead, we had baseball players dropping up to cook the prizes they bagged while out hunting. Hunting season was as hectic as the baseball season."

Yet, most of the final baseball season must have been somber. For the Browns lost 100 games in 1953 and finished last. Attendance stagnated at just over half a million fans. This time there was no secret that Veeck was headed out of town—Baltimore. He was certain, his friends among the other owners told him, that they would permit him to leave this time.

More than thirty years later it may seem strange that no one attempted to halt the departure, that no civic group sprang up, no mayor chastised Veeck, no congressman called for an investigation. Yet, many fans were outraged, at the least.

As a matter of fact, Mayor Raymond R. Tucker seemed to pass it off as just one of those business decisions a company has a right to make. The mayor's correspondence is now in the archives at Washington University in St. Louis, where Peter Ruger, the school's general counsel, made the following letters available. Ruger was surprised at how little heat the move generated from city officials.

The letters often vilified Veeck but brought no sense of loss from the Mayor. On September 14, 1953—sixteen days before the Browns officially quit—Tucker wrote to a Don O. Pyke:

"Although this matter may definitely be a 'hot potato,' I still cannot see why I should participate in this in any way.

"For your information, since becoming Mayor I have received only one request that I intercede in this matter and that was an anonymous telegram. . . ." But the next page in the file shows a Western Union telegram signed by a Bob Rodgers that reads, in part, "DON'T WAIT UNTIL LAST SECOND WHEN IT'S TOO LATE TO DO ANY GOOD ACT PROMPTLY AND GO ALL OUT TO HAVE VEECK SELL CLUB TO ST. LOUIS INTERESTS. GET INJUNCTIONS ETC."

In a July 23 letter the mayor's aide wrote to another fan who wanted to keep the team in St. Louis, "[The Mayor] is completely lacking in authority in such matters and has been unable to obtain any information from Mr. Bill Veeck as to his plans for the 'Browns.'

"If you feel that efforts should be made by the business interests to keep the 'Browns' in St. Louis it is suggested that you call your views to the attention of the St. Louis Chamber of Commerce, 511 Locust Street."

On and on the mayor went in this vein, while letter after letter and card after card came into his office, pleading with him to step in. Ironically, when Veeck finally did get the American League to agree with him to move the club, they did it on the condition that he get out—of baseball. He could move the club, all right, as long as he wasn't running it. They allowed the Browns to move, but only if Veeck sold it to Baltimore interests. In this way the owners would get rid of two embarrassments: the St. Louis Browns and Bill Veeck.

Again, the Yankees led the assault. In trying to analyze why the Yankees hated him so, some thought back to the winter of '48, after the high-flying Veeck had seen his Indians capture the World Series in Cleveland. During a Hot Stove League dinner honoring Boudreau in Chicago, Veeck took the microphone on the dais, on which sat Yankee officials and Joe DiMaggio. The great ballplayer was in the middle of a contract dispute with the Yankees. Veeck referred to DiMaggio as a player of such magnitude "that he deserves anything he can get out of the Yankees—even more than $100,000."

But Veeck didn't stop there. He announced that the Yankees would finish third in 1949. And who would win the '49 pennant? Why his Indians, of course, with the Red Sox finishing second.

Of course that got the desired rise out of the Yankees' humorless general manager, George Weiss. The next day a steamed Weiss phoned Veeck and screamed at him that, while the Yankees were trying to sell tickets for the 1949 season, here was Veeck in effect telling the fans not to bother, they didn't have a chance. Not only that, Veeck was getting involved in the Yankees' negotiations with DiMaggio.

"I wouldn't come out to your town and say any such things," Weiss told Veeck.

"Then why don't you call up the papers and tell 'em I'm a jerk?" a delighted Veeck replied.

Weiss haughtily responded he would not dignify Veeck's remarks by calling attention to them.

Click.

Rudie Schaffer, his longtime business associate, actually moved to Baltimore from St. Louis, so sure were they that the Veeck operation would soon follow.

"The Yankees particularly stood in Bill's way," says Schaffer. "He was just a brash young fellow and he was always trying to poke holes into the Yankees, and he would say things about the Yankees and their personnel—particularly about George Weiss and others that were in the management of the Yankees. You know, when you say things publicly about someone, the recipients don't take kindly to you for those things. So that was, shall we say, a way of getting even for all those nasty little pokes he took at them."

Count the ways he made fun of them:

"Their baseball knowledge, the way they conducted their high-and-mighty business. He would attack them on a personal basis. At league meetings there'd always be a confrontation between the Yankees and Bill, either he was opposing them or they were opposing him. They were taking turns all the time. The Yankees at the time were a dominant force. While Will Harridge was the president of the league, the Yankees really were running the league."

The Yankees, and some other owners, were not the only people who found Veeck less than amusing. His style irritated Sidney Salomon, Jr., who owned 20 percent of the Browns and was a very powerful Democrat nationally and a friend of President Truman's. Salomon had grown wealthy in the insurance business. He was low-keyed in his dealings and wore expensive, dark business suits.

Shortly before his death in 1986, Salomon reflected on Veeck, who in his public posture, at least, had always spoken highly of Salomon: "I didn't go along with his way of thinking, but that's just one man against another man," said Salomon. "He lost his interest in St. Louis. I don't think he bought the team with the idea of moving it, but eventually he lost interest."

Why?

"Oh, you'd have to know Bill Veeck. He lost interest because he wasn't getting too much praise."

In the three years they were together, Salomon and Veeck often clashed—over the midget ("I told him it was taking advantage of baseball in the wrong way"), but mostly over Veeck's insistence on leaving St. Louis, which was Salomon's city and power base. "There were some owners didn't like him," said Salomon. "But some called me and asked me to go easy on him, that he was a better personality than I gave him credit for." Finally, when it came time to leave, said Salomon, "I fought against it, and didn't want it to happen. There was no alternative because Veeck had control."

Salomon contended that his close friend Del Webb actually was responsible for bringing Veeck into the Browns. Salomon was close to Webb and Topping, the other major Yankee owner. Yet, Salomon recalled the time that Veeck took Webb's new hat, grabbed it, said, "I don't like it"— and stomped on it.

"I said to him, 'Veeck, this isn't a way of making friends.'"

Veeck replied, "You've got to have a sense of humor."

Salomon claims that once the team was sold "we never discussed anything or ran across each other. It was a closed book as far as I was concerned." Salomon saw a Bill Veeck different from the way most others did: "I think he was an unhappy man. He had ways of letting things get the better of him. I think he meant well."

How did Salomon know Veeck was unhappy?

"He was always buying and selling and didn't care who he bought from or who he sold to."

The 1953 season had barely ended when the Browns were sold to Baltimore interests for $2.4 million. But Veeck, who had gone into the meeting assuming he was still the Browns' owner, learned that everyone had turned on him. When the three days' of meetings had started, the Tigers owner, Spike Briggs, proposed that Veeck be allowed to move the franchise to Baltimore. The proposal was even seconded. Veeck believed he was on his way. But when it came to a formal vote, it didn't work out. You can move the Browns, they told him, but you're not going with them.

"For the time being, at least, that's the end of Veeck in big-league baseball," wrote the Chicago *Daily News* sports editor, John P. Carmichael. "They didn't care whether they bought him out or froze him out. Just so they got even with him, after five years, for disturbing the old, established order of things... for thumbing his nose at brassier hats... for making enemies."

Chapter 8

Gadfly.

That was the role he really desired now that he was out of the ownership business. "Whatever little bit of money he might have been able to take out of the Browns carried him for a little bit," says his old friend and public relations partner, Marsh Samuel.

Veeck now made himself available to anyone who wanted to know what was wrong with the state of baseball, or sports. He also hooked up with P. K. Wrigley to explore bringing major-league baseball to Los Angeles, where Wrigley owned the minor-league team and thus had the territory. Samuel describes the role as "consultant." An Associated Press report said Veeck was "employed by" Wrigley. Veeck always made a point of denying that he actually "worked" for Wrigley. Rather, he described it as a sort of association.

But within three months of selling the Browns, Veeck was in California and sitting down with Governor Goodwin J. Knight to discuss building a stadium or two large enough for big-league teams. Besides Los Angeles, how about San Francisco?

Veeck had both places covered. For in addition to working with Wrigley in Los Angeles, Veeck's good buddy Rudie Schaffer was the nominal head of a group attempting to buy the minor-league San Francisco Seals.

Veeck, of course, denied that he was associated with Schaffer in this venture, but he conceded, "It's possible that if Rudie gets the franchise, I will wind up with him. We have a habit of staying together."

So Veeck had two irons in the fire when he approached the governor. This may have been the first time private sports teams dangled a franchise and asked local government to build them a place to play. Veeck may have been cynical about other owners who liked to claim they were sportsmen. But he had become busy brokering teams himself.

Now it is commonplace. Although County Stadium in Milwaukee—where the Braves moved from Boston—was built with municipal funds, it was constructed with the idea of luring a team and well before any deal actually was made.

Veeck explained to Knight that baseball was considering moving to Los Angeles and San Francisco—but that private capital couldn't possibly build a ballpark. If something could be done, said Veeck, financially troubled clubs might move out to the Coast, or perhaps the area would even be ripe for expansion, with the leagues expanding from eight teams to circuits of ten or twelve clubs.

How would these be paid for? Veeck suggested that the state, or a public agency such as an authority, could float bonds and then retire them with the rent from the teams.

Some people wondered whether fans would turn out in San Francisco because of the cold weather. Why, fans were staying away from Seals Stadium. Veeck didn't see that as a problem. "Heat the place," he said. "They do that at racetracks in the East all the time."

But could San Francisco really draw major-league-sized crowds? he was asked.

"Sure, look at Milwaukee," said Veeck. In that city's first major-league season, it broke the National League attendance record. That should not have been surprising to anyone familiar with Milwaukee baseball, which was revived during World War II by Bill Veeck.

Although the West Coast now is a baseball megalopolis, with six teams stretching from San Diego to Seattle, Veeck was too early. He left California. And then, according to Schaffer, "bought a ranch somewhere. He enjoyed the wide-open spaces. He needed to recuperate a little bit, health-wise."

The ranch was on 47,000 acres a little north of Albuquerque, New Mexico. Actually, he probably didn't really own all 47,000 acres, says his son Peter, but had the right to use the land.

To a man wedded to a telephone, this was a strange place to be. For there was no phone at the ranch. And people were forever trying to get in touch with him. But this was the setup:

The phone was on a weathered utility pole five miles from the ranch.

Twice a day Veeck would drive to the phone and call the local operator (he actually lived in a place called Glenwood) for messages. And what would happen if there were an emergency? The operator asked the caller if he or she wanted a personal messenger—for a fee—sent to the ranch so that Veeck could come to the phone or return the call.

He enjoyed telling the story of a call he received from another baseball official who wanted his opinion on a possible player deal. This was an important deal, with big salaries involved, but the caller couldn't hear Veeck speaking.

"Talk louder," he told Veeck, "it sounds like a tornado is going through your living room."

"It's no tornado and I'm not talking from my living room. I'm out in the middle of the sticks, and I'm holding on to this pole for dear life. There's a heck of a dust storm blowing and I think I just saw one of my steers go flying by."

While he was out on the farm, late in 1955, he was asked by Salomon to take over the new Miami team in the International League. The Miami team actually was the Syracuse club and was being taken down South. Veeck was enthusiastic about the venture of taking baseball to that resort town and told a reporter that Miami "at its worst will be five times as good a baseball town as Syracuse."

Yet, in his biography, Veeck pokes fun at Salomon for having been stuck with a bummer of a franchise—which he supposedly bought against Veeck's advice.

Veeck tried, and failed, to get into major-league baseball. A bid for the Tigers was turned down. He still attempted to get a Los Angeles syndicate going. Finally, he became a p.r. man.

The vehicle was his childhood buddy, Marsh Samuel, who already had a well-connected firm. "In 1957 he called me one day and said he'd like to go into a little public relations work, and Cleveland would be the place to do it," recalls Samuel.

Samuel did not have a large operation, but Veeck wanted to bring in Jim Gallagher, who had been the Cubs' general manager. Samuel seemed a little concerned that a one-man business now suddenly would have three people, but Veeck assured him there'd be enough money for everyone. Veeck was going to bring in the Indians as a client.

He did. But the Indians balked at his suggestions. The Indians' attendance had shrunk to among the lowest in baseball—nearly 2 million less than in Veeck's golden year of 1948. When he joined the p.r. firm the Indians were attracting barely 700,000 fans. Veeck tried to hype the gate but management wouldn't take his suggestions. He threw out the Indians as an account. Now there were three mouths to feed in the firm. Gallagher subsequently left for the Phillies and the p.r. operation became a two-man partnership until Veeck left in 1959 and bought the White Sox. The club had not won a pennant since 1919—when it also threw the World Series and became known as the Black Sox.

Naturally, with Veeck looking it over forty years later, it was a team in turmoil—at least in the front office. The Comiskeys—younger brother, older sister—were feuding.

In Milwaukee during World War II Veeck had found a disintegrating park housing a deadly dull team. In Cleveland he revived a club and a city that had last seen a pennant in 1920. In St. Louis he gave the bored fans a small fling at fun, but ultimately lost out. Now he was trying to gain control from a brother-sister act that was the talk of Chicago, a tarnished royal family squabbling in public.

The Comiskeys went back, way back. Even before they created the White Sox 59 years earlier. In the team's history, the family had been the only people to control it.

The Comiskeys made an impact on Chicago after settling there in 1848. John Comiskey was a county clerk, then an alderman in the old Tenth Ward. He told his son Charles that plumbing was a fine occupation for a young, strong lad, and apprenticed his son.

But Charles Comiskey loved baseball, a pastoral game that was becoming popular across a muscle-flexing America. He became a free-lance player, moving around the Midwest, wherever a team needed a first baseman.

Then, in the 1880s, he joined the St. Louis Browns of the American Association, the "renegade" league that was challenging the established National League. In 1883, Comiskey finished fourth in batting at .297. He played first base in the same era as Cap Anson, who overshadowed not only the hitters of his time, but also anyone else playing the position. In 1886 the Browns defeated the National's White Stockings in what was the forerunner of the modern World Series.

Comiskey played until 1894, and in his thirteen seasons batted .266. He had one peculiarity as a hitter. He never liked to walk—in 1,385 games he walked only 197 times, an average of about once every 30 at-bats.

But it was as an owner that he made his mark on American baseball. His determination to run a team, and to make it big-league, was largely responsible for the creation of the American League. That, of course, led to the World Series—and this country's Septembers haven't been the same since.

After his playing career ended, Comiskey got in on the ground floor of another upstart league, the Western League, and gained a franchise in St. Paul, naming the team the Saints. In 1900 the league changed its name to the American League—although it still was a minor league—and Comiskey moved his team, with some difficulty, to Chicago. Because his team was not part of a major league, he did not want to anger the Cubs. So Comiskey agreed to place his club on the South Side—and not to use the city's name in business dealings.

The team was holed up in a small wooden park at Thirty-ninth and Wentworth. The Cubs were pleased. Why, what right-thinking Chicagoan would venture into that neighborhood to see minor-league baseball? One reporter covering the opening game labeled the field "unfit to play on." Meanwhile, the sportswriters nicknamed the team "the White Stockings."

The next year, led by the American League president, Ban Johnson, and Comiskey, the "minor" American League tagged itself a major league and announced it was a rival of the entrenched Nationals. The White Sox quickly established themselves as a legitimate contender for Windy City fans by winning the American League's very first pennant in 1901.

Now fans began to wonder: Which was the better team, the Cubs or White Sox? James Hart, the Cubs' owner, refused to consider an intracity rivalry. But in 1903 they began their famed City Series. The upstart Sox held the Cubs to a draw, and Hart immediately claimed that one of his pitchers had thrown games to the Sox.

The teams were to meet only once in the World Series. The year was 1906 and it was such a momentous time for the city that both clubs led their leagues in attendance—the Cubs, winning by 20 games with their double-play combination of Tinker to Evers to Chance.

And the White Sox? They produced a late-season 19-game winning streak to defeat the Yankees despite the fact that not one batter hit .280 for the season. They were to earn their historic nickname of the "Hitless Wonders." They even went on to defeat the Cubs by 4 games to 2 in the Series.

By 1910 the Sox were ready for their own new park, and they moved into one of the few nonwooden stadiums in the United States. It was on Thirty-fifth Street and Shields Avenue and they called it Comiskey Park—where it remained the longest-lived ballpark in major-league history. White

Sox management seventy-six years later told the city it was time to build a new park or face the prospect of the team leaving.

Despite the new park, Comiskey's team floundered and failed to draw more fans than before. So in 1915 he signed five new players, including Shoeless Joe Jackson. The team quickly became competitive, winning the World Series in 1917, and in 1919 again captured the pennant with Jackson batting .351 and Eddie Cicotte winning 29 games and Lefty Williams adding 23.

When the Sox lost the Series to the underdog Reds, people explained that the Chicagoans were tired from their grueling pennant race with the Indians. This was followed by a best-of-nine-game series. Jackson batted .375 in the Series, but Cicotte managed only a 1-2 record while Williams was 0-3.

The next year Comiskey learned that his stars had conspired to lose the World Series, and eight players were banned for life by Judge Landis, who took over the newly created post of Commissioner of Baseball.

The 1920s were downward spirals, not only for Comiskey's White Sox, but for Bill Veeck, Sr.'s Cubs. If there were territorial bragging rights to be won, they weren't accomplished until 1929, when the Cubs won their first pennant for Veeck. But the White Sox floundered, preoccupied by the scandal that would not go away.

After the story broke, following the 1920 season, the White Sox failed to get out of the second division for the rest of the twenties. Their losses, the taint that surrounded his team, collapsed Comiskey. He was described as brokenhearted and disillusioned when he died in 1931, a year before Veeck, Sr., passed away.

His son, J. Louis, and Harry Grabiner, the general manager, took over the team and began a long process of rebuilding. They developed a young pitcher in Monty Stratton. He captured 15 games in 1937 and 15 more in 1938. But following a hunting accident, his leg was amputated and Stratton was finished, although his name was revived almost twenty years later when Jimmy Stewart portrayed him in the movies. The White Sox, anchored by Luke Appling, had become a solid contending club but fell apart after Stratton's injury. That was compounded by J. Lou Comiskey's death in 1939.

Now, Grace Comiskey, his widow, was the Comiskey in charge. She had a son and a daughter, but she ran the club and was described not only as the "First Lady of Baseball," but the creator of the only feminine reign in American League history. The will left by J. Louis Comiskey doled out shares of stock to his children. They would each get some when they reached the ages of twenty-one, thirty, and thirty-five.

Grace had a falling-out with Grabiner in 1945 and he left for the Indians, where he was to hook up with Veeck a year later. By the late 1940s her son, Chuck, took a firm hand in the team and he hired Frank Lane as general manager and Paul Richards as manager. This was a team that in 1950 stole a total of 19 bases.

But the next season, under Richards, they became heralded as the "Go-Go" Sox and led the majors with 99 stolen bases. Minnie Minoso led the league with 31 while batting .324, and Jim Busby and Chico Carrasquel helped provide other excitement as the fans at Comiskey Park chanted "Go! Go! whenever a White Sox runner got on base.

Yet, internal wrangling among Chuck Comiskey and Lane and Richards was constant, and Lane eventually left, as did Richards. New, good young players arrived, though—particularly Luis Aparicio at shortstop.

Grace Comiskey died in 1956. But her daughter Dorothy inherited 500 more shares than did Chuck, the younger brother. Very quickly the children battled over control just when it appeared the White Sox were on the verge of breaking the Yankee dynasty. The siblings were tied up in court while the club never appointed a president to replace Grace Comiskey.

Veeck dabbled in several ventures. He had already lost a bid to buy the Tigers in the 1950s, and a deal fell through to take over the Ringling Brothers circus. Now, Mrs. Dorothy Comiskey Rigney wanted to get out of the White Sox. Veeck was interested, and so was Charles O. Finley, a Chicago insurance man who had made a fortune after he suffered a heart attack. Recuperating, surrounded by doctors, he thought about disability insurance. That was just what the doctors needed. He became rich and famous selling insurance tailor-made for physicians. He was interested in spending some of that money to buy a baseball team.

Veeck, though, got the option first to buy Mrs. Rigney's majority interest for $2.7 million. "I would definitely keep the White Sox permanently in Chicago," he said. "I am not intersted in obtaining the club to make a quick profit. I am interested only in developing a championship team for Chicago."

Attendance had plummeted to about 800,000 from more than 1.1 million in 1958. The payroll for players—and coaches—was about $610,000. Finally, on March 10, 1959—after Charles Comiskey's last-minute attempt to buy his sister out for $500,000 more than Veeck offered—the deal was made.

For the first time since the Old Roman, Charles Comiskey, founded the team, the family no longer was in control. Yet, the family was still around. Chuck owned his 46 percent. And Dorothy Comiskey's husband, John Rigney, was a White Sox vice president.

Veeck brought in Greenberg, along with half a dozen other owners, and then announced he was going to Opening Day "to see what we've bought." He apparently didn't think much of the White Sox's chances. In an article in *The Saturday Evening Post*, early that season, Veeck was quoted as saying, "I hate to admit this, but we cannot beat the Yankees."

What made it even worse, Veeck admitted, is that George Weiss, the general manager, "is one of my least favorite people." Veeck, though, didn't put the antipathy on a personal level. It wasn't that Weiss had done anything to Veeck, you understand. It was because "Mr. Weiss is completely devoid of a sense of humor and the milk of human kindness. I suppose a good part of my antipathy to him is jealousy. The fellow is the best operator in baseball, but cold fishes always irritate me. It's fun to deflate and annoy them. The madder they get the more fun you can have with them." That, of course, was typical Veeck—setting up the straw man to ignite him with a spark.

Yet, Veeck told the interviewer, he had always liked Casey Stengel. And here Veeck said something that, once again, opened a window to Veeck's ego: "Casey has been one of my favorite guys ever since I hired him as my manager at Milwaukee fifteen years ago. It's always enjoyable and educational listening to him."

Actually, Veeck didn't hire Stengel, but did fire him. The story was unearthed in the book *Stengel, His Life and Times*, by Robert W. Creamer. The author explained in an interview that he dug up the following letter in Milwaukee, where Stengel had been hired in 1944 to replace Charlie Grimm—who had gone to the Cubs—while Veeck was in the Marines.

When Veeck found out that Stengel was the new manager, he was furious. Veeck wrote the following letter to Grimm—a part-owner of the Milwaukee club—and other team officials:

"I learned an hour ago the identity of our new manager. I've waited an hour to write this, hoping to cool off. So far it hasn't been too successful. To say I'm very disappointed is putting it mildly.

"I'd like to have a complete explanation of where Stengel came from. Who suggested him? For how much and how long? I don't want anything to do with Stengel, nor do I want him to have anything to do with anything I have a voice in.

"I will now proceed to elucidate the above:

"First, Stengel has never managed a winner. In my humble opinion, he is a poor manager.

"Second, he has been closely connected with Bob Quinn and the operation of the Boston Braves. This in itself is enough to damn him. [Stengel had managed the Braves the previous six seasons, never getting them higher than fifth.]

"Third, I don't believe that Stengel is a good judge of ballplayers so can be of no value in amassing future clubs.

"Fourth, from what I know of Stengel he is tight-fisted and this will not prove acceptable.

"Fifth, from my observation, Stengal is mentally a second-division major leaguer. That is, he is entirely satisfied with a mediocre ball club as long as Stengel and his alleged wit are appreciated.

"Sixth, I have no confidence in his ability and rather than be continuously worried, I'd rather dispose of the whole damn thing.

"Seventh, Stengel doesn't fit in at all with the future—and I'm looking, as usual, for the long haul.

"If these aren't reasons enough, I don't like him and want no part of him. If Stengel has an iron-clad contract and it will be expensive to break I guess that we'll have to be stuck with him. If not, replace him immediately with Ivy Griffin."

And so Stengel was a lame duck in Milwaukee—where he was in the process of winning a pennant.

Now, with Veeck's return to baseball, the Stengel-led Yankees were the bugaboo he had to overcome. The Bronx Bombers had won the last four pennants. In fact, they were the only American League team to win a pennant since 1947, except for the Indians of 1948 and 1954.

The White Sox were not the Hitless Wonders of another era, but they still stroked fewer homers than any other team in baseball. They loved to run, though, and put opposing pitchers off guard.

The day before the season opened, Veeck was still trying to wrest control of the daily operations from Chuck Comiskey. Veeck was trying to get another seat on the board to replace Comiskey's sister. That seat would effectively give Veeck veto power over Comiskey.

In any event, Veeck turned out at Detroit the next day for the season's opener. There, in thirty-seven-degree weather, he wore a blue suit but no topcoat. He made four radio appearances before the game, and during the game cops and vendors and fans came over to congratulate him on his new team.

Veeck kept his offhanded appearance throughout the game, which ran on and on. In fact, it lasted four hours twenty-five minutes and finally ended in the fourteenth inning. Then, Nellie Fox, of all people—he hadn't hit a home run all of 1958—blasted a two-run shot to give the Chisox a 9-7 victory.

This was a Chicago team that knew it could win, and so did manager Al Lopez. During the second half of 1958 they posted the best winning percentage in either league. "We can win it all this year," Lopez said on the eve of the opener.

Lopez wasn't the only one who was confident. "The players were the players of the previous administration. But Veeck created a mood," recalls Bill Gleason, who was covering baseball and other sports for the Chicago *American* then. "There was never a Chicago team during the fifties—when they had very good ball clubs—that believed the team could win it. He changed that whole atmosphere, particularly in the clubhouse. For the first time ever I heard a Sox player talking about winning the pennant. Warren Brown, who was a columnist, would go to spring training every year and come back muttering and fuming about the players on the White Sox talking about their aspirations—which was to finish second behind the Yankees.

"Veeck came in and he just excited the entire city. There was a feeling that never was here before—that this man wanted to win."

He took over the Bards' Room, the press and old boys' hangout, and Veeck turned it into something more: It was a place where baseball, and life, were to be discussed in an atmosphere of truth-seeking, helped by a steady flow of beer. In Cleveland he was forever seeking places to run to. But in Chicago they came to him at the Bards' Room. And it said something about the relationship that Veeck established between himself and newspapermen (women weren't allowed in the press box, nor were there even any female writers to ban).

"It went back to the Old Roman," recalls Gleason. "It was originally called the Woodlands Bards' Room. The Old Roman, Charles Comiskey, had an estate up at Eagle River, Wisconsin, and in the off-season he used to have the baseball writers up there for hunting and fishing. He just transferred the rustic room to Comiskey Park and made it the press room. Presided over by Ernie Carroll for fifty years. Often, Bill would be there till five o'clock in the morning. He was there not as a public relations gesture but because he enjoyed it."

In those late (or early) hours, Gleason and a buddy, Joe Mooshil of the AP, would sit and drink and argue with Veeck. They'd discuss baseball philosophy and Veeck would come out with a "what-if" trade and Mooshil or Gleason would tell him the potential deal was rotten and Veeck would tell them they were crazy.

"Bill was hard of hearing in one ear, but he could hear himself speak, so he used to talk in a low voice. You'd have to strain yourself, get to within three or four inches of Veeck's lips to hear him. He had jungle rot in the ear, and with his middle finger he was always tweaking at his ear because the jungle rot was bothering him."

With all the hours they spent together, two incidents have become forever part of Gleason's memories of Veeck. One says something about Veeck's relationship with people, how he cared for the fans. The other showcases the humor in baseball and the absurd that Veeck enjoyed so much.

"In his first regime, he still had the leg below his knee, and he was remarkably agile. He was always up in the press box, as Frank Lane [the White Sox famed general manager in the years before Veeck took over] used to be. Unlike Frank, Bill didn't shout and exclaim and threaten to fire the manager. He just liked to be up there. One night the ticket office put two huge groups next to each other—one from East Chicago, Indiana, and one from Whiting, Indiana. Side by side in the upper deck, just outside the press box. If you've been in Comiskey Park, you know on humid nights is when the fights break out.

"And this night, these people—ethnic types—they just didn't like each other. There's a rivalry there that goes back to high school sports. Whiting is a refinery town and East Chicago is a steel-mill town. They're very large people, Poles, Lithuanians, Hungarians. And the beer...those times they were selling beer in bottles and cans, and the vendors would just bring five cases of beer and set them up in the aisles next to these people. About the fifth inning the inevitable happened—the greatest gang fight I've ever seen. Even the women were involved. The women were hitting the guys with umbrellas.

"People were rolling around the aisles, over the seats, and Veeck decided that he would be the peacemaker. And there was a window on the right side of the press box and Veeck jumped out of the window onto the seats below, and I said to myself, 'Well, I've got to see this.' So I followed him. He was gimping up the aisle toward this melee, and he tapped this big guy on the shoulder. He wanted to say something to him in his role as peacemaker, and this guy turned about and whistled a right hand and knocked Bill right on his ass.

"And the guy looked down and he says, 'Oh, my God, Bill, I didn't know it was you. Sorry.' And he went right back into the fight."

The other incident Gleason so fondly recollects occurred during the 1967 World Series. Gleason and Veeck were sitting in the press hotel in Boston one night with Al Barlick, the senior National League umpire. "Across the room from us there was a group that included a couple of American League umpires. One of the guys was very loud. He had had too much to drink. And Barlick, he had a crewcut, an old coalminer down from southern Illinois, he says to us, 'Wait a minute, gentlemen, I'll be right back.'

"And Veeck says, 'This is gonna be historic. This is something you don't want to miss.' So Barlick strides across the room and he points a finger at the umpire and he says, 'YOU'RE OUT OF HERE!' and the guy says, 'Al, what do you mean?' And Barlick says, 'You know what I mean. You're out of here. Go to your room.'

"Bill says, 'Well, just as I said. That's historic. That's the first time in history an umpire threw another umpire out of a bar.'"

Gleason's relationship with Veeck continued over the years, from the first tenure in Chicago, to the "convalescing" years in eastern Maryland, to the return to the White Sox, to the days in the bleachers once again at Wrigley Field.

Veeck's first turn with the Sox was to end after barely two years. One day Gleason and Warren Brown visited Veeck in his apartment on South Lake Shore Drive overlooking Lake Michigan. Veeck was ill—suffering coughing fits and then blacking out.

"We stayed there about two hours," says Gleason, "and we came down the elevator and went out into the sunshine and Warren said to me, 'Bill, we're never going to see him alive again.' And I felt the same way. I thought this was absolutely the last visit. Of course none us knew what was wrong with him. And that's what I wrote after his death last January—'We got a 25-year bonus.'"

Strange that there was. Everyone surrounding Bill Veeck has stories regarding his disdain for doctor's orders.

To say simply that Veeck was a chain-smoker fails to capture the enormity of his habit. "In the apartment, in the home I visited him at in eastern Maryland, where he went to convalesce, everywhere in the house— I've never seen anything like it—everyplace, in the bathrooms, on every table—there were packages of cigarettes, which Mary Frances put around so he wouldn't have to be searching for them," says Gleason.

"The guy was larger than life. One night we had just finished dinner, and this was when the Braves were trying to leave Milwaukee. Bill was an adviser to the attorneys for the city, which was trying to keep them there.

He was on the phone practically all night, to 3 A.M. We sat up until five. We were there at that same table drinking beer, and I have something of a reputation as a beer drinker. But after the first two hours I started going to the bathroom quite frequently. This man, in eight hours—he went once.

"Another time, we had a big discussion in the Bards' Room with Ernie Carroll. He was the authority on the eating and drinking habits of everyone who came into the Bards' Room. They had a lot of Falstaffian figures in there. So one night we had a big discussion on who was the most prodigious beer drinker. I nominated George Connor, former Bear, Notre Dame All-America. "Ernie looked out at us and said, 'Connor was second, Bill Veeck was first.'"

The '59 White Sox really weren't Bill Veeck's team, but he made it his. Much of it had been put together by Frank Lane, dubbed Trader Lane, who had run the team as general manager until his continued feuding with Grace Comiskey chased him out. He moved over to the Indians.

The Chicagoans that Veeck took over had only two players who would hit home runs in double figures—Sherm Lollar and Al Smith. It had thirty-five-year-old Earl Torgeson at first, thirty-one-year-old Nellie Fox at second, thirty-four-year-old Lollar catching, and thirty-one-year-old Smith in the outfield. The pitchers included thirty-nine-year-old Early Wynn, thirty-two-year-old Billy Pierce, thirty-five-year-old Turk Lown, and thirty-eight-year-old Gerry Staley.

But the manager was Al Lopez, and he not only had experience, he was clever enough to figure out how to use the talent he had. He worked hard.

Lopez was always working hard because, it seemed, he was always chasing the Yankees. First, he managed the Indians, replacing Boudreau, in the years after Veeck sold the team. Lopez managed the 1954 Indians that interrupted the Yankees' perennial string of pennant winners. Now, in 1959, it was time to shove aside the Bronx Bombers once again.

"Everybody took it for granted that the Yankees would win again," recalls Lopez from his home in Tampa. "I kept saying, 'I know, I know,' to those writers from New York—Red Smith and Frankie Graham and Arthur Daley. They used to come up to spring training and kid me all the time and they'd ask, 'How you gonna catch them this year? You're always saying you're gonna catch them.' Naturally, nobody figured we would.

"When Bill took over the team he said, 'If Al Lopez could win the pennant with that club, I'll go down to Michigan and Lake and eat crow.'

I think the next year he went down there. I don't know if he ate crow or pheasant, but he went down and ate something.

"He worked harder than any owner I knew of. They had a private office for him, but he just went outside the office and had a big desk put out there. He put phones in there and anybody who walked in, he could just see him working. He didn't touch the team that year, but that winter we made some trades. He thought maybe we could win another pennant or two if we could get some hitting in the line-up. And we made some deals. He gave away some young ballplayers that turned out to be good ballplayers because he thought that by getting some power we could win the pennant again."

Veeck's reputation as a trader and Yankee-killer has grown, more or less unchallenged over the years, because the teams that beat the Yankees in that era were teams that Veeck was associated with. Certainly he was instrumental in the success of the '48 Indians, although by no means did he develop the team. The nucleus was there, and had been there. But he did engineer some of the key moves.

Yet, when the 1954 Indians also won, there was barely any relationship to the team that Veeck had been associated with, but in the public's mind he still was the man whose teams halted Yankee dominance.

The 1954 Indians, though, had only three regulars—Al Rosen, Larry Doby, and Bobby Avila—who could properly be credited to Veeck. Among the starting pitchers there was the redoubtable trio of Bob Lemon, Early Wynn, and Mike Garcia to arrive during Veeck's tenure.

None of the key players of the pennant-winning 1959 White Sox—with the possible exception of Ted Kluszewski, who batted 101 times after he arrived in a trade on August 25—could be considered as Veeck's boys. Of course Veeck arrived while spring training was going on and the club was set.

"We didn't have any power. We had great fielding, good pitching, good speed," recalls Lopez. "I had two guys in the bull pen that did a great job—Turk Lown and Gerry Staley. And Early Wynn and Bob Shaw had a great year for us. Wynn ended up winning 22 games and Shaw was a big surprise. We didn't expect anything from him." Shaw, acquired in a trade the previous year, posted an 18-6 record in the pennant-winning season.

"We had speed—Aparicio stole 56 bases, which was tops in the American League, and we had Jim Landis stole some bases. Then, in the middle of the year, we got Ted Kluszewski from Pittsburgh. I thought that was a great acquisition. You know we had Lollar batting fourth, our catcher.

He was our power hitter, and he was the only power hitter in the line-up, and by getting Kluszewski it kind of lifted us morally."

Lopez had spent spring training not only managing and devising ways his light-hitting boys could win but also by trying to build their confidence that this, finally, was to be the year someone beat the Yankees—the Yankees of Skowron, Richardson, Kubek, Bauer, Mantle, Berra, McDougald, Howard. But what the Yankees didn't have in 1959 was pitching, except for Whitey Ford and, occasionally, Art Ditmar and Duke Maas.

"This was the feeling you try to get into a club, that you can win. The Yankees had a heck of a club. They were the best team in baseball all those years, by far. Even the year that we beat them in Cleveland, we won 111 games and they won 103 games—more games than in any other year that Stengel managed."

Lopez's White Sox weren't in the same class as the '54 Indians. But Chicago went on to win the pennant by five games over the Indians—with the Yankees trailing in third place, 15 games behind.

"I enjoyed managing the '59 club more than I did the Cleveland club that won more games," says Lopez. "I had to manage more in Chicago. The Cleveland club, we didn't have to steal, to grab a run here and there, whichever way. I think we won 41 games by one run with the White Sox that year."

The Yankee dominance really had come to a crash on May 20, when they sank into last place—below, even, the Senators. The Sox, meanwhile, took over first place on July 28 and preserved the edge with a key 4-game sweep of the Indians the final days of August.

Chicagoans learned to be patient waiting for their team to score, to wait for one of the 113 stolen bases that would lead the majors. Certainly there wouldn't be many homers—only 97, by far the fewest in the big leagues. So there were doubles by Nellie Fox and Jim Landis, walks to Torgeson and Aparicio—and saves from Lown and Staley. The thirty-five-year-old Lown led the league with 15 while Staley, thirty-eight, produced 14. It was a good thing they did. Wynn, at thirty-nine, rarely could finish a game, yet he started more than anyone else in the American League and hurled the most innings.

The White Sox didn't make that first pennant in forty years easy. They were coasting in late September and hoped to clinch the flag at home against Detroit. But in successive days over the weekend the Tigers scored 5-4 victories, and Comiskey Park heard boos scattered through the stands. Was this going to be another cruel season for Chicago, Lopez turning in another also-ran, as had fifteen managers who preceded him?

Two days later the Sox were in Cleveland, where Wynn was sent to the mound for the pivotal game. The Indians were in second place, now being orchestrated in the front office by Frank Lane, the man who had created the Go-Go Sox.

Wynn made it until the ninth inning, when he loaded the bases with one out, holding on to a 4-2 lead. Lopez made a change, thirty-eight-year-old Gerry Staley in for the thirty-nine-year-old Wynn. Staley threw one pitch, the ball was grounded to Luis Aparicio. He grabbed it, stepped on second, threw to first—double play, the Sox had won the pennant. Wynn, who had been in the locker room dragging on a cigarette and listening to the game on radio, jumped to his feet and shouted, "One pitch!"

The Sox left Cleveland for Chicago for the victory parade, the city's first since the Cubs' pennant of 1945—but the Sox's first since 1919, after which so many dreams died.

State Street was packed from the curbs to the storefronts. People waved from windows showering confetti and scraps of paper and ticker tape (today's "ticker-tape" parades more likely contain shredded paper). The parade wended its way south on State from Wacker Drive to Adams, west to La Salle, then north, through the heart of the financial district to City Hall. At the head of the parade, Veeck and Comiskey were joined by Mayor Richard Daley, who called himself "the Number One Sox Fan," a South Sider who had grown up near Comiskey Park.

They were accompanied by six bands, marching units, a large truck painted with the sign "Go, Go Sox," and a funeral car bearing the remains of a dead Indian. The chief of the police's traffic division said he had not heard such noise or seen so many people so jubilant since the day World War II ended.

Winning the pennant meant, of course the World Series. And that meant Veeck had a chance to get back at the Yankees. He had been waiting for years, but they always were winning pennants.

"You know, the Yankees, when they were winning pennants, they were very careful who they gave good seats to," says Lopez. "I think every club was allotted 200 tickets, but clubs the Yankees weren't very friendly with—and they weren't very friendly with Bill Veeck—they'd give them tickets up in the third tier.

"And in the '59 World Series he said, 'I'm going to get even with those guys. I don't know if I'm going to get another chance.' So he put 'em up in the top tier, as far away from home plate as he possibly could.

"I don't think he got along too good with Weiss. But it's not a bad idea. If you're going to pick on somebody, might as well pick on some big guy."

The 1959 White Sox drew more fans—more than 1.4 million—than any team in Chicago had previously attracted, but they fell victim in the Series to the Los Angeles Dodgers, whose West Coast dynasty was starting.

After the Series, Veeck began a series of trading blunders. Trying to repeat as a pennant winner, he believed the team was desperate for power. He was willing to sacrifice young players to get this instant fix. He knew that the Yankees were working on acquiring the young slugger Roger Maris from Kansas City. The Yankees would be tougher in 1960.

Veeck loved his old players—old not only in the sense they once played for him, but also had grown a few whiskers. So in the off-season Veeck acquired thirty-three-year-old Roy Sievers from the Senators and thirty-seven-year-old Minnie Minoso from the Indians. And he also tried to convince Lopez that Satchel Paige, who would be fifty-four years old during the 1960 season, merited a return.

"He had Sievers with the Browns," says Lopez. "He liked Sievers personally, and he brought back Minnie Minoso from Cleveland. We gave up some young players—Callison to Philadelphia, which turned out to be a good ballplayer, for Freese. We gave Romano to Cleveland for Minoso and we gave Earl Battey and Mincher to Washington."

All the players Veeck acquired for the 1960 season were gone from the White Sox after 1961, their careers ended two years after that. But Johnny Callison, John Romano, Earl Battey, and Don Mincher all had careers that extended well into the 1970s.

"We made deals that really hurt us. You can't trade away young guys. Any time you do that to your ball club, it's not going to show right then, but three or four years from then."

Lopez refused to listen to Veeck on one deal, though: bringing back Paige, who had been out of the majors for six years. "He was like a godfather to Satchel Paige. He thought Satchel Paige was the greatest pitcher in the world. I thought that Satchel was great, but I just didn't like his habits. He'd show up whenever he felt like it. I didn't think this would go good with the club. It would disrupt the rest of the guys. The morale on the club wouldn't be good.

"It's all right for a club that's down, not fighting for the pennant. But we were always going for second place or the pennant and I didn't want a fellow like Satchel in there because it was going to disrupt everything we were trying to do—to have discipline and to have everybody on time. Satchel did what he wanted to do. So I always turned Bill Veeck down on Satchel Paige. Even after Bill left Cleveland and Hank Greenberg was there, Bill would call Hank and tell him to take Satchel, that Satchel could help the Indians.

"Bill had one thing wrong with him—it was that he fell in love with players and he hated to get rid of some guys that weren't good ballplayers. But he wanted to keep them around because he loved them."

Veeck was able to convince Lopez to implement another idea. Breaking with tradition, Veeck made off-season news when he splashed his players' names across the backs of their road uniforms. "After all," Veeck pointed out, "it cost us only about $200 to have the names put on the uniforms, so why keep the fans in the dark?"

The club did not need names on home uniforms, he contended, because everyone knew the players. He did not add, however, that for those who didn't, it was necessary to buy a program.

It was believed that this was the first time names were put on the backs of baseball uniforms. Observers wondered just how this would sit with the players, steeped in baseball tradition. Kluszewski, though, said, "It's a good thing I've got a good broad back."

One of Bob Shaw's shirts came back with the named spelled "Show." He pointed out that the club already had a pitcher named Wynn, now all it needed was someone named "Place."

That season, Veeck unveiled another innovation to help visibility— the exploding scoreboard. It soared 130 feet over center field. Ten electric towers raised and lowered at Veeck's whim. It was gaudy, it was grand, it was bothersome to the opposition and adored by the fans. And it came about in a completely nonbaseball way, as only Veeck would have it:

"I was daydreaming one day," he explained. "And, for no reason at all, I started thinking of a play by William Saroyan that I saw maybe fifteen years ago. It was called *The Time of Your Life*.

"There was a guy in there who didn't have a line of dialogue. He kept playing a pinball machine all through the play and finally he hit the jackpot or whatever it is they get on a pinball machine.

"Well, it was the funniest sight I ever saw. I never forgot it. The machine practically exploded. The American flag was unfurled; battleships fired guns; music blared. It was really something. It was just so silly, you know, that it was unforgettably funny.

"I began to imagine something like that on a big scale, like a scoreboard. I got the Spencer Display Company in New York and we worked the thing out."

He worked it out in such a way with the advertisers that the $300,000 item would pay for itself in just seven years.

The board went into action when a White Sox player hit a home run—although those were not exactly daily events. At that point, though, Veeck gave the order and someone in the bull pen pushed a button. The effect was staggering. There might be the sound of two trains rushing toward each other—and then the crashing noise of a collision, of screaming whistles and screeching metal. Or there were foghorns, battle sounds, a cavalry charge on a bugle. How about the 'William Tell Overture'? The lights on the scoreboard twinkled or ran crazily in a circle.

Then came the fireworks. The turrets moved into position and each of them sent off an explosion. The whole effect lasted thirty-two seconds.

When Veeck heard that Jimmie Dykes, the Tigers' manager, was going to protest, Veeck wondered, "What are they going to protest? What are we trying to do to baseball, make it like tennis?"

Since it made noise only when something good happened for the Sox, Casey Stengel and his Yankees decided to throw their own celebration for one of their accomplishments. Unknown to Veeck, Stengel brought in a supply of sparklers. And sure enough, that game a Yankee blasted a home run. As he trotted the bases, the Yankee dugout suddenly came alive like a small July 4 party—everyone up and down the bench was holding a little sparkler.

Actually, Veeck claimed he planned something just for the Yankees. He spoke to a pigeon fancier in the Bronx—who operated not far from Yankee Stadium—and planned to bring in a hundred birds. They would be concealed in the scoreboard, to be released when a Yankee hit one out.

And where would these birds fly?

"Back to the Bronx with the news, of course," Veeck replied. "For those who can't make it nonstop, we'll arrange for them to stop in Cleveland."

Too bad he never got around to trying it. But he did do something on the board for the opposition—a twenty-second clock. The rule at the time, to speed up a game that was having attendance problems, was that a pitch had to be delivered twenty seconds after the ball was returned to the pitcher. But the countdown started in blinking lights on the huge board only when a rival pitcher was on the mound.

Meanwhile, Veeck also tried an innovation in the time-honored act of the umpire dusting home plate. Veeck produced a vacuum cleaner that dusted off the plate. The umpire would step on a trigger built into the ground and a jet of air would swirl the dust around.

It was the scoreboard, though, that gave Veeck a kick. "All my life I've heard of gadgets which did everything but whistle 'Dixie,'" he said. "Well, I've finally got the perfect squelch to wise guys. This board of mine does do everything. It even whistles Dixie."

And while Veeck tinkered with the grand old game, Chuck Comiskey quit as the Sox' executive vice president. His departure ended sixty years of having a Comiskey in the front office. The thirty-three-year-old Comiskey wrote a formal note of one sentence: "I sincerely wish Manager Al Lopez and the players and the club continued success and am confident that Al and our players will win the American League pennant and the World Series for the City of Chicago this year."

Although Lopez got 28 home runs out of Sievers—the second-highest figure ever reached by a White Sox batter, only one under the club record—and Minoso led the league with 184 hits and batted .311, the club fell to third. Early Wynn, now forty years old and still pitching every fourth day, managed 13 victories. He was one of four hurlers to post that many on the club, which was led by Billy Pierce's 14. But the bull pen floundered.

Meanwhile, Baltimore—Veeck's old St. Louis Browns—got out of the second division for the first time, helped by their remarkable pitching staff. The Orioles wound up second.

And the winner? The Yankees, resuming their dynastic stretches. They slugged 193 home runs with Mickey Mantle producing 40. Roger Maris added 39, lead the league in runs batted in, and was voted the most valuable player.

Still, the Sox shattered their own attendance record by drawing more than 1.6 million fans.

Veeck, though, was having strange symptoms. He seemed to be dying. His uncontrolled coughing spells became more frequent. Finally, he was diagnosed as having a brain tumor. His friends assumed it was just a matter of time. He coughed, then he passed out. Eventually he wound up at the Mayo Clinic. There they discovered that blood vessels in the brain had been damaged, probably from the frequent expansion and contraction caused by his continual cough. As a result, blood wasn't flowing freely to the brain, creating an oxygen loss—and the blackouts. The cure: Get out of baseball.

He did not go gently.

No sooner did the '61 season open than Veeck rehired Eddie Gaedel. In fact, he hired Gaedel and five other midgets. The idea was for the Sox Six to perk up Opening Day attendance by selling hot dogs.

But after working the game, Gaedel, the group's spokesman, wrote a letter of resignation to Veeck. Gaedel explained that he and his colleagues had aching feet. Within two months Veeck sold the team, and within ten days of the sale, Gaedel was found dead.

Veeck survived. He sold a team that was about to finish fourth, and which had dropped almost 500,000 in attendance in 1961. In June, though, he sold the Sox to Arthur C. Allyn, Jr., whose father had been an original partner of Veeck's.

The announcement of the sale was made with Veeck's regrets, and noted only that he was "ailing." Even those around him didn't understand exactly what was wrong, and the public could not guess.

"This [sale] was solely because of the necessity for Bill to become completely disassociated from baseball while he is fighting to regain his health," said Allyn.

He had been ailing for a year, since the seventh amputation on his right leg in June 1960. This was the one that sent him into dark moods, for it was cut off above the knee. That affected him more than the other operations, for now an element of control had been lost.

Since tranquility was ordered, tranquility he bought—a big, old house on eighteen acres on the bank of Peach Blossom Creek, two miles from Easton on the famed Maryland eastern shore. Veeck labeled it "Tranquility." It was to be his base for almost a decade, until he was unable to sit around anymore.

Chapter 9

Tranquility was sixty miles from Washington and sixty miles from Baltimore. He moved in with the five children (one more was yet to be born) from his marriage to Mary Frances, several dogs, and many tropical fish.

Slowly he regained the fifty pounds he had lost in only a year. He stopped driving a car. He told friends he was going to bed at normal times, although that unlikely regimen soon ended. (Recall Bill Gleason's drinking with Veeck—who continued to smoke—until five o'clock in the morning.)

The city of Easton is prerevolutionary, its homes often furnished in Early American. Veeck described his furniture as Early Early American, made by the Indians in the Southwest and transported from his New Mexico ranch.

On the estate, Veeck spent hours at a time in a greenhouse where he worked with seeds and bulbs and flowers. This was barely a few months after he sold the Sox. In time he was to spend more time working the telephone. When he was free of the phone, he might keep busy by refinishing Early American furniture he picked up at local secondhand stores. He stocked the guesthouse rooms with his refinished furniture. The children had a tree house.

A hint of what was to come was the guesthouse. It was remodeled so that it could accommodate a dozen overnight visitors—hardly conducive to the sort of quiet the Mayo Clinic doctors had ordered.

137

Veeck enjoyed gimmicks. He installed a beer tap connected to a keg in his wall so that he could tell friends it was like drinking at a bar. He had a game room in an adjacent building that he called the "studio." He filled the room with his collection of hundreds of records that were played on a huge Seeburg automatic jukebox. Hank Greenberg sent him a folding motor scooter to be used in getting around the eighteen acres.

He quickly went to work. That included the final editing of a book that he collaborated on with Ed Linn, a well-regarded sportswriter who had done many prominent articles for *Sport* magazine.

The book came out in 1962 and it was to make Veeck's name prominent again. It had the rhyming, easy-to-remember title of *Veeck—As in Wreck*. It appeared a year after Jim Brosnan's ground-breaking account of a baseball campaign called *The Long Season*, and heralded the start of a new way of looking at sports.

Veeck's book was greeted with a half-page review in the Sunday *New York Times*, which titled it "Odd Man Out." Alfred Wright, a senior editor of *Sports Illustrated*, was the *Times* reviewer. He enjoyed it, but also contended that too much of the book found Veeck tilting at the Yankees and Commissioner Ford Frick. Veeck certainly took advantage of the book's 380 pages to lash out at the Yankees.

Wright concludes, "Bill Veeck can be vastly amusing when he tells us what he thinks and what he remembers, and somewhat less entertaining when he cavils over his pet obsessions. Yet the feeling persists that this brave, outspoken and pixyish man is a bracing tonic for a sport that often takes itself too seriously."

How seriously Veeck was not to realize for a few years—until he tried to get back into baseball. The Establishment was not amused with the book. What didn't they like about it? Perhaps Wright's review yields clues:

"Midway through this autobiography, Bill Veeck, the baseball impresario, tells us, 'In the past fifty years, there have been only two rules changes affecting the game on the field. One of them directs the players to bring their gloves back to the dugouts between innings instead of leaving them out on the field; the other is so revolutionary that I forget it....'

"It is, in a way, strange that Veeck should have become the hair shirt of his fellow entrepreneurs, for he grew up in the ivy-clad traditions of Wrigley Field in Chicago.... But one does not read very far in the younger Veeck's story before learning... that this energetic and playful man has little sympathy with the conventions of life and baseball.

"Veeck tells us in no uncertain terms that his overriding antipathies are directed against the management of the New York Yankees and the present commissioner of baseball, Mr. Ford Frick... based, one gathers... on his refusal to adopt many of the innovations Veeck believes would enliven the game.

"When he is not unburdening himself of his grievances against the Yankees and [Del] Webb and Frick, Veeck tells an entertaining story about his years as a baseball owner.... Following this story as it unfolds, anecdote after anecdote, is much like sitting with Veeck or some other talented raconteur through a few long nights in a saloon."

Precisely.

The book had a memorable last few paragraphs:

"Sometime, somewhere, there will be a club no one really wants. And then Ole Will will come wandering along to laugh some more.

"Look for me under the arc-lights, boys. I'll be back."

Almost twenty-five years later I asked Ed Linn about the reception the book received. "Few people realize what baseball did to him for that," said Linn.

Now that Veeck had become a literary lion, he was in demand as much as ever—speaking, writing. Indeed, he started writing a syndicated column that the Chicago *Sun-Times* ran in the early and mid-1960s. He also commuted several times a month to Chicago, where he taped ten radio shows at a time. He went on speaking engagements an average of six times a month. He read five books a week.

Usually, his columns were about sports. But after President Kennedy's assassination in November of 1963, Veeck wrote a paean to the American television industry and its coverage of the event.

Veeck and his son Mike, who was then twelve years old, had stood on line for more than seven hours to pass the coffin. It was hard for Veeck with his wooden leg. He rarely was on his feet for even a few hours at a stretch normally, and because he remained so active he was forced constantly to soak his stump.

Yet, he waited on line. Finally an usher recognized Veeck and told him to come along and get into a special V.I.P. entrance. Veeck refused. He and his son waited.

"I'm not here for any special treatment," Veeck told the usher. "I'm here because our President died."

Later, Veeck wrote of the moment, "I didn't know Mr. Kennedy, at least not personally.... Yet each of us honestly felt that we had gathered together to pay honor to a friend. Not the 'friend of the people,' 'friend of mankind' variety, but a close personal friend to us...." He went on to compliment television for its sensitive coverage of the event, and as an "example of how a great nation accepts a great loss."

Generally, his pieces were about the lighter side of sports, thin essays on such subjects as Yogi Berra or the Chicago Bears. The newspaper pieces had none of the sharp edge that marked the book, but that, of course, was prepared with a professional writer.

In retirement, Veeck became an American folk hero, a growlly-voiced, burr-headed iconoclast who received visitors and pontificated on the state of America. That included baseball, of course. But now the major American newspapers and magazines were sending their major writers to this unusually beautiful part of Maryland.

One day in the late 1960s, Paul Zimmerman of the New York *Post* decided to visit Veeck. The Yankees were playing the Orioles in Baltimore, not far from Veeck's retreat. Zimmerman, now with *Sports Illustrated*, is among the more cynical newspaper writers I have met. Also, a guy who enjoys good talk.

To this day he recalls with startling clarity and emotion his one and only meeting with Veeck. Zimmerman wrote about the trophy room—a cigar-store Indian, a squat little bronze statue of Honus Wagner, an ancient wooden figurine of a ballplayer. Zimmerman recounted how Veeck had this innovative idea that baseball people scoffed at—a permanent pinch hitter for the pitcher ("Not as crazy as it sounds," contended Veeck. "It would keep a DiMaggio or a Williams or a Mantle or a Mays around for a few more years"). Today, of course, that is known as the designated hitter.

"This was '68," says Zimmerman. "I'd say it was the most memorable interview I've ever conducted in my life. I've never gotten over it. As I was talking to him I knew that whatever I was going to write was going to be inadequate because there was no way I could cover this man in one column or a magazine piece or even one book, unless it was a real fat one.

"What really made a memorable impression was that I lost my critical perspective totally within the first ten minutes. Scared me because I was no longer a journalist—I mean, I was just an admirer and I never had my critical instincts so completely wiped out so quickly."

Zimmerman noticed that on Veeck's mantel there was a figurine of a duck dressed in a hunter's outfit, wearing a jacket and hat and with a gun tucked under his arm. Next to the figure was a sign that read "Legal Limit—Six Hunters."

Veeck chuckled when Zimmerman asked him about the duck. This

was hunting territory, especially duck hunting, and Zimmerman recounts
Veeck's story:

"He was in this bar. He said he liked to check out the neighborhood,
the environment, and he'd go to the bars in the neighborhood, and he
was in this bar that was frequented by all these yahoos. They were talking
about hunting, and bragging, and finally, very quietly, Veeck said, 'I live
near here and I've got a lot of acreage. Any one of you hunters like to
engage in a little contest, I'll be very happy to oblige you. You start at one
end, I'll start at the other. You take whatever weapon you want. I'll take
my B.A.R. [which I had in the service] and we'll stalk each other. We'll
put $10,000 on it, and the survivor collects the money.'

"He said a hush fell on the group and they all started to back away.
I said, 'Would you really have done it?' and he said, 'No, of course not,
but they didn't know that.'"

Zimmerman's conversation with Veeck took them to literature, to
wines, to football, to the labor movement.

"I remember Mary Frances told me that one time when Finley was
having trouble—he was trying to pull some stunts and the league was
blocking him—he called up Veeck and Mary Frances answered the phone
and he said, 'This is Charlie Finley and I'd like to talk to your husband—
I'm a rebel just like your husband.' And she said, 'You might be a rebel,
but you're nothing like my husband.'"

America was catching up to Veeck, it seemed. In so many ways, baseball eventually adopted the very things they had fought Veeck on. Now,
the country was even coming around to Veeck's way of dressing—the tie
was becoming an artifact with the emergence of the turtleneck.

He claimed that the only time he had ever worn a tie was in the Marines. "The necktie," he explained, "is uncomfortable, completely use-
less, no enhancement of beauty and a mark of serfdom. The first guy who
put on a necktie did so because he wanted to hide a dirty shirt. Even the
word "necktie" has unpleasant connotations. When they strung up a horse
thief in the Old West, they always called it a 'necktie party.'"

Over the years he won some necktie battles and lost others. "I won at
Toots Shor's and '21' in New York," he said. "I won at the Pump Room
in Chicago. I simply told them I didn't wear neckties and if they didn't
like it I would leave. The only decisions I have lost have been at a couple
of snooty country clubs where people went to show off their fancy clothes."

No sooner did he give an interview on ties in 1968 than he proposed a realignment of baseball, creating divisions based on regional rivalries. Since shortly after the turn of the century there had been two baseball leagues, virtually unchanged. When new clubs arrived in the 1960s, they simply were added to the existing leagues, creating a pair of ten-team leagues.

Veeck suggested that all of baseball should be reorganized in divisions to create natural geographic rivalries. Thus, the Mets would leave the National League to move to the Eastern Division in the American, where they would be the Yankees' rivals.

This is how Veeck's league would look:

National League

Southern Division	*Western Division*
St. Louis	Anaheim
Atlanta	Los Angeles
Cincinnati	Oakland
Houston	San Diego
Kansas City	San Francisco
Philadelphia	Seattle

American League

Eastern Division	*Midwest Division*
New York Mets	Pittsburgh
New York Yankees	Minnesota
Baltimore	Detroit
Boston	Cleveland
Montreal	Chicago Cubs
Washington	Chicago White Sox

"The plan makes too much sense for baseball to understand," he said.

"You'd have natural division rivals, like the White Sox and Cubs, the Yankees and Mets, the Orioles and Senators. And look at the bonanza out West, like San Francisco and Oakland for starters. The only way they can survive in that area is to play each other. But that rivalry would be nothing compared to the one in Southern California among the Dodgers, the Angels, and San Diego."

He knew it was nothing but a nice dream: "I couldn't tell anybody how to run the game even when I was one of the owners."

Veeck was constantly sought after. Although four deals fell through to buy baseball teams—including repeated false hopes involving the Washington Senators—it seemed it really was people in other sports who wanted him.

In fact, who knows what might have happened to the National Football League if the irrepressible Billy Sullivan had had his way? Sullivan was the founder of the New England Patriots, a man who loves a story and loves a storyteller.

He had known Veeck since 1948, when the Indians and Braves met in the World Series. Sullivan was the Braves' publicist at the time, and in his way an innovator too. Sullivan believes he was the first in the National League to put out a team yearbook, and he admired Veeck's ways. Their relationship remained strong over the years, with mutual respect.

It didn't even diminish when Veeck put the midget up to bat. For a true baseball character named Donald Davidson had worked for Sullivan. Davidson was a dwarf. After Veeck sent Gaedel to bat, Davidson chided him for "lowering the value of midgets."

By 1966, Sullivan was running the Patriots, which were based in Boston but playing wherever they could find a stadium open for business. The Patriots were part of the fledgling American Football League, engaged in a war with the National Football League.

This was a critical year. The battle was heating. Both leagues were starting to throw around money for the top collegians. The A.F.L. president, Joe Foss, was stepping down and the league needed someone of authority, presence, and public acceptance to continue the struggle with the entrenched N.F.L.

"Milt Woodard, who was the assistant to Foss, said to me he had a name he wanted to suggest—Bill Veeck. I said, 'Great.' So I went about quietly trying to line up the votes. I went to the meeting with, I thought, four votes in my pocket. But Al Davis already had gotten the people he needed, so he won and became commissioner. I often think that that was the beginning of my problems with Davis."

Davis won the election on April 8, but within two months there was a merger of the leagues—and Pete Rozelle was named commissioner. Davis was out, and he never forgave those who had not accepted him.

By 1968, Veeck was ready to return to full-time work. Suffolk Downs, the Boston racetrack, was in trouble and was sold to a shadowy New York group named Realty Equities Corporation. Veeck was named president and chief officer of the track.

"I am not going to bring a carnival to the track," he said.

That was precisely what horse racing needed, though. The average age of the horseplayer, Veeck quickly found out, was about fifty. He paid his money and entered a tumble-down plant. This was a sport going nowhere, but unable to change. Of course it had never had a Bill Veeck around before, either.

Veeck was fifty-four when he joined the track and announced, "I'm going to stay with it. I figure this is the last go-around for me. They're going to have to cart me out of here."

Racetracks had played a major role in his baseball dealings, Veeck confided to Red Smith. "It was at a racetrack," Veeck said, "that I unloaded Hal Peck on Larry MacPhail and I outsmarted Mark Steinberg, a St. Louis tycoon."

Peck, of course, was the outfielder who had shot off some toes on his foot. But at a racetrack encounter with MacPhail, then running the Brooklyn Dodgers, Veeck convinced MacPhail to buy the wounded Peck.

"Steinberg was going out to Del Mar just to have a good time for himself at the races—and I stiffed him in as my largest partner with the Browns. You can see that racetracks are very important."

Getting into racing offered Veeck a chance—and he missed very few— to explain what was wrong with baseball. "It seems to me that if horses run around the track nine times a day, that's got to generate some excitement. It's not very often these days we get to see ballplayers run around the bases nine times in one day, you know.

"Oh, I'm not one of those who insist there has to be a lot of hitting in baseball and a lot of runs scored. What bothers me is that it now takes half an hour longer than it did a few years ago to play the same game. It isn't as though they'd changed the game and added quality to justify the additional time. All they've added is tedium."

Veeck received $50,000 a year, plus a percentage of the profits, to try to transform this grimy track, which had become known as "Sucker Downs." It had barbed wire on the fences and if you wanted to go to the bathroom, you had to put money in the pay toilet. Veeck tore down the barbed wire, he let the public go to the bathrooms for free, he gave the place a face-lift. Now, he had to get the people in.

Bob Varey, a newspaperman, joined Veeck at the track in the public relations department. "He didn't know a lot about horse racing, to tell the truth. He was more of a promoter."

Still, Varey recalls the Halloween they had racing. "If you brought a black cat to the track you could get in free. At least that's what he proposed. But it never came about because of the A.S.P.C.A. They moved in and told him he couldn't run this promotion. They said what the hell you gonna do with three or four thousand cats? Where you gonna keep them? Where you gonna feed them? What are you gonna do with them?"

Veeck had less trouble with the animal authorities on his Ben Hur Chariot Race Night. This was going to be one of those Romanesque extravaganzas, greater than anything DeMille produced.

"He sent an agent out to Hollywood. The MGM studios were having an auction, and they were auctioning a lot of their sets," recalls Varey. "They auctioned off five chariots which they used in the *Ben Hur* movie. The agent bought the chariots, but actually he needed six. So his friend owns Caesar's Palace, and he contacted him and he bought one from him."

To spread the word for what he was going to do, Veeck involved all the disk jockeys from the Greater Boston area. This not only generated publicity, but it reached the sort of people that he realized racing needed— a younger crowd.

"He decided he was going to have the disk jockeys drive the chariots. So he had them over one day before the races to test them out. Then he found an outfit in New York State that rented horses for special occasions. These were big draft horses, something like 1,600 or 1,700 pounds, like the Budweiser horses. And he put the disk jockeys in the chariots to run around the track. Most of these guys were scared shitless. They couldn't handle these horses. So he still had the Ben Hur races, but he hired some drivers and had the disk jockeys stand in the chariots holding the whips."

How else to bring in people? The Boston Bruins won hockey's Stanley Cup, so anyone named Stanley could get into Suffolk Downs for free. And if you were named Stanley Stanley, why you'd also get a free lunch and be guaranteed a winning daily-double ticket. Speaking? He addressed the Florence Crittenton League, which raised money for unwed mothers. He spoke two hundred times a year.

"Then he used to have Lucky License Plate days, where they'd write down the guy's license plate and then give him enough hot dogs for a whole summer's cookout, and then they'd give another guy a bunch of Coke and they'd tell the guy with the hot dogs to get together with the guy who had the Coke. Screwy things like that."

Or like Turkey Day, with the lucky people going to the winner's circle, where the live turkeys sat. The thing was, you had to catch the turkey yourself.

Veeck not only took the locks off the toilets (he was photographed in one paper personally dismantling them), he did away with the distinction between grandstand and clubhouse. Instead of a $1.00 general admission and $2.00 clubhouse fee, he threw open the whole place for $1.50.

Attendance began to grow and the sort of people who turned out were different from the traditional patrons that racing attracted. That used to be the pensioners, or the barbers and bartenders on Mondays. Instead, by golly, they got Harvard kids when the Crimson marching band was on display, and there were Boston University students too.

Veeck blew some promotions. His most expensive failure was the Yankee Gold Cup. He decreed in 1969, after only about six months on the job, that the richest grass event in the history of American racing should be held at good old Suffolk Downs. The race excited no one except the owners of the horses that shared in the added purse of more than $200,000—the "added" meaning the track put up most of the money. It was never staged again.

"On-the-job training can be expensive," Veeck said good-naturedly of the fiasco.

Typical of Veeck, though, he didn't hang around long. Only two full seasons. But they were special, and he created a legacy.

"His last year there," says Varey, "for the first time in maybe ten or twelve years, Suffolk Downs averaged a million dollars a day in handle, and they averaged about 12,000 people. And they haven't done it since. It was only the fifth time in the history of Suffolk Downs, which opened in 1935, that they averaged a million a day."

Veeck, though, suddenly made the announcement that he was leaving. He picked a dramatic setting, one guaranteed to bring in an inordinate amount of publicity—the Boston Baseball Writers dinner in January of 1971. "He brought the house down. He was the keynote speaker. He upstaged the whole dinner," Varey recalls.

Veeck left because, as usual, he was involved with an undercapitalized outfit. "Realty Equities was in cosmetics, leisure, and they had a real bad year, and what they were doing was they were taking fresh money out of the track," explains Varey. "We used to joke that they sent a guy from

New York with a black leather bag to Suffolk Downs. And Bill couldn't pay his bills. The track started to go down. He couldn't pay the telephone bills. He couldn't pay the oil bills. In fact, they lost the harness-meet license. The state took it away because they weren't financially stable enough to run a harness meet. There hasn't been harness racing there since."

Veeck also had continual battles with the state legislature. He wanted children to attend the races ("I'm not ashamed of what I do. I think my kids are entitled to see what their old man is up to").

Annoyed that he couldn't get the support of elected officials, he said, "There are no amateur politicians in this state." Strong words from someone brought up in Chicago.

Yet, through it all, he demonstrated his affection for the common man, the one who could use his toilets for free, and who, if he got lucky, could chase a turkey around the racetrack.

After Veeck put in a thousand lightweight folding chairs for people who wanted to sit anywhere they pleased, he said, "I was told the chairs would be stolen in a week. I think we lost two in the first month. Treat people right, and they'll treat you right."

Veeck installed an apartment at the track, although his family still lived in Maryland. "He had his own bedroom, his own living room, which was adjacent to his office," Varey remembers. "He put in a bathroom there. He put in a whirlpool, built special with steps leading up to it, with a little railing, so he could soak his leg. Of course he took the wooden leg off. That wooden leg, he had an ashtray built into it. Wherever he was, he'd sit there with his legs crossed and pull his pants leg up and put his ashes in the ashtray."

When Veeck left he put his reflections down on paper. They resulted in a book called *Thirty Tons a Day*—the amount of manure shoveled daily at the track.

Veeck continued to define the American scene, to be a part of the changes of the age, even from his Maryland retreat.

"The people around here don't know how to take me," he confided. "I'm something of an Ishmael in this part of the country. I didn't realize that it was still part of the traditional South until I started working to get a biracial housing complex built here. We got it through, but it didn't endear me to the people."

Shortly after he quit the racetrack, he was dismayed when the annual Hall of Fame voting was announced. Once again no provision had been made for honoring the black ballplayers who performed before they were accepted into the major leagues.

"If it's baseball's Hall of Fame, not just the major leagues', how can they keep out Satchel Paige, Josh Gibson, Cool Papa Bell, Smokey Joe Williams?"

Other aspects of baseball outraged him—the reserve clause, for example. This was the heart of baseball's favored status with the courts. It bound a player to a team for life, because even when his contract was over, he was "reserved" to the team for the following season. In other words, every time a contract was over, the only one he could sign a new one with was his existing team.

Curt Flood challenged this venerable code. The Cardinals' outfielder refused to accept being traded to Philadelphia. The suit was held in New York in the spring of 1970. And Veeck was there—testifying, of course, for the little guy, for Flood.

But Veeck also told the court that the reserve clause should be replaced gradually. This would not only give the players more freedom, it would not harm the owners either. In a little more than five years, it was to come to fruition—but not quite the way Veeck envisioned, and ultimately it was to drive him out of baseball.

But this June day in 1970, Veeck was at center stage and waxing philosophical in a federal courtroom. Veeck spoke for two hours. Perhaps his key point was that a sudden, complete elimination of the reserve system would be "chaotic." Some long-term relationships were needed, he explained, to prevent dislocation of the national game.

Baseball's lawyer, Victor Kramer, cross-examined Veeck. Kramer seemed to be after not so much what Veeck was saying now but what Veeck had said previously, especially in his anti-Establishment *Veeck— As in Wreck*.

Veeck had precedent for his suggestions of an orderly retreat for baseball. He cited the DuPont antitrust case, in which the government ordered the corporation to divest itself of General Motors stock but gave it time so as not to dislocate the market.

Veeck had two interesting alternatives to the reserve clause. One was the "Hollywood" contract, under which a club could "reserve" a player's use for, say, a seven-year period. This was based on the one-time contracts that aspiring movie performers signed. In Veeck's plan, each year the club could renew its option on the player in return for a scheduled raise. At any time the club and player could agree to tear up the existing contract and write a new seven-year deal.

The other was a "football" contract, under which a player could play a season without a contract and be a free agent at the end. But Veeck understood that this didn't work in football, because when the player was free, the commissioner arbitrarily could set a recompensation price that the new club would pay to the old club.

In Veeck's approach, actuaries would determine how much the club had spent developing the player it was losing, and this "just recompense" would be the price the new club would pay.

He described the ballplayer's condition—precluded by the draft from picking his original team and by the reserve clause from moving to another—as "human bondage."

Veeck interspersed his hard-nosed, practical ideals with the lyrical: "Everyone," he said, "should have the right, at least once, to determine his future."

How about a baseball strike? What did Veeck say about that?

When one loomed in 1972 he told the Chicago *Sun-Times*, "...the players...have gone too far. Too far and too fast....The players are currently being paid what I would have to say are inflated salaries." He made the point that the fans were not behind the players and that "this, in itself, should worry the athletes. Because rarely has management in baseball done anything that would merit the fans' support."

Strange to think that Veeck was, in some ways, agreeing with his former colleagues, the owners. But he was on track in getting back into baseball now. A team from Washington again had moved—this time the Senators went to Texas. Veeck was not to buy the Senators. Instead, he again found a near-bankrupt Chicago franchise. The White Sox were for sale again.

Chapter 10

The White Sox were in trouble. Boy, were they in trouble. John Allyn—who had bought the team from his brother in 1969—was near bankruptcy. The American League was holding frantic meetings to figure out how to save the franchise. Should the league take it over or—the unthinkable—move it someplace else? Say Seattle?

Chicagoans were getting edgy over this possibility. Mayor Richard Daley, whose South Side roots were entwined with Comiskey Park and whose political base had started in the area, said he would never allow the beloved "Pale Hose" to leave.

But by 1975 fan support had dwindled. In a disappointing season that saw the team fall to 22 1/2 games out of first in the second division, attendance plummeted to only 770,800. Each of the previous three seasons of hope had lured more than 1.1 million fans.

In the summer of '75, Veeck began plotting his return to Chicago and reacquiring the Sox, the team he had sold fourteen years before. His prophesy from the last line of his book—"Sometime, somewhere, there will be a club no one really wants. And then Ole Will will come wandering along to laugh some more"—was coming true.

The problem was that while everyone in baseball knew there had to be an American League team in Chicago, most of the other owners didn't want Veeck to run it. "People were still against him because of things he had done before," concedes Lee MacPhail, who was the league president then.

Yet, along came Veeck.

Roland Hemond was the White Sox general manager. He knew about the imminent removal of the Sox to either Seattle or Toronto. He knew Veeck was trying desperately to put together a financially stable group. And he knew that when Veeck came in, Veeck would be his own boss. So Hemond was surprised one night at eleven o'clock when he got a call from Veeck, who was staying in the same hotel, the Executive House.

"What are you doing? Why don't you come upstairs and talk a little baseball?" said Veeck.

"I'd go to the restaurant there, Club 71, and that's where I got to know him. He'd ask me a lot of questions—if he bought the club what deal would we make with this club or that club?"

They talked for months, through the end of the season, and got to know each other's thinking. They devised a master plan for improving the Sox. Finally, by December, Veeck had lined up more than forty investors. He was ready to make his move with the league.

He brought in someone a little different this time—the first black man into major-league ownership. He was John Harold Johnson, the owner of *Ebony* and other black-oriented publications. Johnson was part of a group of about thirty-five Chicagoans, each of whom put up $100,000 as part of the 80 percent of the team that Veeck would buy from Allyn for about $11 million.

Veeck needed approval from nine of the twelve American League owners. The owners turned Veeck down. They claimed his capitalization was weak and faulty, too much of it based on dubious tax-shelter gimmicks. It wouldn't stand up in day-to-day operations. That probably was true. There was also another side.

Gene Autry—known as "the Cowboy" and now owner of the California Angels—was one of those voting against Veeck. Autry explained, "I have to vote against a fellow who runs down baseball, then reenters it."

Actually, the owners gave Veeck another week to come up with a better financing deal. They believed—they said—that he was underfinanced, that he wouldn't have enough money for operating expenses. They wanted him to find another million dollars.

"I'd rather not know who voted against me. No, come to think of it, I would like to know. Then I wouldn't be suspicious of everybody," quipped Veeck.

Veeck now looked around for money. He squeezed $10,000 more from a supermarket owner. He got others to up their stake. But finally he had to get the money from himself—he yielded the fee he had earmarked for putting the package together. That cost him about $750,000. And the money he did raise for his initial stake was partly financed when he sold his Maryland home. At the last minute another $250,000 was raised when a friend of Mayor Daley's, who also was a food concessionaire, bought into the group.

It had become a civic affair. Jack Brickhouse, the Chicago television personality, actually helped get Veeck together with his new investor. He was Patrick L. O'Malley, and his reasons for becoming involved spotlighted what a team can mean to a city. "We wanted to do our part to save this franchise for Chicago," explained O'Malley. "I've seen what happened to other communities losing sports teams. I remember back when New York lost the Dodgers and Giants, and the city really lost some of its sports heritage."

So Veeck brought in his new financing and the owners took another vote at their annual meeting in Hollywood, Florida. This time the Tigers' owner, John Fetzer—who detested Veeck—came to his defense in an impassioned plea. He reminded the other owners that they had established the financial guidelines and Veeck and his group had met them.

"We told them to go out and do it, and they did it. Now we can't cry over spilt milk," argued Fetzer.

"Look, I don't like it any more than you do that we're allowing a guy in here who has called me a son of a bitch over and over. But, gentlemen, we've got to take another vote."

They did. It was 10-2 for Veeck and he was in. Finley stormed out of the meeting, his hopes thwarted of moving his Oakland team to Chicago. After calming down, Finley told a group of reporters, "I'm very happy for Veeck. I consider him an ally. He has refreshing ideas. You might say misery loves company."

Veeck's friends were overjoyed. "There were tears in my eyes, I think there were tears in Bill's eyes too. I never thought I would see it happen," recalled Bob Fishel.

The news rang through Chicago like a blessed event: Veeck was back, the White Sox were staying. In the newspapers and on television, Veeck was praised as the man who had saved the Sox for Chicago, had allowed the city to keep its identity not only as a two-team town but as a major-league city. None of this losing-a-team business. Nothing like what happened in New York City almost twenty years before. Bill Veeck kept Chicago healthy.

"It's wonderful," said a South Sider named Mary McNicholas when she learned the Sox were staying. "But I'm surprised in a way. I thought those owners would try to goof up Bill Veeck. I hoped to myself that he'd sit them on their ass."

Everyone knew how the league had forced Veeck to come back with more money—and how the rascal had done it!

"I'll bet anybody in the place a drink he'll draw a million fans this year," said her husband, Tom. "I didn't want the Oakland A's to come here. Another team, it wouldn't be the same. It wouldn't be our team."

Now the months of preparation with Hemond paid off.

"There was bedlam late that night with press conferences," recalls Hemond. "I went over to Bill, who was surrounded by all the TV and radio people, and I whispered in his ear and told him the Phils are prepared to make the trade. I had really made the deal earlier in the day but couldn't announce it until Bill took control because we were trading Jim Kaat, and he was Allyn's favorite player. The Phillies were interested in Kaat and he had won 20 or 21 games for us, but he was getting up in age. Little did I know he'd pitch another eight, nine years.

"Anyway, when I told him we were ready he said, okay, announce we'll be making a trade in forty-five minutes and have a press conference. And the news media said, gee, how could you make a trade so fast?"

It was more than a trade. It was something like a wholesale exchange of quality players. Kaat and a minor-league infielder were sent to the Phillies for three players under the age of twenty-five. All had been number one draft choices—Alan Bannister, Dick Ruthven, and Roy Thomas. This was only the beginning.

Bowie Kuhn had been the commissioner since 1969, so he had never before dealt with Veeck on their current levels. Kuhn had replaced William Eckert, a retired general who had been dubbed "the Unknown Soldier" when he was hired. His tenure as Ford Frick's replacement was brief. The owners fired the general.

It had always been troubling to Kuhn that he was thought of as a stiff, humorless sort. He was a tall, scholarly lawyer with a formal way of speaking, but he had his sense of humor and it distressed him that the press and public never were able to see that side of him.

Of course to Veeck, Kuhn represented authority. And while he was more intelligent than Frick—the last commissioner Veeck had dealt with—and grasped the issues, Kuhn still was commissioner.

Kuhn wound up disliking Veeck, making it abundantly clear in an autobiography called *Hardball: The Education of a Baseball Commission* er, which he wrote with Martin Appel and which was published early in 1987 after two years of work.

Marty Appel had become vice president of public relations for WPIX-Channel 11, a huge independent television station in New York. Some years earlier, though, he had been the Yankees' publicist—the heir apparent to Bob Fishel.

"Bowie saw him as a guy who was always going to bait authority, whether it was ridiculing Ford Frick or making up his mind that he wasn't going to get along with Bowie Kuhn," says Appel.

Kuhn quickly came to this conclusion the very day that Veeck took over the White Sox. The only common ground they had was that they both liked the old ballparks.

"Bowie, figuring it was the right thing to do, made arrangements to have a private one-on-one meeting with Veeck in Bowie's suite at the Diplomat Hotel. They met for a couple of hours. It was very strained, very difficult to have a conversation with Bill. Bowie tried to bring up subjects of mutual interest—he mentioned how baseball had never been very successful in attracting black fans, and he wondered if Bill had any ideas. Veeck seemed, more than anyone else, to be successful in courting the black audience. Bowie thought maybe Bill could work on that in Chicago and share some ideas with the other owners.

"But then the next morning was when Veeck set up shop in the lobby of the hotel—you know, selling ballplayers. Bowie was just offended by it. It was at the time of the Messersmith thing [the suit for free agency] pending in the courts, and the Catfish Hunter thing [in which the pitcher got out of his contract with Finley] had happened the year before and it was the last thing that anyone wanted—to portray baseball being like an old-fashioned slave market. And here was Veeck doing business as usual, as though he still had his head in the sand and treating the ballplayers as if it was a slave market.

"Bowie said—and he hated to say it—that Veeck almost got what he deserved because, of all the owners, he was the one always sort of suggesting there shouldn't be a reserve clause, and shortly after he bought the White Sox came the Messersmith decision."

First, though, came the honeymoon, starting with the outrageous trading post in the lobby of the Diplomat. Hemond will never forget the operation:

"In the morning I'd gone down to the lobby of the Diplomat Hotel. It's a circular lobby with a central area and had high-backed leather chairs and some round tables. It looked like a little arena in the middle. So I'm sitting in the chair looking out at the lobby and I said to myself, 'Geez, this would be a good place to make deals from today.' I remember when I met Bill he told me not to worry about keeping my job. 'One thing, working for me, Roland—I want you to let your imagination run rampant. Propose anything you want.'

"Well, he told me to propose anything that might come to mind, so I went up to his room. He was coming out of that tub, you know, from soaking that limb, and I said, 'Bill, I was down in the lobby and I think it would be fantastic for us to put up a sign that says "Open for Business." And we could wheel and deal there.' And he says, 'That's great! What are you waiting for? Get it up.'"

So Hemond went to the lobby, found a bellman who printed a sign, and, to give the whole area an authoritative look as befits the National Pastime, stuck an American flag on a desk. The thing is, it worked. Everyone was attracted to the enclave—rival general managers, television announcers, newspaper reporters, visiting ballplayers.

"I sat in the chair and immediately Phil Seghi of Cleveland, and Dan O'Brien, who was with Texas at the time, and Dick O'Connor of the Red Sox, Patterson of Pittsburgh—they all came over. And Phil Seghi says to me, 'I know you've been talking to the Braves about a possible deal and I'd like to get involved. I know you want Brohamer. If you can get Blanchard I'll get you Brohamer.' I started making appointments to talk trades. Then I called Bill on the house phone and told him what Seghi proposed, and Bill came down and sat in one of those high-backed chairs.

"Gabe Paul came around. He was with the Yankees at the time, and we ordered milk shakes and hamburgers and no one left. Bill stayed in the chair."

Deals were proposed and deals were made as the midnight deadline approached. The Sox traded Ruthven—just acquired from the Phillies—and Dan Osborn and Ken Henderson for Ralph Garr and Larvell Banks.

"Let's just announce it right here," Veeck told Hemond as they sat in the lobby.

Conventioneers were now surrounding the railing over the little arena. One of the baseball people looked at the scene and said, "They're running a meat market down there. It's awful." Hemond told Veeck, and Veeck replied, "Don't worry about what people say, Roland, it's working."

Hemond quickly looked for Seghi, and informed him the Sox had Banks. Now, how about Brohamer? Deal made.

Phone calls started to come into the lobby because there was a jack right next to the desk. Not everyone wanted to be seen in the lobby making deals with Veeck while the camera lights were on and tipsy conventioneers shouted encouragement. So some general managers went up to their rooms and called Veeck in the lobby over the house phones or on the private phone near his desk. The phone was called the White Sox Hot Line.

Chief Bender of Cincinnati called and said he was looking for a left-handed pitcher and he might trade Clay Carroll for Rich Hinton. Veeck okayed the deal as relayed by Hemond, but when Hemond phoned Bender back, the Reds now wanted a minor-league catcher thrown in.

That distressed Veeck. "They proposed the deal and now they won't make it," he said. "What's happened to this game since I left?"

Finally, Veeck decided to make the deal but needed Carroll's approval because the pitcher had tenure. It was now 11:30 P.M., thirty minutes from the midnight trading deadline.

Joe Reichler of the commissioner's office had been dispatched to the lobby headquarters to make sure Veeck did not breach the deadline. After just one day on the job, Veeck was already receiving special attention from baseball's highest office.

Meanwhile, a storm had knocked out phone lines near Carroll's Virginia home. Finally, they got through.

There was more wheeling and dealing and Veeck told Hemond just to make the announcements, that it would all be straightened out in due time. Hemond had been under a tight money restraint in previous years, but this was different.

"I know, Roland, you're not used to spending money. But let's be extravagant tonight," Veeck told him.

Just then the phone rang. It was Bing Devine of the Cardinals confirming a deal.

"It's a minute to midnight!" Reichler shouted to Hemond. "You've got one minute."

Hemond quickly told Devine to listen and Hemond called out for the assembled crowd, "We've traded Bee Bee Richard for Buddy Bradford and Greg Terlecky," and Reichler said, "Midnight, that's it."

The Sox had made four trades in an hour and fifteen minutes, six overall since Veeck had taken over twenty-four hours earlier.

Every deal seemed to have been made under hurry-up circumstances. There was one that started on a cruise hosted by Calvin Griffith, the owner of the Minnesota Twins. At the cocktail party Hemond got into a conversation with Harry Dalton, the general manager of the California Angels. They struck a deal. But Hemond had to get Veeck's approval. Before the ship pulled out, Hemond jumped off the boat and ran across the highway looking for Veeck at a restaurant.

"I asked the maître d' and he said Bill was on the dance floor, and he was there dancing with Mary Frances. She had flown in to help celebrate the fact he had been able to buy the club." On the dance floor, Veeck okayed a trade of Bill Melton and Steve Dunning for Jim Spencer and Morris Nettles.

Now, twenty-four hours later, all the trades completed, Veeck and Hemond sat down. Hemond had virtually undergone a personality transformation.

"I was delirioulsy happy, and Bill looks at me and says, 'Roland, you really look happy. How would you describe it?' And I said, 'Bill, when we have a newborn child at home, that's got to be tops. But this is pretty darn close.' And he said, 'That's the way you'll be the rest of your life.'"

It was typical Veeck. He had the ability to make people he liked enjoy themselves more than they had ever believed they could.

"He had an understanding of life," explains Hemond. "The joyous moments, capturing it, nursing it, caressing it. That's why he meant so much to me. When you see all the adversity, the pain, that he went through, but he never complained."

But events soured for Veeck quickly. For thirteen days after taking over the White Sox the game of baseball changed under him. It came with the so-called Messersmith decision.

The historic change, mandated by the arbitrator Peter Seitz, read in part: "The grievances of Messersmith and McNally are sustained. There is no contractual bond between these players and the Los Angeles and Montreal clubs.... The clubs had no right or power...to reserve their services for their exclusive use...beyond the renewal year...."

Thus, Andy Messersmith and Dave McNally became free—and so did every other ballplayer when his contract ended. Free agency had begun, an era in which a player would be free to sign with anyone he wanted when his contract was up. This was the freedom that Veeck had argued for when he testified in Curt Flood's trial, or wrote outraged dissertations on the venality of the owners. But Veeck had always cautioned that the change shouldn't happen suddenly.

It happened too suddenly for him and his organization. Now, players were free to go to the highest bidder. He had nothing to bid with. He barely sneaked in under the other owners' financial guidelines and his working capital probably was not more than a million dollars.

That soon would be a year's salary for some ballplayers.

Hemond's introduction to Veeck's working hours was long and sometimes painful but always tinged with expectation. Hemond's problem was
how to keep up with Veeck and how to say no. That difficulty reached its
height during spring training for the '76 season.

Veeck had a routine, He might get to bed at three or four in the morning, but he would get up at six to soak his stump, which had gotten irritated because of the attached prosthesis. Veeck would leave his front
door open before he went into the tub.

Hemond would come by with the newspapers and coffee at seven and
the day would begin for the two of them, Veeck soaking, reading, and
shaving at the same time. Before he got out of the tub he would give
Hemond a dozen items to look into.

It wasn't the morning that gave Hemond trouble. It was the night.
"He'd go on and on. He had tremendous stamina. In spring training I'd
tell him, 'Bill, I'm going to dinner with some friends.' He'd say, okay,
and when I came back I'd see the shades to his room would be open, the
lights would be on, the door was open, and he'd be waiting for me because he always had ideas and plans and promotions, and I'd think, geez,
I could use some sleep."

Getting it wasn't easy. Hemond would crawl behind some bushes so
that Veeck, if he happened to look out the window, wouldn't spot him
sneaking into his room. "I'd brush my teeth in the dark," says Hemond.
"I'd jump into bed—and then a few minutes later the phone would ring
and I'd be debating whether to answer it. And I'd think, geez, maybe my
wife is calling and there's something wrong at home. Instead, Bill would
be on the phone and he'd say, 'Oh, you're back? Come on over. We've
got a few things to talk about. There's always time to sleep.' So I'd spend
two, three hours more with him.

"But you were anxious to get up in the morning because you didn't
want to miss anything. And you hated to leave because it was fascinating
listening to him. His great friend, Hank Greenberg, used to come visit
him in spring training, and we used to put Greenberg in a connecting
room and I used to think, 'Thank God for him showing up. Now I'll get
a little breathing room for four or five days.'"

How better to celebrate the American Bicentennial than with the Spirit
of '76? And there was Veeck, with a real—not a prop—wooden leg helping the White Sox celebrate America's birthday on Opening Day by toot-

ling a flute, wearing a bandanna around his head, and gamely walking across the field with two cohorts. His return to Chicago was official.

The place needed some spirit. Back in the press box on the first day, he happened to look at the nearby announcers' booth during the seventh-inning stretch. Harry Caray, the Sox's colorful announcer, was singing "Take Me Out to the Ball Game."

"No one would hear it," says Caray. "I was just singing for myself. Without me knowing it, he put a microphone in the booth and everyone in the place heard me. Veeck said to me, 'For thirty-five years I've been looking for a guy to sing this.' I was flattered. Then he said, 'I need a guy who can't sing so the other fans aren't intimidated.'"

Caray singing "Take Me Out to the Ball Game" became one of the loudest and most popular minutes of every baseball game at Comiskey Park. He was to spend a total of eleven seasons with the Sox, then move over to the Cubs in 1982, handling the play-by-play over WGN. Caray achieved what Veeck never could.

"The crucial thing about him," says Caray, "is that Bill Veeck never had a chance to manage a club he really should have managed—the Cubs. After he retired from the White Sox, he didn't go to their games—he went to the Cubs."

But that was some years down the road after Veeck returned to Chicago for the 1976 season.

According to Kuhn's biographer, Marty Appel, Veeck already was behind the times. It wasn't simply free agency that had changed things. "Bowie says that when Veeck came back, his marketing concepts were primitive," according to Appel. "He hadn't advanced with the times. The game had grown much more sophisticated from a marketing point of view. Bill was still doing the things he did twenty years before. He had no real plan for how he was going to market his product in a very sophisticated city. By then clubs were actually hiring nonbaseball people to advise them on marketing strategy to make themselves part of the twentieth Century."

Veeck's old-fashioned hands-on style was still welcome in the press box, though. He sat there and kibitzed with the writers, turning the place into a sort of round table of baseball. Of course that didn't stop him from still hating the Yankees.

One day he was sitting in the press box behind Appel, who as usual had a phone to his ear. Appel was talking to George Steinbrenner. "When George was in Florida, he wouldn't be able to listen to the game," recalls Appel. "So he'd frequently call the press box and ask for the p.r. guy on the press-box telephone, and he'd tie up the phone for as long as it took to get a pitch-by-pitch, play-by-play account. It was as if I was the radio announcer. So what could I say to George—'I can't do this?' I'd just do the play-by-play figuring sooner or later somebody would just ask me to hang up. Veeck was behind me and he was aware of what I was doing. And he hated George."

So Veeck finally had enough. He just walked over to Appel, put his finger on the button, and disconnected the phone, muttering about the Yankees. Steinbrenner thought Appel had hung up on him.

Veeck's arrival may have stirred attendance—it picked up by about 140,000 fans—but even with the new manager, Paul Richards, and all the dealing, the Sox had a worse season than they did in 1975. They slumped to last, won only 64 games, and finished 25 1/2 games out of first. It was, in fact, their second-poorest season in twenty-five years. Their home-run leaders were Jorge Orta and Jim Spencer, and they struck only 14 apiece. Ken Brett had the best percentage among pitchers, and he was 10-12.

Yet, it was a team that had the remarkably fine reliever Rich (Goose) Gossage. The trouble was you don't waste him in a relief role if there are no games for him to save. Veeck convinced Richards to employ Gossage as a starter.

"We're not going to have that many leads," Veeck reasoned. He was right.

Clearly, something had to be done after the season ended. This free-agency business would kill the underfinanced club in the long run. And the slappers they had for hitters...well, it was no way to excite fans.

The '76 season was a washout, while other teams had entered the free-agent market and shelled out money for Reggie Jackson or Joe Rudi or Bobby Grich.

Now, with 1977 looming, Veeck had a couple of potential free agents himself—and he knew he wouldn't be able to afford them. Not only that, he couldn't compete in the marketplace for the burgeoning number of quality players who were becoming available.

The Sox did, however, have several quality players. They couldn't be counted on in the long run, though. "If Bucky Dent and Rich Gossage and Terry Forster stayed with us in '77, they would have become free agents," explains Hemond. "So Bill was looking down the line and he knew he wouldn't be able to afford them, so he figured, if he can't sign them, he'd be better off trading them."

Then Veeck made a remarkable decision, a brilliant strategic move. He decided, just like that, that the White Sox were going to change their image. They would become power-hitters instead of banjo-hitters. "Let's put some pop in the park," he told Hemond. "We'll bring some new excitement to Comiskey Park."

First, he needed some power-hitters. He struck on an unusual idea. The free-agency system that had messed him up was going to save him. "He said we'll rent a player for a year," says Hemond.

It was to be no longer than that—Veeck couldn't afford long-term commitments. Now he had to find ballplayers who would be willing to sign for just one year. In all, he signed thirteen players—a record that still stands. None rated multimillion-dollar headlines.

They were players who had to prove themselves—who needed to have good seasons in 1977 in order to sign lucrative long-term contracts. The people in this group included Oscar Gamble, Richie Zisk, and Eric Soderholm.

"Soderholm was another story in itself," says Hemond. "Bill was always willing to take a chance with someone who was coming off a bad injury. It was synonymous with his life of overcoming adversity. He relished that. He loved giving somebody a chance. He would recognize the person who had a problem and, with dedication, overcome it.

"Soderholm had a very bad knee injury in Minnesota. He was buying a new home and slipped in the hall while it was being constructed. He was let go by Minnesota. I remember he came by the park and Bill was in the hospital—you know, he was hospitalized so many times in those five years I was with him. I think then he was having a breathing problem.

"Soderholm said, 'I'd love to go down on the field.' I think there was snow on the field and he stood at third base and imagined himself coming back. Then we drove out to the hospital to see Bill. You could see the relationship building beautifully. We signed Soderholm and he was named the comeback player of the year, hit 25 home runs, really helped our club."

The Go-Go Sox of 1977 suddenly became known as the South Side Hit Men. They slugged homer after homer—192 in all, more than any Chisox team had previously. Gamble blasted 31 and Zisk added 30. Under the new manager, Bob Lemon, the Sox actually grabbed first place and held the lead from July 1 to August 11.

With the booming home runs came instant victories. And a tradition was born in Comiskey Park—the curtain call. Fans never before had seen their heroes pop so many home runs. Suddenly games that seemed out of reach were in Chicago's hands. The crowds savored these moments and didn't want to lose the new sensation.

So invariably after a clutch home run, the crowd would chant for the player so long and so loud that he simply had to go back onto the field, doff his cap, wave.

There were new players in Zisk, Gamble, and Soderholm, not to mention Lerrin LaGrow and Steve Stone. And in addition to Lemon, there were new coaches in Larry Doby, Bobby Knoop, and Stan Williams.

The combination of enthusiasm and home runs worked only up to a point. Without any real depth on the pitching staff (Ken Kravec's sky-high earned-run average of 4.10 was tops on the club), the Sox eventually stumbled. Still, they produced 90 victories for the first time in twelve years and moved up to third. In the process they drew a club record of 1.657 million fans.

Veeck was named the Major League Executive of the Year by *The Sporting News*. It was the second time he captured the honor. Twenty-nine years earlier he had taken it when he ran the Indians. And seven years before that he had been named the Minor League Executive of the Year for his success in Milwaukee.

Veeck, meanwhile, never forgot the problems he had buying into the White Sox the second time. After he finally did, he would not attend league or joint meetings. This he asked the club's chairman, Bill DeWitt, to do.

The flush of the 1977 season was to fade virtually as soon as the campaign ended. Gamble left for San Diego and Zisk took off for Texas. Veeck thought that, perhaps, he might be able to draft players. He seemed to draft everyone who was available, but baseball wasn't going in that direction anymore. Teams were trying for quick fixes—the Yankees signing Reggie Jackson, for example. The players that Veeck got through the draft were merely fill-ins, bodies to man a position.

That didn't mean Veeck still couldn't have any fun. Take his spy-in-the-sky caper, which involved the Yankees, of course. Billy Martin was managing and, looking for an advantage, he employed Gene Michael as his eyes from on high. Michael would sit in the press box and communicate with Martin over a walkie-talkie. Michael might notice, for example, that the outfielders were playing too deep for a certain hitter, or he spotted a flaw in the opposition's defensive alignment.

This particular day, though, Veeck had enough of Yankee spying. He complained to Jerome Holtzman, the Chicago writer, that Michael was managing from the press box. That was breaking the code of neutrality.

In all of sports, no group of writers has control over their environment like the baseball writers do. In fact, press boxes are considered the writers' domain and a haven for neutrality. Before many games there is an announcement: "No cheering in the press box." An owner can't send his friends up there and the best ticket in the place doesn't help you get in if you don't have the proper credentials. Holtzman kicked Michael out, Michael remembers. He remembers it with a sense of humor, honed in two stints as a Yankee manager.

"I had to sit in the stands to scout, and this clown, a guy wearing a clown costume, sits on my lap, and Harry Caray comes over to interview me. Veeck was somewhere laughing," says Michael, a lean, former Yankee infielder known as Stick. He is convinced that Veeck sent both the clown and Caray after him.

Caray recalls the incident this way: "Stick was in the stands talking on a walkie-talkie and it was getting out of hand. He was sitting near the edge of the balcony. I thought the fans would throw him over. They started to surround him. I quieted them."

Whatever, the affair became known as the spy-in-the-sky, another moment in Veeck's career that touched so many other people and, to this day, makes them smile. Even Michael.

With the loss of their better free agents to greener pastures, so to speak, the White Sox needed to jack themselves up for 1978.

Veeck filled his training camp in Sarasota with a strange mixture of motivated men: minor leaguers hungry for the big money, discarded or injured players like Ron Blomberg, desperate for a chance to get back into the system, and stars traded from other teams.

They included players such as Bobby Bonds, traded because he was playing out his option. Veeck didn't expect to sign these people again once they were "free" at season's end. But he knew they were hungry to prove a point—just as those he had signed in 1977. They needed one big season before auctioning themselves off.

"It's an interesting experiment," Veeck said. "It's kind of like Las Vegas. They'll bet you're wrong. That's what we're doing—we're letting the other teams take the high-priced talent in the open market and we're betting they're wrong.

"Why are they wrong? Because high-priced talent breaks down too."

So Veeck assembled the biggest army of players of any training camp in the spring of 1978: sixty players. Of all sorts. "I also happen to believe in rehabilitation," he said, "so we took the lame, the halt, and the blind too."

The Sox, though, reverted to type. They fell badly under .500 in 1978 and Lemon was dismissed just before the midway point of 1978, with the Sox mired at 34-40. It was to be a season in which the highest batting average on the club was only .273, the most homers 20, the most runs batted in 72.

The way Doby remembers it, Veeck reluctantly turned over the club to him when Lemon was fired—reluctant because Veeck didn't want Doby saddled with a bad club. He would be only the second black manager in big-league history, after Frank Robinson.

The team did no better under Doby the rest of the '78 season, producing only a 37-50 record, next to last in the six-team division. And with the disappointment of the season came stirrings from many of the forty-six other owners that maybe this wasn't any way to run a ball club, that maybe they should get out. Money was becoming scarce, even with a solid attendance that reached nearly 1.5 million fans. The continuing problem was quality players for the long haul.

Meanwhile, Veeck's physical problems continued—indeed, seemed to be escalating. He estimated he had gone through thirty-three surgical procedures, including his latest, an operation to fuse vertebrae that had been affected by the constant thumping of his peg leg.

Even his "good" left leg had a plastic joint. He had other problems—partial paralysis of the hands, complete deafness in one ear, partial in the other. By now he had to give up tennis, a game he played with powerful aggression once he reached the ball.

He had rigged his wooden leg so that he could make a point in conversation if he had to. Sometimes, as a salute or as a joyous gesture, he would swing it straight up in the air, making it stand at attention while a startled onlooker would gasp.

"I figured it out," he said, "and I've spent four and half years of my life in hospitals. Every year at the end of December, Illinois Masonic Hospital does their books. If they're in the red they call me up. I put them over the top." And he smiled and took another drag on his Salem Longs.

Doby said they both cried when he was fired after the 1978 season. Doby, though, returned to spring training with the team in a poorly defined role while Don Kessinger would be the new manager for 1979.

"I wouldn't say Kessinger didn't like me," says Doby now. "But that is the right word. I was never put in the position to coach. I guess because of Bill he'd just have me hanging around. I'm not a hang-arounder. Bill told me to stay, but that would have been like going through the same things I went through when I first started. So I left."

The '79 season would prove to be an embarrassment to Veeck when one of his promotions backfired. It provided the ammunition that his critics didn't hesitate to use. And it altered Veeck's perception of the fan, the one he had always held in esteem and had said would be nice if only you were nice to him. For not only had the game he grew up with changed, along with the players, but the people watching the game were different too. That was brought home one night during the Disco Demolition fiasco.

And what about the announcers? Veeck had approved the hiring of Jimmy Piersall, one of the most intriguing characters in baseball history. As a rival outfielder he threw a ball in anger at Veeck's exploding scoreboard; he squirted home plate with a water pistol; watered down the infield between innings; spent time at a hospital after suffering a breakdown with the Red Sox in 1952; ran around the bases backward after hitting a home run with the Mets.

He became nationally prominent with the movie version of his autobiography, *Fear Strikes Out*, in which Anthony Perkins, of all people, played Piersall. Perkins threw a baseball like a little girl throwing a rubber duckie. Piersall remarked ruefully he didn't have much better luck when they produced a television movie of his life. This time Tab Hunter played Piersall.

To say the least, Piersall's tenure as Veeck's announcer was stormy—in some ways as zany as anything Piersall produced as a player. There was the time Piersall called Mary Frances "a colossal bore."

According to one account, Veeck sent his son Mike—who worked in the club's promotion department—to challenge Piersall to a fight. The fight never took place but an argument did. According to the report, Piersall then was led into Bill Veeck's office, where Piersall broke down crying. Veeck's anger apparently softened and Piersall was given two weeks off.

Piersall disputes that. He recalls that "Mike Veeck came up with somebody else and grabbed me from behind. But his dad had nothing to do with it. Bill Veeck fought his own battles. Bill Veeck never said one word to me about my statement."

Small wonder, though, that Piersall and Mrs. Veeck did not get along. He was—and still is—outspoken. She was, meanwhile, always protective of her husband and his image.

"One time, in a *Sport* magazine article, they asked me about Bill

Veeck," recalls Piersall. "And I said, 'Well, he's never proven to me he's been a success,' and, oh, boy, Mary Frances really got pissed. I said, 'Well, that's my opinion.' He's been on losers that never really were a success. In Cleveland he took over players already good. In Chicago, actually, he tore that club down. His forte was communication with the press, communication with the public, and his promotions."

Piersall is ambivalent in speaking of Veeck. For Piersall also wants the record kept straight, that Veeck should not be blamed for things he didn't do. According to Piersall, the 1979 fiasco Disco Demolition was in fact a Mike Veeck promotion "okayed by his dad." Perhaps, but Bill Veeck always took the blame for what happened that night in 1979.

Veeck was always trying to raise the tone of the fans, whether it was having the "Hallelujah Chorus" ring out on his gee-whiz scoreboard or every patron coming in one night receiving a copy of the current best-seller.

So the disco promotion was simple: He offered a reduced-price ticket to every spectator who bought a disco record to the game. The idea was the record would be carted away and destroyed, a fate, said Veeck, that particular form of music deserved.

"It was," remembers Piersall, "a very scary night. We had a full house. The people were supposed to leave the records at the gate. Instead, a lot of them brought their records in. They were throwing them everywhere, on the field."

Fans were burning the records and surged onto the field between games of the doubleheader. The behavior of the crowd stunned Veeck. He did something very unusual. He went onto the field for one of the few times in his baseball life. Although he had always been visible, and although he often spoke to a crowd, he rarely actually set foot on the playing field. He looked at the baseball field as someone else's domain. This time, though, he went down and appealed to the fans who were running around. His talk didn't help. Finally, the second game had to be postponed.

Had people changed that much since his first, crazy promotions? Veeck was unsure. He would not attribute what happened solely to the fans. "It was a promotion that was far too good," attracting a larger crowd than expected. "We were caught with our drawers around our ankles," he said, "and you can't run very fast that way."

This was the first time he had to confront the legacy of the 1960s. "Why would people be less violent in the ballpark if they're more violent in the streets?" Veeck asked. "Possibly as a result of the sixties and seventies there is less respect for the law, for people in authority. 'Do your own thing' is the quote, I believe."

Kessinger got the chance to manage for 106 games before he was dismissed with the team going nowhere. He was replaced by Tony La Russa—a thirty-four-year-old who had graduated from law school the year before and was studying for his bar examination. The Sox played .500 ball for him the remainder of the '79 campaign, but still finished fifth in the division.

It was apparent that 1980 was going to be the end of the baseball road for Veeck, sixty-six years old, short of money, and with not enough talented players. His illnesses seemed to be coming with increasing frequency, his falls more serious.

After speaking at a South Side high school alumni reunion following the 1979 season, he slipped on a wet floor. He broke his left kneecap, which needed two pins to hold it together.

That hardly prevented him from rolling up his sleeves and going after the Yankees early the next season—his last in baseball. It was mid-April, and a night game against the Yankees in Comiskey Park was knocked out by rain, sleet, and snow. Veeck merely rescheduled the game for the following day at 4:45 P.M.

But that forced a postponement of the Yankees' welcome-home dinner in New York scheduled for Thursday night. The dinner also benefited summer camps of the Catholic Youth Organizations.

"Thousands of kids are going to be deprived of going to camp, all because of the wishes of Mr. Veeck to play the game at 4:45," complained Steinbrenner, who complained to both Kuhn and MacPhail, but the league rules gave the White Sox the right to play the game at the rescheduled time.

"He can complain all he wants, and I'm sympathetic," said Veeck, holding out an olive branch. "But I'm also interested in my own welfare. I want to stay alive. To lose a day with the Yankees is expensive for us. Whether they have 1,200 people going to a banquet, we have 10,000 or 15,000 fans who want to see a ball game. I can't accept responsibility for the weather." Now, putting some thorns in the olive branch, Veeck added, "If George wanted to use some influence, why doesn't he talk to the weatherman and do something about the weather?"

But La Russa could do little with the team that he inherited. It was a sluggish 1980 season, with the Sox winning only 70 games and finishing in fifth place, 26 games out of first.

Chapter 11

Veeck was Chicago, wasn't he? He and Mayor Daley and George Halas. The name Veeck had been Chicago baseball since the boys came home after World War I. But few people in Chicago have ever realized that Veeck—the man who came back to town to save the team—finally got so desperate to sell his floundering franchise that he actually had an agreement to move the club to Denver.

The man he was going to sell to was Marvin Davis, a fabulous businessman whose own life had been as varied and interesting as Veeck's. Davis had everything, even girth. He was a three-hundred-pounder who settled in Denver in the 1950s after leaving Brooklyn, where he grew up near Ebbets Field. His father, known as Blackjack Davis, had been an amateur boxer, and went into the clothing business, where he reached everlasting fame as the co-inventor of corduroy. His son became an oil wildcatter, then started to acquire things—Twentieth Century-Fox, for example. He even made a couple of failed bids for CBS. He was one of the world's wealthiest men, his fortune, privately held, allowing him to stay out of the public eye when he wished. What he didn't have was a baseball team. A friend of his knew one of Veeck's four dozen owners, who said the team was for sale.

Davis's speaking style is matter-of-fact, unemotional, as if he were recounting the selling of a pair of pants in a retail clothing store. He of course remembers well the time in 1980 he had a baseball team—at least in principle.

"We had a meeting with Veeck," recalls Davis. "He came to Denver. He said he'd like to sell the team. We negotiated with them. We came up with a price."

But that wasn't all. In the past, when Veeck had sold, he had left the team completely. This was different, though. "He was very funny," says Davis. "He wanted to go with the team, which we agreed. He wanted to go with the team as an assistant. I said, fine, let's sit down. Our guys went down to look at the books in Chicago. Our offer was fifteen, sixteen million as I remember.

"We shook hands on the deal. He was excited about it. We took a drive out to the stadium. We were going to play right in Mile High Stadium. You push a button and the stands move back for baseball."

So Veeck was moving to Denver, baseball team and all. It had come about because of some rather complicated deals involving a pair of Oakland sports teams—Finley's A's and Al Davis's Raiders.

Finley had hoped to move his team to Denver and had made a deal with Marvin Davis. The Oakland Coliseum Commission was going to let Finley out of his contract for $4 million—the American League would put up $1 million, the San Francisco Giants would put up $1 million, Finley would ante up a million and so would Marvin Davis. The Giants then would play part of their home schedule in Oakland, which would obviously improve their attendance situation. And Oakland still had the football team.

But just at that time there were stirrings from the Raiders. Al Davis was unhappy with his Raiders contract. He wanted the Coliseum to install luxury boxes. Because the home football teams don't share with visiting clubs the revenue from these boxes, Davis could have taken in another $2 million a year. And while he was negotiating for a better lease and improvements, he started talking to Los Angeles about moving the Raiders there. Los Angeles was available for an N.F.L. team, since the Rams had left for Anaheim the year before. Not only would Los Angeles build him boxes, the city also had something Oakland never could hope to possess: a few million people with a potential windfall for cable television.

Now, Oakland was faced with losing not only a baseball team but a football team as well. Not only was Oakland forever marked, in the words of Gertrude Stein, as the city where "there is no there, there," but it wouldn't even have a major-league team.

"My deal with the A's was all set and then all of a sudden they got religion out there and decided they're not going to let the team go," says

Marvin Davis. "Al Davis steamed them up. I was very disappointed because I thought I had a ball club and the town was hysterical."

According to Marvin Davis, he sold, unsolicited, $5 million worth of
tickets for A's games that never were held but that would have been used
by fans to see the Denver White Sox instead. "People just came streaming
in. They wanted baseball. They still do to this day, very badly. People
reserved tickets, they'd send me a check made out to 'Marvin Davis, baseball owner.'"

Marvin Davis recalled he told Veeck, "'Bill, you got a deal.' He said,
'Great. I'll deliver.' Then he couldn't deliver."

What killed the White Sox transfer, according to Davis, was that people in Chicago and the league "were determined not to let the team out
of Chicago." Still, Davis has fond memories of the deal he made, of his
brief moment as owner of the Denver...er, Chicago...White Sox.

"I was amazed when Veeck came to the office, how bad he looked
with the one leg, dressed horribly. Open-neck shirt. He was no Beau
Brummel, let's put it that way. To me, he was a legend in baseball. I
always remembered the midget and everything else.

"He came in, and it was a very cold meeting to start with, but the guy
had a great personality. It warmed up near the end. We became close
friends. He put his arm around me, I put my arm around him. We all
became very happy. I enjoyed him at the end. But at the beginning, well,
I think he suffered on a long trip even though we flew him in our plane.
I think he suffered on the trip. He looked like he was chock full of pain
when he walked into the office.

"But when he walked out, he felt better. We gave him some food, a
soft drink, we made him feel good and he got happy with the surround-
ings. He started ambulating a little bit more. He was a great guy. I had
a lot of fun with him.

"Actually, I was on the hook. I loved baseball and Denver didn't have
a team. I've been watching baseball since I was a kid. When I was a kid
I used to sit out there in Brooklyn, I think it cost a quarter in the bleachers
those days. We lived near Prospect Park, on Ocean Parkway. I moved to
Denver thirty-two years ago, but I love baseball."

And Davis got to like Veeck?

"You couldn't help but like him, he was a lovable guy. He was full
of shit, you know, with his stories, with this and that. To me, I love
anything about baseball. He saw my love for it, he told stories, we laughed.
We sat for six hours. He told me stories with the midget, with this and
that. Lot of fun. He really wanted to move to Denver. It would be a new

experience, a new this, a new that. So we both kept yelling at each other, how great it's gonna be. But it never came to pass."

And why would Davis, who has all the toys he wants, also want a baseball team?

"My wife don't let me eat peanuts in the living room," he explains.

In that summer of 1980, Veeck then began negotiating for the sale of the Sox with a man who started the shopping-mall boom in the United States—Edward J. DeBartolo, Sr. DeBartolo would keep the team in Chicago.

DeBartolo owned hotels and office complexes, racetracks, and land. He entered the construction business during the Depression when he was thirteen and prepared estimates for his stepfather, a master mason and general contractor who could not read English. In 1948, at the age of thirty, DeBartolo founded his own company, then plunged into an uncharted business—building shopping centers in suburban neighborhoods around his native Youngstown, Ohio. When that worked he gradually stretched to other areas of the Middle West.

Then he tried another idea: the enclosed shopping mall. By the 1960s he had branched out into thoroughbred race courses because he saw the real estate as undervalued. He eventually bought the San Francisco 49ers football team for his son, Edward, Jr., to run, and also bought the Pittsburgh Penguins hockey team.

Now, Veeck and DeBartolo struck a deal—the seventy-one-year-old DeBartolo would buy the Sox for $20 million. Of course, he would keep the team in Chicago. All Veeck needed to complete the deal was the approval of ten of the fourteen other American League owners. And why wouldn't they give their consent? Here was a multimillionaire who would not come in merely to move the team someplace else.

But the owners didn't consent. Only eight owners voted to approve the sale. The reasons the deal didn't go through, said those who voted against it, was that DeBartolo owned racetracks and he lived in Ohio, not Chicago. Absentee ownership was always anathema to the league, they said. It seemed not to matter that Charlie Finley had never moved to the cities where his A's played—either to Kansas City or Oakland—but had remained in Chicago.

The league said it would take up the matter again in two months, at the annual meeting. Meanwhile, Veeck still had a ball club to run—indeed, a ball club to build.

His health, though, had reached the point where mini-visits to a hospital didn't halt his problems. On Labor Day he quit smoking—"after four packs a day for fifty years," he announced. And as soon as the season ended, he spent five weeks in a hospital being treated for emphysema and pneumonia.

No sooner was he out of the hospital than he began to sweat out the DeBartolo situation. He also rehired La Russa. Meanwhile, in a few days the free-agent draft would be held. La Russa and Veeck wanted the plum of the draft—the San Diego Padres' star, Dave Winfield. Although he batted only .276 in 1980, Winfield was a versatile performer who obviously would be even better with a contender.

Looking back, it is apparent that Veeck never would have been a serious bidder for Winfield. At the time, though, Veeck was furious at what Winfield did. Winfield began a letter-writing campaign designed to insure that the Yankees had a chance to select him in the draft. He sent letters to fifteen of the twenty-six major-league teams—including the White Sox—and advised them "in your own self-interest not to waste a first-round draft choice on me," because he had no intention of signing with them.

The letter was a shock not only to Veeck but to the city of Chicago. For here was a player who said in his letter that he wanted to play for a club in a metropolitan area where his work through the Dave Winfield Foundation for Children could be "most productive," and for a team that was a contender.

"I've been seeking that level of competition for some time," he wrote. "I must rule out certain teams and communities while trying to determine my future."

Thus, with a few words, he downgraded America's Second City— and, of course, its American League team. So at the news conference in Chicago to announce the rehiring of La Russa, an irate Veeck rose to Chicago's defense. He said that, though he had intended to draft Winfield, he would not do so now because "we don't want him in our town." It was a clever strategic ploy—finding a common enemy. Veeck surely knew he never could have matched the extraordinary $1.6 million annual salary Winfield eventually was to receive from the Yankees as he became the highest-paid athlete in sports history. Instead, Veeck claimed, "We're never going to waste a draft choice on a .276 rumdrum."

If Veeck was angry then, his ire exploded in a few more weeks in Dallas. For the second time in two months, the American League rejected DeBartolo's attempt to buy the White Sox. This time the margin of defeat was even wider. Veeck needed ten votes. At the October meeting he got eight. Now, he got three.

"It's capricious and very unfair," charged Veeck, who still managed a quip. "I can understand their throwing me out now and then, but I can't understand this. I'm ashamed of the American League."

To DeBartolo's allies it seemed that DeBartolo was being excluded because he was in the sort of business that seemed the stuff of crime stories. But DeBartolo has never been tinged with unseemly associations, not by baseball's security division, which investigated him thoroughly, nor by the National Football League's security operation. Both leagues' security is run by former FBI agents who maintain solid pipelines to the Bureau. If DeBartolo had been even faintly associated with criminal elements, that would have come out.

Kuhn and MacPhail claim this was never an issue—actually the mob connection was mere speculation by the news media, who created the specter of a witch-hunt simply because DeBartolo was Italian. When De-Bartolo was rejected, though, he himself raised the issue.

"It's unbelievable to think," DeBartolo said after the defeat, "that we live in a country where there are still prejudices and people would create doubt about the viability of the free-enterprise system. I spent three and a half years in the service, built my business, worked hard. Then, to have fourteen people and the commissioner of baseball sit in judgment on me is wrong."

The showdown took place in a closed meeting of the league's owners. Edward Bennett Williams of the Baltimore Orioles and Bud Selig of the Milwaukee Brewers were against approving DeBartolo, an ironic turn. Here were two cities that got franchises because of Veeck, in a sense. DeBartolo pleaded his case for seven minutes, then was excused for the vote.

MacPhail tried to couch in diplomatic terms the reason the vote had gone against DeBartolo. But the bottom line was that the owners did not believe DeBartolo would divest himself of his racetracks and move to Chicago. "His offer came very late, and there was no guarantee when or if that would happen," said MacPhail.

The owners had a history of being burned by new owners who came in promising to become part of the community. It happened most notably with Finley. "My mind was open," claimed Calvin Griffith of the Minnesota Twins. "But seeing is believing. It's one thing to say something, another to do it. Charlie Finley was always promising to move to Kansas City too."

Kuhn agreed that DeBartolo failed to get support because of the racetracks and the fact he didn't live in Chicago. But Kuhn also cited De-Bartolo's "pressure tactics" as an underlying negative. From the beginning, DeBartolo had held up the threat of a lawsuit if he didn't get the club.

"In our first meeting," Kuhn said, "he mentioned litigation. I told him not to approach it that way. He then put pressure on various people in baseball, and that sat bad with certain owners."

Enter again, Jerry and Eddie, the new wave of baseball owners.

Jerry Reinsdorf, not yet forty-five years old, was born in Brooklyn and attended Northwestern University law school. He stayed in Chicago after graduation and eventually got into real estate, heading one of the country's largest investment firms.

He hadn't seen his old friend Eddie Einhorn in twenty years, since they had been classmates at Northwestern Law. Einhorn, a native New Jerseyan with a sidewalks-of-New York speaking manner, had gone into show business. A year out of law school, he founded the independent sports network TVS, which rose to prominence televising N.C.A.A. basketball games. He wound up joining CBS Sports and was executive producer of *Sports Spectacular*. He also demonstrated sensitivity when he won an Emmy as producer of *The Gossamer Albatross, Flight of Imagination*, a film about the creation of an airplane powered by a young man using bicycle energy.

"All of a sudden I got this call from my old law-school mate whom I hadn't seen or talked to in twenty years," recalls Einhorn. "He was calling me that he had a chance to buy the White Sox. He knew I had been interested in buying a team because I had tried before to buy the Padres, when Ray Kroc bought them. He told me he had a deal with Veeck. Jerry had another guy in with him named Bill Farley. They wanted me for the marketing."

But not so fast.

"All of a sudden Jerry calls me up and says we didn't get the deal, DeBartolo got it. Then he calls me back the very next day and says, 'We're not dead yet. The league might not approve DeBartolo.'"

But after the league ousted DeBartolo's bid, it then withheld approval from Farley. It didn't want him either.

"Now Farley's out of the picture, so I said, 'What does that mean?' It means I have to run the White Sox. So that's how I came into the thing. I quit CBS, and all of a sudden it became the Einhorn-Reinsdorf group instead of the Farley-Reinsdorf group." The bid was successful, and for $20 million Jerry and Eddie became the new owners of the White Sox.

But a strange thing happened to the sixty-seven-year-old Veeck. He divorced himself from the team, as if it never existed for him, as if his two tenures as president were merely fill-ins for other things in his life. What Veeck did as he approached the age of seventy was to go back to the Cubs.

His disaffection with the Sox's new owners was immediate. Reinsdorf became the chairman of the board—and Einhorn now was the president of a major-league baseball team. He ran the team. But it would be without any advice or affection from Veeck. For no sooner did Einhorn become president of the Sox, just a few days before spring training was to begin in 1981, than he said the wrong thing at his opening news conference.

"We basically never talked again," Einhorn concedes. "I did something at the conference that apparently got him angry. I said something to the effect—I don't remember the words—that we intend to run a very high-class operation, et cetera, et cetera. And he took offense to that as meaning that he didn't run a high-class operation. I didn't mean that at all, but he never forgave me for that."

But that wasn't all Einhorn said. He also described the team as in shambles. It was a club without enough employees, with no money to pay for adequate front-office help, for marketing. But it was in the television and radio markets that Einhorn was shocked. Veeck was a man who knew what the public wanted and what the public should pay for it. Yet, Einhorn could not believe what he found.

"They had incredibly bad radio and television contracts. They were getting the lowest television rights of any team in baseball—in the second-highest market."

You mean, less than the Athletics, for example?

"Oh, yes. The Sox were getting $6,000 a game. We now get $80,000. I built it up right away to $15,000. I'm not knocking him. If he could have done it, he would have. But the thing is, he was money-strapped and he couldn't have a staff to do it. I never blamed it on him, but he always resented the way it came out in the paper. We never talked from that day on. Some polite 'Hello's.' Until the day he died, we never talked."

It wasn't only over the fact that Veeck believed Einhorn belittled him. Einhorn—this guy from television—was changing the park, for God's sake. He was changing the way Veeck had always done business.

"Like, we had Golden Boxes, a more exclusive section. Then we put in the luxury suites, which he never liked. We did things to bring the team into the modern age, which he interpreted as...I mean, he was a guy that liked to sit in the bleachers, and any things that brought out—

I don't like to call it 'class'—really modernizing, he resented. When he adopted the Cubs, he went back to the bleachers. Now, as soon as he went back to the Cubs, they had the bleachers reserved—so he wouldn't go to the games there, either. He wound up not going to any games. That's the way he was.

"He called his ballpark the world's largest outdoor saloon, and was proud of it. We came in immediately and tried to change that image. And we succeeded in making it a family place to be. It was a dangerous place. You know, I was attached to Comiskey Park. I was a vendor when I was going to law school, I sold there during the World Series in 1959, so I was attached to it. But when I was there in those days they used to say it was unsafe around the park. The joke was, when I came back—it was unsafe *in* the park.

"The neighborhood wasn't that bad but in the park it was bad, and I mean bad. They had attracted, with Harry Caray and his beer...we had the biggest beer consumption of any team in the major leagues, and it was a wild place, a young place. You heard of that Disco Demolition. I did a lot of speaking the first six months, and what I found was that a lot of White Sox fans would not come to the ballpark any more. They didn't like the atmosphere. We increased security. We got rid of Harry Caray, who fed all that stuff, and Jimmy Piersall, and we virtually changed it all around.

"Some people didn't like us for it. But we sold more season's tickets than they ever had in history. We broke all-time attendance records—and not just broke them, but by half a million. I felt we did a very good job, but Veeck never liked it. He wouldn't even come to the play-offs. We asked him to throw out the first ball when we made the play-offs. He wouldn't do it. The fiftieth anniversary All-Star Game, he wouldn't come out."

Just a few days after Veeck sold the team he reflected on what had happened to him and baseball. He now aligned himself with an old adversary, Calvin Griffith, the owner of the Minnesota Twins, whose family ties went back to Washington and the Senators of World War I, when Veeck's father was building the Cubs.

Veeck now contended that he and Griffith were the last of a breed, owners whose only business was baseball, but who were forced to compete for players against teams subsidized by giant corporations with an endless infusion of money.

This all came about, he explained in a Chicago interview, because of "catastrophic changes" to his game as a result of free agency. "That brought an end to Calvin and myself," said Veeck. "We are doomed. We are the last dinosaurs in a forest where there are no more trees to feed on."

Ironically, Veeck's estrangement from his old team grew as the Sox got better. In fact, the Reinsdorf-Einhorn connection made the Pale Hose an instant contender, to Veeck's chagrin. And they did it by employing the same quick-fix methods that the Old Master himself had found useful for the short haul.

First, though, Reinsdorf believed that the cure to the Sox's ills would be a long-term commitment, an infusion of money into scouting, and a farm system and player development. And it would probably work somewhere down the line. On the other hand, Sox attendance had declined steadily after Veeck's second season of 1977, when there was a run for the pennant—a loss of 167,000 fans the next year, followed by a loss of 211,000, followed by a loss of 80,000. Reinsdorf's speeches to the fans were filled with promises of a brighter future, but Einhorn wasn't willing to wait.

"I've been in sports," says the practical Einhorn, "and I said, 'Jerry, I've got news for you—this is going over like a dead elephant, a lead balloon. They've heard this bullshit before. We're going to have to go out and show them, do something.'"

What they did was go after the most attractive free agent they could find. There was one ready-made: Carlton Fisk. He had been the Red Sox anchor as catcher since 1972. He was a nationally recognized hero since that moment in the twelfth inning of the sixth game of the 1975 World Series against the Reds—when he "waved" his home run fair and then ran around the bases taking leaps of joy every other step.

The thing was now, would Fisk be willing to come to Chicago?

"All I heard was that no one wanted to come to the White Sox," recounts Einhorn. "We called ourselves the Rodney Dangerfield of baseball. We had no respect because of the image we had."

So, quietly, Einhorn called up Fisk's agent, Jerry Kapstein. Einhorn and Kapstein had known each other from Einhorn's television days. This was going to be a very sensitive situation. If Fisk turned Einhorn down, the Sox would retain their image not only as losers, but as a pariah.

"I'll come and talk to you," Einhorn told Kapstein, "but I want to know if I really have a chance. Don't use me. This is our first big thing as new owners, and if I screw it up, I'm going to look really bad."

Instead, they not only talked, Fisk signed.

The way Einhorn remembers it, "The reaction of the town was in-sane—just as I thought it would be. No one thought the team—the Chi-cago White Sox, who in 1977, when Veeck didn't have the money to handle free agency, got all these guys on one-year deals and lost them all—couldn't believe a quality player like Carlton Fisk would go to the White Sox.

"When I saw the reaction after I signed him, I said, 'Holy shit, let's get some more.' This was the way. And I said, 'Roland, get me a list of who's available.' And then next thing was, Luzinski was available. I closed the deal the morning of the N.C.A.A. basketball championship, which I had been at for twenty-five straight years, and I said, 'Hey, I'm a baseball guy now. Basketball's over.'"

The magic continued even after the honeymoon of the signing end-ed. For as dramatic effect would have it, the Sox opened the season in Boston. In his return to Fenway Park, Fisk clobbered a three-run homer in the eighth inning and the White Sox scored a 5-3 victory. Then, four days later, they opened at home. A record home-opener crowd of more than 51,000 greeted him and they saw Fisk nail a grand-slam home run to help defeat the Brewers.

Blessed with this fast start, the fans returned and the team continued to do well. But this was also to be the strike season of '81. When the strike ended, though, the Sox returned home in first place on September 1. Then they went into a tailspin. Still, they produced a better-than-.500 season of 54-52. Although the season was cut short by more than a third, Luzinski still powered 21 homers and Fisk produced five game-winning hits, although his overall production was below his Red Sox years. He caught more games than any other catcher in the American League, and established a stable base.

"Some days we had walk-ins of 20,000 fans. We were averaging 27,000 a game when we were going good. It was the most insane thing you ever saw. We didn't know how many people were in the park some days," says the hyperbolic Einhorn. "Chicago had been the Second City sportswise, and no ownership had ever been this aggressive."

Perhaps. Veeck was still around, though, reminding people of an-other era. And even though the Sox did even better in 1982, Veeck had now adopted—and been adopted by—the Cubs. He was sixty-eight years old, a Gray Eminence. But he sat without a shirt in the bleachers at Wrigley Field, where baseball remained a glad game played only under the sunlight. Now, in a twist, he was the Cubs' only link to the old days. For the year before, the same year Veeck had sold, William Wrigley had sold his Cubs, ending the longest continuous reign by one family in the history of baseball. *The New York Times* recorded a visit with Veeck that spring. He explained that, even though he carried a lifetime pass in his wallet to any ballpark in the majors, he preferred to pay his own way. "I pay for my tickets so I can complain,". he explained.

People constantly came over to talk, and if people wanted him to call them back, he asked the female assistant with him to note it on the yellow legal pad she carried.

"I can't say I really miss it very much," he said while watching a game against the Expos. "A lot of people I did business with I'm delighted to miss. I miss having to sign those checks like I miss the bubonic plague. I miss a lot of people, a lot of conversation, a lot of lies being told and the ones you are telling."

A young man came up and asked Veeck what he was doing these days.

"I'm a bum," Veeck replied.

A vendor reminded him, "Say hello to Mary Frances." Veeck asked another vendor about the day's receipts.

Veeck saw a television light in the grandstand. It reminded him of the time in '38 or '39 when he sold a lot of mirrors for the fans in the bleachers to hold when an enemy batter came to the plate.

Veeck rose during the seventh-inning stretch when Harry Caray—he had moved over to the Cubs' broadcasting booth from the White Sox—led everyone in singing "Take Me Out to the Ball Game."

"Another gag that worked," said Veeck. "I suppose it's poetic justice for me to be sitting in the bleachers which I helped build," he suggested. "I planted the ivy, literally. I wired the scoreboard."

Later, as he sat in the courtyard of the Bleachers, a saloon across from the park, a young man approached him. He also had lost a leg. The pair spoke about treatments and artificial legs.

Then a young boy came up to Veeck's table. The youngster wondered who Veeck was and what he did.

"I used to operate baseball teams," Veeck explained.

"Which ones?" said the boy.

As Veeck left to return to his car—a 1958 Ford Thunderbird—he spotted the young man who had lost his leg.

"When you get well," said Bill Veeck, "we'll race."

Veeck avoided the Sox in 1983, the year of the golden anniversary of the first All-Star Game, the year the Sox won their division by 20 games.

For the first time in Chicago history, a team had attracted two million fans.

"The irony was that in a Cubs' town—and this is a Cubs' town—we won, and then the next year the Cubs won and the Bears won the year after," says Einhorn. "I'm not saying he resented our success, but he never wanted to be a part of it. I tried to make up, I tried to explain what I meant but he never wanted to hear it. He was always the hero and we were always the bums [when Einhorn complained of the stadium and that he might be looking to move]. That's the irony of it. But that's life. What can I yell ya?"

There was more surgery for Veeck late in 1984. He had a malignant tumor in his right lung. Now, with Veeck seriously ill, many people championed his entrance into the Baseball Hall of Fame. The eighteen-member Veterans Committee of the Hall had never mentioned his name at its annual meeting. The committee was limited to selecting two people a year from the ranks of old-time players, executives, umpires, and Negro League players, and one of those picked had to be a former player. The committee had been created with the idea of bringing in a former player or official who, for some reason, had been overlooked in his time.

One committee member was Buzzy Bavasi, a longtime front-office official of the Dodgers and Angels. "Bill's a little like Leo Durocher," Bavasi explained. "He made a lot of friends, and he had a lot of people annoyed at him." In other words, Veeck wasn't getting in just yet.

It was suggested to Larry Doby—who was championing Veeck for the Hall of Fame—that perhaps Veeck didn't belong because he didn't produce consistent winning numbers. "You want to see a statistic?" shot back Doby. "Let the people vote and see what happens."

In Veeck's last years, Asher J. Birnbaum, the editor-publisher of a Chicago-area magazine named *North Shore*, asked Veeck to write a monthly column. It was called "Cleanup Man."

The month he died, January 1986, Veeck wrote a poem called "Where Did It Go?"

It began:

> Where did it go? I looked away
> And suddenly it seemed
> There wasn't any time at all
> To do the things I'd dreamed...."

He regretted that he would "never fly with Wendy nor hunt with In-
jun Joe...nor see the White Whale blow."

Yet, he concluded:

> So now I sit and ponder long
> Who, when and where I'll be.
> But when it all is said and done
> I'd rather just be me.

CARMEL CLAY PUBLIC LIBRARY